Contents

Introduction iii

How to use this dictionary iv

A–F 1

G–M 136

N–S 221

T–Z 257

Appendices 258

Introduction

Discover the power of words with this new edition of the **Oxford Junior Illustrated Dictionary**. The pages are contemporary, clean, bright, and colourful, which makes it easy to find the words you need. The text has been carefully aimed at primary school children aged 7-9 years, has been created using the Oxford Children's Corpus, and tested extensively in the classroom with teachers and children. Language is brought to life in example sentences from the best children's authors such as *Roald Dahl, Philip Pullman, JK Rowling*, and *Jacqueline Wilson*.

You can explore language further with the guide to spelling, punctuation, grammar, and vocabulary building at the back of the book.

If you love learning about new words and language, and if you want to find the meaning of a word that isn't in this dictionary, try a bigger dictionary, for example, the Oxford Primary Dictionary.

www.oxforddictionaries.com/schools

How to use this dictionary

alphabet
on every page the alphabet is divided into four sections, with the letter you are in highlighted, so you can find your way around the dictionary quickly and easily

catch words
guide you to the correct place to find the word you need, they show the first and last word on the page

pronunciation
helps you to say the word, remember that this is not the way to spell it

headword
in alphabetical order, in blue, it shows you how to spell a word

label
gives you context for the word so that you can understand how and when to use it

word class
what type of word it is, for example, noun, verb, adjective, or adverb

A B C D E F G H I J K L **M** **N** **O** **P** **Q** **R** **S** T U V W X Y Z

need noun plural needs
1 Your needs are the things that you need.
2 If someone is in need, they do not have enough money, food, or clothes.

needle noun plural needles
1 a thin, pointed piece of metal with a hole at one end that you use for sewing

2 A knitting needle is a long, thin stick that you use for knitting.
3 The needles on a pine tree are its thin, pointed leaves.

negative adjective
1 (in grammar) A negative sentence is one that has the word not or no in it. Rebecca is not very happy is a negative sentence .
2 (in mathematics) A negative number is less than 0.

neighbour noun plural neighbours
(say nay-ber)
Your neighbours are the people who live near you.

nephew noun plural nephews
Your nephew is the son of your brother or sister.

nerve noun plural nerves
The nerves in your body are the parts that carry messages to and from your brain, so that your body can feel and move.

nervous adjective
If you feel nervous, you feel slightly afraid. To tell the truth, Jack felt a little nervous, because it isn't every day you find a Scarecrow talking to you. — Philip Pullman, The Scarecrow and his Servant

nest noun plural nests
a home that a bird or small animal makes for its babies

net noun plural nets
1 A net is a piece of material with small holes in it. You use a net for catching fish.
2 (in ICT) The net is the Internet.

netball noun
a game in which two teams of players try to score goals by throwing a ball through a round net on a pole

nettle noun plural nettles
a plant with leaves that can sting you if you touch them

network noun plural networks (in ICT)
a group of computers that are connected to each other

never adverb
not ever I will never tell a lie again!

new adjective newer, newest
1 Something that is new has just been made or bought and is not old. I got some new trainers for my birthday.
2 Something that is new is different. We're moving to a new house.

news noun
The news is all the things that are happening in the world, which you can see on television or read about in newspapers.

newspaper noun plural newspapers
A newspaper is a set of large printed sheets of paper that contain articles about things that are happening in the world.

next adjective
1 The next thing is the one that is nearest to you. My friend lives in the next street.
2 The next thing is the one that comes after this one. We're going on holiday next week.

nibble verb nibbles, nibbling, nibbled
When you nibble something, you eat it by biting off a little bit at a time.

nice adjective nicer, nicest
1 Something that is nice is pleasant or enjoyable.
2 Someone who is nice is kind.

nickname noun plural nicknames
a friendly name that your family or friends call you

niece noun plural nieces
Your niece is the daughter of your brother or sister.

night noun plural nights
the time when it is dark

nightmare noun plural nightmares
a very frightening dream

nil noun
nothing, the number 0

nine noun plural nines
the number 9

nineteen noun
the number 19

ninety noun
the number 90

no
1 interjection You use no when you want to give a negative answer to a question. 'Would you like more cake?' 'No, thank you.'
2 determiner You use no to mean not any. I have no balloons left.
3 determiner You use no to mean not. I've asked that they come to the meeting no earlier than six o'clock.

nobody pronoun
no person There's nobody here.

nocturnal adjective
Nocturnal animals move around and feed at night.

nod verb nods, nodding, nodded
When you nod, you move your head up and down to show that you agree with someone.

noise noun plural noises
a sound that you can hear, especially a loud or strange one
noisy adjective If something is noisy, it makes a loud sound. If someone is noisy they make a lot of loud sound. My brother's music is so noisy that I have to shut my bedroom door when I do my homework.

noisily adverb
If something is done noisily, it is done with a lot of sound. He eats noisily.

a b c d e f g h i j k l m **n** o p q r s t u v w x y z

138

139

definition
what the word means and if a word has more than one meaning, then each meaning is numbered

other forms
different forms so that you can see how to spell them

example sentence
shows how the word is used, which helps you to understand the meaning

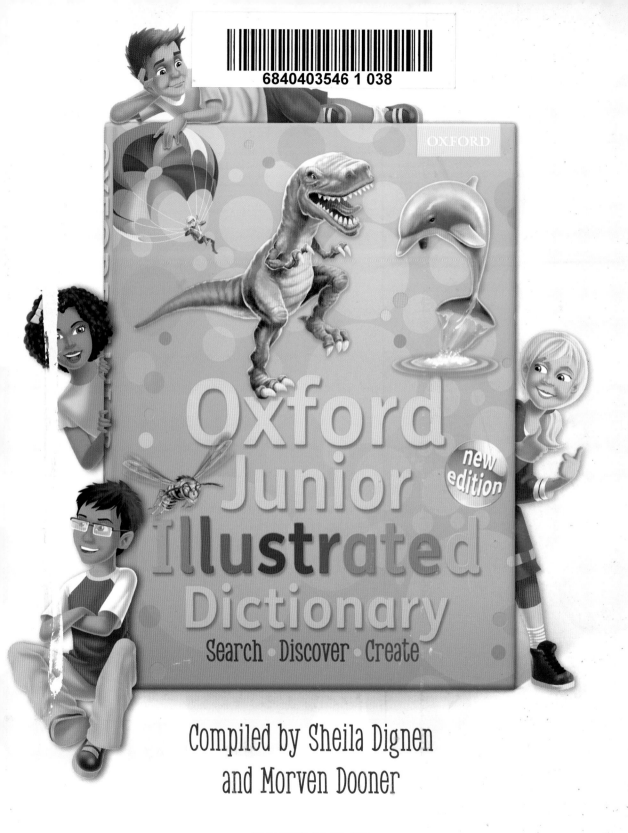

OXFORD

Oxford
Junior
Illustrated
Dictionary

new edition

Search · Discover · Create

Compiled by Sheila Dignen
and Morven Dooner

OXFORD
UNIVERSITY PRESS

OXFORD
UNIVERSITY PRESS

Great Clarendon Street, Oxford OX2 6DP

Oxford University Press is a department of the University of Oxford.
It furthers the University's objective of excellence in research, scholarship,
and education by publishing worldwide in

Oxford New York

Auckland Cape Town Dar es Salaam Hong Kong Karachi
Kuala Lumpur Madrid Melbourne Mexico City Nairobi
New Delhi Shanghai Taipei Toronto

With offices in
Argentina Austria Brazil Chile Czech Republic France Greece
Guatemala Hungary Italy Japan Poland Portugal Singapore
South Korea Switzerland Thailand Turkey Ukraine Vietnam

© Oxford University Press 2011

Database right Oxford University Press (maker)

First published 2003
New edition 2007
This new edition 2011

All artwork by Dynamo Design Ltd.
Photos: Shutterstock, OUP and Photos To Go
Page 80 (flea) © Nigel Cattlin/Alamy
Page 128 (maze) © Millets Farm Centre.

British Library Cataloguing in Publication Data available

ISBN hardback 978-0-19-273259-0
ISBN paperback 978-0-19-273260-6

10 9 8 7 6 5 4 3 2 1

Printed in Singapore

Paper used in the production of this book is a natural,
recycleable product made from wood grown in sustainable
forests. The manufacturing process conforms to the
environmental regulations of the country of origin.

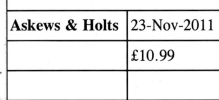

TEACHERS
For inspirational support plus
free resources and eBooks
www.oxfordprimary.co.uk

PARENTS
Help your child's reading
with essential tips, phonics
support and free eBooks
www.oxfordowl.co.uk

Aa

a, an determiner
One of something. You use **a** when you are talking about something that starts with a consonant *a tree, a bus, a dog,* and you use **an** when you are talking about something that starts with a vowel *an orange, an apple, an umbrella.*

abandon verb abandons, abandoning, abandoned
If you abandon someone, you go away and leave them and never go back to them.

abbreviation noun
plural abbreviations
a short way of writing a word *Dr is an abbreviation for doctor.*

ability noun *plural* abilities
If you have the ability to do something, you can do it.

able adjective
1 If you are able to do something, you can do it.
2 Someone who is very able is very good at doing something.

about preposition
1 on the subject of *I like reading books about animals.*
2 more or less, but not exactly *There are about 25 children in my class.*

above adverb, preposition
1 higher than *In a plane, you often fly above the clouds.*
2 more than *The film is only for children above the age of 12.*

abroad adverb
When you go abroad, you go to another country.

absent adjective
Someone who is absent is not in a place. *Why were you absent from school yesterday?*

absolutely adverb
completely

absorb verb absorbs, absorbing, absorbed (in science)
To absorb liquid means to soak it up.

accept verb accepts, accepting, accepted
If you accept something, you take it after someone has offered it to you. *My aunt offered me a drink, and I accepted politely.*

access verb accesses, accessing, accessed (in ICT)
When you access information on a computer, you find it and use it.

accident noun *plural* accidents
1 When there is an accident, something bad happens and someone gets hurt.
2 If something that you did was an accident, you did not do it deliberately.
accidentally adverb When you do something accidentally, you do not do it deliberately. *I accidentally knocked a glass of water over my books.*

a
b
c
d
e
f
g
h
i
j
k
l
m
n
o
p
q
r
s
t
u
v
w
x
y
z

A
B
C
D
E
F
G
H
I
J
K
L
M
N
O
P
Q
R
S
T
U
V
W
X
Y
Z

account noun plural accounts
1 If you give an account of something that happened, you describe what happened.
2 If you have a bank account, you keep money in a bank and can take it out when you need it.

accurate adjective
Something that is accurate is exactly right or correct. *He gave the police an accurate description of the thief.*

ache verb aches, aching, ached
(rhymes with *bake*)
If a part of your body aches, it hurts.

achieve verb achieves, achieving, achieved
If you achieve something, you manage to do it after trying very hard.

acid noun plural acids (in science)
An acid is a chemical. There are many different kinds of acid. Lemons contain a type of acid which makes them taste sour. Some acids are very strong and can burn your clothes and skin.

acid rain noun
Acid rain is rain that is polluted with gases from cars and factory chimneys. Acid rain can harm plants and animals.

acrobat noun plural acrobats
someone who entertains people by doing exciting jumping and balancing tricks

across preposition
1 from one side to the other *We walked across the road.*
2 on the other side of something *The park is across the river.*

act verb acts, acting, acted
1 When you act, you do something.
2 When you act, you take part in a play.

action noun plural actions
1 When there is a lot of action, a lot of exciting things are happening.
2 An action is something that you do.

active adjective
If you are active, you are busy doing things.

activity noun plural activities
1 When there is a lot of activity, people are busy doing things all around you.
2 An activity is something enjoyable that you do for fun.

actor noun plural actors
a person who acts in a play or film

actress noun plural actresses
a woman who acts in a play or film

actually adverb
really *I thought it was a wolf, but actually it was a dog.*

add verb adds, adding, added
1 (in mathematics) When you add numbers together, you count them together to make a bigger number.
2 When you add something, you put it with other things or mix it in with other things. *I added some more sugar to the mixture.*

address noun plural addresses
1 Your address is where you live.
2 Someone's email address is the set of letters or numbers that you use to send them an email.

adjective noun *plural* adjectives
(in grammar)
An adjective is a word that tells you what someone or something is like. Words like *short*, *small*, and *dirty* are all adjectives.

admire verb admires, admiring, admired
1 If you admire someone, you like them and think that they are very good. *Which famous person do you admire the most?*
2 When you admire something, you look at it and think that it is nice.

admit verb admits, admitting, admitted
If you admit that you did something wrong, you tell people that you did it.

adore verb adores, adoring, adored
If you adore something, you like it a lot. *I adore ice cream!*

adult noun *plural* adults
someone who is grown up

advantage noun *plural* advantages
something that helps you to do better than other people

adventure noun *plural* adventures
something exciting that happens to you

adverb noun *plural* adverbs
(in grammar)
An adverb is a word that tells you how someone does something. *Furiously, carefully,* and *peacefully* are all adverbs.

advert noun
An advert or **advertisement** is a picture or short film that shows you something and tries to persuade you to buy it.

advertise verb advertises, advertising, advertised
To advertise something means to tell people about it so that they will want to buy it.

advice noun
If you give someone advice, you tell them what they should do.

advise verb advises, advising, advised
If you advise someone to do something, you tell them they should do it. *Suri's dad advised us to stay away from the river.*

aeroplane noun *plural* aeroplanes
a large machine that can travel through the air and carry passengers or goods

affect verb affects, affecting, affected
To affect something means to make it different in some way. *Will the rain affect our plans?*

affection noun
Affection is the feeling you have when you like someone.

afford verb affords, affording, afforded
If you can afford something, you have enough money to pay for it.

afraid adjective
If you are afraid, you are frightened.

after preposition
1 later than *We got home after lunch.*
2 following someone, or trying to catch them *The dog ran after me.*

afternoon noun *plural* afternoons
The afternoon is the time from the middle of the day until the evening.

again adverb
once more *Try again!*

against preposition
1 next to something and touching it *He leant against the wall.*
2 on the opposite side to someone in a game or battle *We've got a match against Luton on Saturday.*

a b c d e f g h i j k l m n o p q r s t u v w x y z

3

A
B
C
D
E
F
G
H
I
J
K
L
M
N
O
P
Q
R
S
T
U
V
W
X
Y
Z

age noun
Your age is how old you are.

ago adverb
Ago means in the past. *I first started dancing three years ago.*

agree verb agrees, agreeing, agreed
If you agree with someone, you have the same ideas as them and you think that they are right. *Amina says this book is boring, but I don't agree with her.*

ahead adverb
in front of someone else *I went on ahead to open the gate.*

aim verb aims, aiming, aimed
1 If you aim at something, you point a gun or other weapon at it. *Aim at the centre of the target.*
2 When you aim something, you try to throw it or kick it in a particular direction. *He aimed the ball into the far corner of the net.*

air noun
Air is the gas all around us, which we breathe.

airport noun plural airports
a place where planes take off and land and passengers can get on and off

alarm noun plural alarms
a loud sound that warns people of danger

album noun plural albums
1 a book to put things like photographs or stamps in
2 a CD with several pieces of music on it

alien noun plural aliens
In stories, an alien is a person or creature from another planet.

alike adjective
Things that are alike are similar in some way. *Although Sarah and I are not sisters, everyone says we look alike.*

alive adjective
Something that is alive is living.

all determiner, pronoun
1 everyone or everything *Are you all listening?*
2 the whole of something *Have you eaten all the cake?*

Allah noun
the Muslim name for God

allergic adjective
If you are allergic to something, it makes you ill, for example it makes you sneeze or gives you a rash. *I'm allergic to nuts.*

allergy noun
An allergy is something that makes you ill when you eat or touch it. It often makes you sneeze or gives you a rash. *I have an allergy to peanuts. I have an allergy to cats.*

alligator noun plural alligators
An alligator is an animal that looks like a crocodile. Alligators are reptiles and live in parts of North and South America and China.

alliteration noun
the use of words that begin with the same sound to create a special effect in writing, for example *five fat fishes*

allow verb allows, allowing, allowed
If you allow someone to do something, you let them do it and do not try to stop them. *We're not allowed to play football in the playground.*

all right adjective
1 If you are all right, you are safe and well, and not hurt.
2 If something is all right, it is quite good but not very good.

almost adverb
very nearly *We're almost home.*

alone adjective
If you are alone, there is no one with you. *It was a strange feeling, being alone in that big house.*

along adverb, preposition
from one end to the other *He ran along the top of the wall.*

alphabet noun
all the letters that we use in writing, arranged in a particular order

a b c d ... *(Roman alphabet)*
а б ц д ... *(Russian alphabet)*
嘎不才的 ... *(Chinese alphabet)*
ا ب ص د ... *(Arabic alphabet)*

already adverb
before now *When we got to the station, the train had already left.*

also adverb
as well *I love football and also tennis.*

alter verb alters, altering, altered
To alter something means to change it.

although conjunction
even though *We kept on running, although we were tired.*

altogether adverb
including all the people or things

aluminium noun
a light, silver-coloured metal

always adverb
at all times, or every time *Joshua is always late!*

amaze verb amazes, amazing, amazed
If something amazes you, it makes you feel very surprised
amazed adjective When you are amazed, you are surprised. *Max looked amazed to see me.*

ambition noun plural ambitions
something that you want to do very much

ambulance noun plural ambulances
a van in which people who are ill or injured are taken to hospital

among preposition
1 in the middle of *Somewhere among all these books was the one I was looking for.*
2 between *Share the sweets among you.*

amount noun plural amounts
An amount of something is a quantity of it.

amphibian noun plural amphibians
An amphibian is an animal that lives some of its life in water, and some on land.

a
b
c
d
e
f
g
h
i
j
k
l
m
n
o
p
q
r
s
t
u
v
w
x
y
z

A
B
C
D
E
F
G
H
I
J
K
L
M
N
O
P
Q
R
S
T
U
V
W
X
Y
Z

amuse verb amuses, amusing, amused
1 If something amuses you, you find it funny and it makes you laugh.
2 To amuse yourself means to find things to do. *We played games to amuse ourselves.*

analogue adjective
An analogue clock or watch has hands and a dial to show the time.

anchor noun *plural* anchors
An anchor is a heavy metal hook joined to a ship by a chain. It is dropped into the sea, where it digs into the bottom to keep the ship still.

ancient adjective (say **ane**-shunt)
Something that is ancient is very old.

and conjunction
a word that you use to join two words or phrases together *We saw lions and tigers at the zoo.*

angel noun *plural* angels
a messenger sent by God

anger noun
a strong feeling that you get when you are not pleased *The old man's voice was full of anger.*

angle noun *plural* angles
the corner where two lines meet

angry adjective angrier, angriest
If you are angry, you are annoyed or cross
angrily adverb If you say something angrily, you are annoyed or cross. *'You fool!' he said angrily.*

animal noun *plural* animals
An animal is anything that lives and can move about. Birds, fish, snakes, wasps, and elephants are all animals.

ankle noun *plural* ankles
Your ankle is the thin part of your leg where it is joined to your foot.

anniversary noun
plural anniversaries
a day when you remember something special that happened on the same day in the past

announce verb announces, announcing, announced
When you announce something, you tell everyone about it. *Tomorrow we will announce the winner of the competition.*

annoy verb annoys, annoying, annoyed
If something annoys you, it makes you angry.
annoying adverb If something is annoying, it makes you angry. *Sometimes little brothers can be very annoying!*

annual noun *plural* annuals
a book with cartoons, stories, and jokes that comes out once a year

annual adjective
An annual event happens once every year. *We have an annual school outing in June.*

another determiner, pronoun
one more *Can I have another biscuit, please? Would you like another?*

answer noun plural answers
something you say or write to someone who has asked you a question *I don't know the answer to that question*

answer verb answers, answering, answered
When you answer someone, you say something to them after they have asked you a question. *I can answer the question.*

ant noun plural ants
Ants are tiny insects that live in large groups.

antelope noun plural antelopes
a wild animal that looks like a deer and lives in Africa and parts of Asia

anthology noun plural anthologies
a collection of poems or stories in a book

anticlockwise adverb
If something moves anticlockwise, it moves round in a circle in the opposite direction to the hands of a clock.

antique noun plural antiques
something that is very old and worth money

antiseptic noun plural antiseptics
An antiseptic is a chemical that kills germs.

antonym noun plural antonyms
a word that means the opposite to another word *Cold is an antonym of hot.*

anxious adjective
If you are anxious, you feel worried.

any determiner, pronoun
1 some *Have you got any orange juice?*
2 no special one *Take any book you want.*

anybody, anyone pronoun
any person *I didn't see anybody at the park.*

anything pronoun
any thing *I can't see anything in the dark.*

anywhere adverb
in any place *I can't find my book anywhere.*

apart adverb
If you keep things apart, you keep them away from each other. *We have to keep the ducks and hens apart.*

ape noun plural apes
An ape is an animal like a large monkey with long arms and no tail. Gorillas and chimpanzees are types of ape.

apex noun plural apexes
the highest point of something

apologize verb apologizes, apologizing, apologized
When you apologize, you say that you are sorry.

apology noun
You say or write an apology when you are sorry for something you have done. *I think I owe you an apology.*

A
B
C
D
E
F
G
H
I
J
K
L
M
N
O
P
Q
R
S
T
U
V
W
X
Y
Z

apostrophe noun *plural* apostrophes
(say a-**poss**-trof-ee)
a mark like this ' that you use in writing

apparatus noun
the special equipment that you use to do something

appear verb appears, appearing, appeared
1 When something appears, it comes into view and you can see it.
2 to seem *This appears to be the wrong key.*

appearance noun
1 Your appearance is what you look like. *You shouldn't worry so much about your appearance.*
2 when something appears *The audience cheered after the appearance of the band on the stage.*

appendix noun
1 *plural* appendixes Your appendix is a small tube inside your body.
2 *plural* appendices an extra section at the end of a book

appetite noun *plural* appetites
If you have an appetite, you feel hungry. *I'm not hungry. I've lost my appetite.*

applaud verb applauds, applauding, applauded
When people applaud, they clap to show that they are pleased. *The audience applauded politely.*

apple noun *plural* apples
a round, crisp, juicy fruit

appreciate verb appreciates, appreciating, appreciated (say a-**pree**-shee-ate)
If you appreciate something, you feel glad because you have it. *You don't seem to appreciate all your toys.*

approach verb approaches, approaching, approached
To approach means to get nearer to something or someone.

approve verb approves, approving, approved
If you approve of something, you think that it is good or suitable.

approximate adjective
An approximate amount is almost correct, but not exact. *The approximate time of arrival is two o'clock.*

April noun
the fourth month of the year

apron noun *plural* aprons
something that you wear over your clothes to keep them clean when you are cooking or painting

aquarium noun *plural* aquariums
a large glass tank for keeping fish and other sea animals in

arch noun *plural* arches
a curved part of a bridge or building

architect noun *plural* architects
(say **ar**-kee-tect)
a person who draws plans for new buildings

area noun *plural* areas
1 An area is a piece of land. *There's a play area behind the library.*
2 When you measure the area of something, you measure how big it is.

argue verb argues, arguing, argued
When people argue, they talk in an angry way to each other because they do not agree with each other. *We always argue about who should tidy our room.*

arithmetic noun
When you do arithmetic, you do sums with numbers.

arm noun *plural* arms
1 Your arms are the long parts of your body that are joined to your shoulders. Your hands are on the ends of your arms.
2 Arms are weapons.

armour noun
metal clothes that soldiers and knights wore in battles long ago

army noun *plural* armies
a large group of people who are trained to fight on land in a war

around adverb, preposition
all round *We spent the afternoon wandering around town.*

arrange verb arranges, arranging, arranged
1 When you arrange things, you put them somewhere neatly so that they look nice or are in the right position. *She arranged the books into two neat piles.*
2 If you arrange something, you make plans so that it will happen. *We arranged to meet at two o'clock.*

arrest verb arrests, arresting, arrested
When the police arrest someone, they take them prisoner.

arrive verb arrives, arriving, arrived
When you arrive somewhere, you get there at the end of a journey.

arrow noun *plural* arrows
a stick with a pointed end, which you shoot from a bow

art noun
drawing and painting

article noun *plural* articles
1 a thing or an object
2 a piece of writing in a newspaper or magazine
3 (in grammar) The words *a*, *an*, and *the* are articles.

artificial adjective (say ar-tee-**fish**-al)
Something that is artificial is not real, but has been made by people or machines. *She thought the artificial flowers looked just like real ones.*

a
b
c
d
e
f
g
h
i
j
k
l
m
n
o
p
q
r
s
t
u
v
w
x
y
z

A
B
C
D
E
F
G
H
I
J
K
L
M
N
O
P
Q
R
S
T
U
V
W
X
Y
Z

artist noun *plural* artists
someone who draws or paints pictures

as conjunction
1 when *I fell over as I was coming downstairs.*
2 because *As it's cold, I think you should put a coat on.*

ashamed adjective
If you feel ashamed, you feel sorry and guilty because you have done something bad.

ask verb asks, asking, asked
1 If you ask someone a question, you say it to them so that they will tell you the answer.
2 If you ask for something, you say that you want it.

asleep adjective
When you are asleep, you are sleeping.

assembly noun *plural* assemblies
the time when the whole school meets together

assistant noun *plural* assistants
1 someone whose job is to help an important person
2 someone who serves customers in a shop

asthma noun (say ass-ma)
Someone who has asthma sometimes finds it difficult to breathe.

astonish verb astonishes, astonishing, astonished
If something astonishes you, it surprises you a lot.

astronaut noun *plural* astronauts
someone who travels in space

at preposition
1 in a place *Tom is at home.*
2 when it is a particular time *I'll meet you at two o'clock.*

ate verb a past tense of eat

athlete noun *plural* athletes
someone who does athletics

athletics noun
sports in which people run, jump, and throw things

atlas noun *plural* atlases
a book of maps

atmosphere noun (say **at**-moss-fere)
the air around the earth

atom noun *plural* **atoms** (in science)
one of the very tiny parts that everything is made up of

attach verb **attaches, attaching, attached**
If you attach things together, you join or fasten them together.

attachment noun
plural **attachments**
a file that you send to someone with an email

attack verb **attacks, attacking, attacked**
To attack someone means to fight them and hurt them.

attempt verb **attempts, attempting, attempted**
When you attempt to do something, you try to do it.

attend verb **attends, attending, attended**
If you attend school, you go to school. If you attend an event, you go to watch it.

attention noun
1 When you pay attention, you listen carefully to what someone is saying, or watch what they are doing.
2 When soldiers stand to attention, they stand with their feet together and their arms by their sides.

attic noun *plural* **attics**
a room inside the roof of a house

attract verb **attracts, attracting, attracted**
1 If something attracts you, you feel interested in it. *A sudden noise attracted my attention.*

2 To attract something means to make it come nearer. *A magnet will attract some types of metal.*

attractive adjective
An attractive thing is pleasant to look at. An attractive person is beautiful or handsome.

audience noun *plural* **audiences**
all the people who have come to a place to see or hear something

August noun
the eighth month of the year

aunt, aunty noun *plural* **aunts, aunties**
Your aunt is the sister of your mother or father, or your uncle's wife.

author noun *plural* **authors**
someone who writes books or stories

autobiography noun *plural* **autobiographies**
(say or-toe-by-**og**-ra-fee)
a book that tells the story of the writer's own life

autograph noun *plural* **autographs**
(say **or**-toe-graf)
When a famous person gives you their autograph, they write their name down for you to keep.

automatic adjective
Something that is automatic works on its own, without a person controlling it.

autumn noun
the time of the year when leaves fall off the trees and it gets colder

available adjective
If something is available, it is there for you to use or buy. *Do you have tennis rackets available for hire?*

a
b
c
d
e
f
g
h
i
j
k
l
m
n
o
p
q
r
s
t
u
v
w
x
y
z

avalanche noun *plural* avalanches
a large amount of snow or rock that slides suddenly down a mountain

avenue noun *plural* avenues
a wide road in a town or city

average adjective
ordinary or usual *What's the average height in your class?*

avoid verb avoids, avoiding, avoided
If you avoid something, you keep away from it. *Rachel didn't speak to me today. I think she's avoiding me.*

awake adjective
When you are awake, you are not sleeping.

award noun *plural* awards
a prize *The girls were presented with an award for their bravery.*

aware adjective
If you are aware of something, you know about it. *I was aware of somebody watching me.*

away adverb
1 not here *Ali is away today.*
2 to another place *Put your books away now.*

awful adjective
Something that is awful is horrible or very bad. *Your coat's in an awful mess.* — Dick King-Smith, *The Sheep-Pig*

awkward adjective
1 Something that is awkward is difficult to do or difficult to use. *The bags were big and awkward to carry.*
2 If you feel awkward, you feel embarrassed.

axe noun *plural* axes
a sharp tool for chopping wood

Bb

baby noun *plural* babies
a very young child

back noun *plural* backs
1 Your back is the part of your body that is between your neck and your bottom.
2 An animal's back is the long part of its body between its head and its tail.
3 The back of something is the part opposite the front. *We sat in the back of the car.*

back adverb
If you go back to a place, you go there again. *He ran back home.*

background noun
The background in a picture is everything that you can see behind the main thing in the picture.

backwards adverb
1 towards the place that is behind you *She fell over backwards.*
2 in the opposite way to usual *Can you count backwards?*

bad adjective worse, worst
1 Something that is bad is nasty or horrible. *We couldn't go out because of the bad weather.*
2 A bad person does things that are against the law.

badge noun *plural* badges
a small thing that you pin or sew on to your clothes

badger noun *plural* badgers
A badger is an animal that digs holes in the ground. It has a white face with black stripes on it.

badly adverb
1 If you do something badly, you do not do it very well.
2 If you are badly hurt or upset, you are hurt or upset a lot.

badminton noun
a game in which people use a racket to hit a very light cone called a shuttlecock over a net

bag noun *plural* bags
something that you use for carrying things in

Baisakhi noun (say by-sa-ki)
a Sikh festival which takes place in April

bake verb bakes, baking, baked
When you bake food, you cook it in an oven.

baker noun *plural* bakers
someone whose job is to make or sell bread and cakes

balance noun *plural* balances
1 A balance is a pair of scales that you use for weighing things.

2 If you have good balance, you can hold your body steady and not fall over.

3 If a piece of writing has balance, it puts forward both sides of an argument, not just one side of it.

balance verb balances, balancing, balanced
1 When you balance, you hold your body steady and do not fall over.
2 If you balance something, you put it somewhere carefully so that it does not fall. *He balanced a coin on the end of his finger.*

balcony noun *plural* balconies
1 a small platform outside an upstairs window of a building, where people can stand or sit
2 the seats upstairs in a cinema or theatre

bald adjective
someone who has no hair on their head

ball noun *plural* balls
1 a round object that you hit, kick, or throw in games
2 a big party where people wear very smart clothes and dance with each other

ballet noun *plural* ballets (say bal-ay)
a type of dancing in which dancers dance on the very tips of their toes

balloon noun *plural* balloons
1 a small, colourful rubber bag that you can fill with air and use for playing with or to decorate a room for a party
2 A hot air balloon is a very big bag that is filled with hot air or gas so that it floats in the sky.

a
b
c
d
e
f
g
h
i
j
k
l
m
n
o
p
q
r
s
t
u
v
w
x
y
z

A
B
C
D
E
F
G
H
I
J
K
L
M
N
O
P
Q
R
S
T
U
V
W
X
Y
Z

ban verb bans, banning, banned
If you ban something, you say that people are not allowed to do it. *They have banned skateboarding in the playground.*

banana noun plural bananas
a long, yellow fruit that grows in hot countries

band noun plural bands
1 a group of people who do something together
2 a group of people who play music together
3 a thin strip of material *We had to wear name bands round our wrists.*

bandage noun plural bandages
a strip of material that you wrap round part of your body if you have hurt it

bang noun plural bangs
a sudden very loud noise

bang verb bangs, banging, banged
1 When you bang something, you hit it hard. *He banged on the window.*
2 When something bangs, it makes a sudden loud noise. *The door banged shut.*

bank noun plural banks
1 A bank is a place where people can keep their money safely. Banks also lend money to people.
2 the ground near the edge of a river or lake *We walked along the bank of the river.*

banner noun plural banners
a long, thin flag with words written on it

bar noun plural bars
1 a long piece of wood or metal *There were bars on the windows to stop people from escaping.*
2 a block of chocolate or soap
3 a place that serves food and drinks at a counter

barbecue noun plural barbecues
1 a party where people sit outside and cook food over a fire
2 a metal frame that you put food on to cook it over a fire outside

barber noun plural barbers
a hairdresser for men and boys

bare adjective barer, barest
1 If a part of your body is bare, it has nothing covering it.
2 If something is bare, it has nothing on it or in it. *The walls of her bedroom were bare.*

bargain noun plural bargains
something that you buy very cheaply, for much less than its usual price

bark noun
the hard covering round the trunk and branches of a tree

bark verb barks, barking, barked
When a dog barks, it makes a loud, rough sound.

barley noun
Barley is a plant that farmers grow. Its seed is used for making food and beer.

bar mitzvah noun plural bar mitzvahs
a celebration for a Jewish boy when he reaches the age of 13

barn noun plural barns
a large building on a farm, where a farmer keeps animals, hay, or grain

barrel noun plural barrels
1 a round, wooden container that beer, wine, or water is kept in
2 The barrel of a gun is the tube that the bullet comes out of.

barrier noun plural barriers
a fence or wall that stops you getting past a place

base noun plural bases
1 The base of an object is the part at the bottom, which it stands on.
2 Someone's base is the main place where they live or work.

basic adjective
Basic things are simple but very important. *You need to learn the basic skills first.*

basin noun plural basins
a large bowl

basket noun plural baskets
A basket is a container that you carry things in. A basket is made of thin strips of straw, plastic, or metal that are twisted or woven together.

basketball noun
A game in which two teams try to score points by bouncing a ball and throwing it into a high net.

bat noun plural bats
1 a small animal with wings that flies and hunts for food at night

2 a piece of wood that you use for hitting a ball in a game
bat verb bats, batting, batted
When you bat in a game, you try to hit the ball with a bat.

bath noun plural baths
(rhymes with *path*)
a large container which you can fill with water to sit in and wash yourself

bathe verb bathes, bathing, bathed
(rhymes with *save*)
1 When you bathe, you go swimming in the sea or a river.
2 If you bathe a part of your body, you wash it gently because it hurts.

bathroom noun plural bathrooms
a room with a bath, washbasin, and toilet

battery noun plural batteries
A battery is an object that contains a store of electricity. You put batteries inside torches and radios to make them work.

battle noun plural battles
a big fight between two groups of people

bawl verb bawls, bawling, bawled
When you bawl, you shout or cry very loudly.

bay noun plural bays
a place on the coast where the land bends inwards and sea fills the space

be *verb* am, are, is / was, were / been, being
1 If you are something, you exist and you are doing something. *I am alive. The dog is in the park. Dad is in the kitchen. I was sitting in the classroom.*
2 You use **be** when something is going to happen. *Football practice is tomorrow. Mum is going to pick me up. We are going to the shops.*
3 You use **be** when you are talking about feeling something. *I am very happy. The teacher was angry that I had forgotten my homework. I have been sad.*

beach *noun* *plural* beaches
an area of sand or pebbles by the edge of the sea

bead *noun* *plural* beads
A bead is a small piece of wood, glass, or plastic with a hole through the middle. You thread beads on a string to make a necklace.

beak *noun* *plural* beaks
A bird's beak is its mouth, which is hard and pointed.

beam *noun* *plural* beams
1 A wooden beam is a long strong piece of wood that supports the floor or roof of a building.
2 A beam of light is a ray of light that shines onto something.

bean *noun* *plural* beans
Beans are the seeds of some plants which you can eat. Sometimes you eat just the seeds, and sometimes you eat the seeds and the pod that they grow in.

bear *noun* *plural* bears
a large wild animal with thick fur and sharp teeth and claws

bear *verb* bears, bearing, bore, borne
1 If something will bear your weight, it will support your body and so you can stand on it safely.
2 If you cannot bear something, you hate it. *I cannot bear to see animals in pain.*

beard *noun* *plural* beards
hair growing on a man's chin *He had white hair and a long, grey beard.*

beat *verb* beats, beating, beaten
1 To beat someone means to hit them hard a lot of times. *It's cruel to beat animals.*
2 If you beat someone, you win a game against them. *Anita always beats me at chess.*
3 When you beat a mixture, you stir it hard. *Dad beat some eggs to make an omelette.*

beat *noun*
the regular rhythm in a piece of music *I like dancing to music with a strong beat.*

beautiful *adjective*
1 Something that is beautiful is very nice to look at, hear, or smell. *What beautiful flowers!*
2 Someone who is beautiful has a lovely face. *He longed to marry the beautiful princess.*

because *conjunction*
for the reason that *My dad was angry because I was late.*

become *verb* becomes, becoming, became, become
to start to be *She became quite upset when we told her about the kitten.*

bed noun plural beds
1 a piece of furniture that you sleep on
2 a piece of ground that you grow flowers or vegetables in *Keep off the flower beds.*
3 the bottom of the sea or a river *The old ship is now resting on the bed of the sea.*

bedroom noun plural bedrooms
a room where you sleep

bee noun plural bees
A bee is an insect that can fly and sting you. Bees use a sweet liquid called nectar from flowers to make honey.

beef noun
meat from a cow

beetle noun plural beetles
an insect with hard, shiny wings

before adverb, conjunction, preposition
1 earlier than *We usually have maths before lunch.*
2 already *Have you been here before?*
3 in front of *The girl vanished before my eyes.*

beg verb begs, begging, begged
If you beg someone to do something, you ask them very strongly to do it. *'Oh Gran, please, please come with us,' Ruby begged.* — Jacqueline Wilson, *Double Act*

begin verb begins, beginning, began, begun
To begin means to start.

behave verb behaves, behaving, behaved
1 The way you behave is the way you speak and do things. *He was behaving very strangely.*
2 If you behave yourself, you are polite and do not do anything that is rude or naughty.

behind adverb, preposition
at the back of *I hid behind the wall.*

belief noun
A belief is something that you believe is true. *He has strong beliefs.*

believe verb believes, believing, believed
If you believe something, you feel sure that it is true. *I don't believe you—I think you're lying!*

bell noun plural bells
a metal object that rings when something hits it

bellow verb bellows, bellowing, bellowed
If you bellow, you shout very loudly.

a b c d e f g h i j k l m n o p q r s t u v w x y z

17

A
B
C
D
E
F
G
H
I
J
K
L
M
N
O
P
Q
R
S
T
U
V
W
X
Y
Z

belong verb belongs, belonging, belonged
1 If something belongs to you, it is yours. *Does this purse belong to you?*
2 If something belongs in a place, it goes there.

below preposition
1 underneath *Can you swim below the surface of the water?*
2 less than *The temperature was below freezing last night.*

belt noun *plural* belts
a band of leather or other material that you wear round your waist

bench noun *plural* benches
a long wooden or stone seat for more than one person

bend verb bends, bending, bent
1 When you bend something, you make it curved and not straight.
2 When you bend down, you lean forward so that your head is nearer to the ground.

bend noun *plural* bends
a part of a road or river that curves round

beneath preposition
underneath *The ship disappeared beneath the waves.*

berry noun *plural* berries
a small, round fruit with seeds in it *You can eat some types of berries.*

beside preposition
at the side of *Dan was standing beside me.*

best adjective
The best person or thing is the one that is better than any other. *Who's the best swimmer in your class?*

better adjective
1 If one thing is better than another, it is more interesting, more useful, or more exciting.
2 If you are better than someone else, you are able to do something more quickly or more successfully.
3 When you are better, you are well again after an illness.

between preposition
1 in the middle of two people or things *I sat between Mum and Dad.*
2 among *Share the money between you.*

beware verb
If you tell someone to beware, you are warning them to be careful.

Bible noun *plural* Bibles
the holy book of the Christian religion

bicycle noun *plural* bicycles
something with two wheels, which you sit on and ride along by pushing pedals round with your feet

big *adjective* bigger, biggest
Something that is big is large and not small.

bike *noun* plural bikes
a bicycle

bill *noun* plural bills
1 a piece of paper that tells you how much money you owe someone
2 a bird's beak

bin *noun* plural bins
a container for putting rubbish in

bind *verb* binds, binding, bound
If you bind things together, you tie them together tightly.

biography *noun* plural biographies
a book that tells the true story of a person's life

biology *noun*
the study of animals and plants

bird *noun* plural birds
any animal with feathers, wings, and a beak

birth *noun*
The birth of a baby is when it leaves its mother's body and is born.

birthday *noun* plural birthdays
the day each year when you remember and celebrate the day you were born

biscuit *noun* plural biscuits
a kind of small, crisp cake

bit *noun* plural bits
a small amount of something *Would you like a bit of chocolate?*

bit *verb* past tense of **bite** *verb*

bite *verb* bites, biting, bit, bitten
When you bite something, you use your teeth to cut it. *Dogs don't like me—they always try to bite me!*

bite *noun*
A bite is a mouthful cut off by biting. *Take a bite from my sandwich.*

bitter *adjective*
If something tastes bitter, it has a nasty sour taste.

black *adjective*
1 Something that is black is the colour of the sky on a very dark night.

BLACK

2 Someone who is black has a skin that is naturally dark in colour.

blackbird *noun* plural blackbirds
A blackbird is a type of bird. The male is black with an orange beak, but the female is brown.

blackboard *noun* plural blackboards
a smooth, dark board that you can write on with chalk

blade *noun* plural blades
1 The blade of a knife or sword is the long, sharp part of it.
2 A blade of grass is one piece of grass.

blame *verb* blames, blaming, blamed
When you blame someone, you say that it is their fault that something bad has happened. *Everyone blamed me for the broken window, but it wasn't my fault!*

blank to blow

blank adjective
A blank piece of paper has nothing written or drawn on it.

blanket noun plural blankets
a thick, warm cover that you put on a bed

blaze noun plural blazes
a large, strong fire

blaze verb blazes, blazing, blazed
When a fire is blazing, it is burning brightly.

blazer noun plural blazers
a type of jacket, especially one that children wear to school as part of their school uniform

bleach verb bleaches, bleaching, bleached
To bleach something means to make it white, or lighter in colour.

bleed verb bleeds, bleeding, bled
If a part of your body is bleeding, blood is coming out of it.

blend verb blends, blending, blended
When you blend things, you mix them together.

blew verb past tense of blow verb

blind adjective
Someone who is blind cannot see.

blind noun plural blinds
a piece of material that you pull down to cover a window

blink verb blinks, blinking, blinked
When you blink, you close your eyes and then open them again quickly.

blister noun plural blisters
A blister is a sore place on your skin that is caused by something rubbing against it. A blister looks like a small lump and has liquid inside it.

blizzard noun plural blizzards
a storm with a lot of snow and wind

block noun plural blocks
1 a thick piece of stone or wood
2 a tall building with lots of flats or offices inside We live in a block of flats near the city centre.

block verb blocks, blocking, blocked
If something is blocking a road or pipe, it is in the way and nothing can get past it. Some parked cars were blocking the road.

blog noun plural blogs
a website on which someone writes regularly about their own life or opinions

blond, blonde adjective
Someone who is blond has fair or light-coloured hair.

blood noun
the red liquid that is pumped round inside your body

blossom noun plural blossoms
the flowers on a tree

blot noun plural blots
a spot of ink that has been spilt on something

blouse noun plural blouses
a shirt that a woman or girl wears

blow noun plural blows
If you receive a blow, someone hits you hard.

blow verb blows, blowing, blew, blown
1 When you blow, you make air come out of your mouth.
2 When the wind blows, it moves along.

blue adjective
Something that is blue is the colour of the sky on a fine day.

BLUE

blunt adjective blunter, bluntest
Something that is blunt is not sharp. *This knife is too blunt to cut anything.*

blur noun plural blurs
If something is a blur, you cannot see it clearly.

blurb noun plural blurbs
a short piece of writing about a book, which tells you what the book is about and why it is good

Blu-ray noun
(trademark) a round, flat disc on which films are stored. When you watch a Blu-ray film, the picture is very clear and colourful.

blush verb blushes, blushing, blushed
When you blush, your face goes red because you feel shy or guilty.

board noun plural boards
a flat piece of wood

board verb boards, boarding, boarded
When you board an aeroplane, bus, ship, or train, you get onto it.

boast verb boasts, boasting, boasted
If you boast, you talk about how clever you are or how well you can do things.

boat noun plural boats
a vehicle that floats on water and can carry people and goods over water

body noun plural bodies
1 Your body is every part of you that you can see and touch.
2 A body is a dead person.

bog noun plural bogs
a piece of soft, wet ground

boil verb boils, boiling, boiled
1 When water boils, it bubbles and gives off steam because it is very hot. *Is the water boiling yet?*
2 When you boil something, you cook it in boiling water. *Boil the pasta for about six minutes.*

bold adjective bolder, boldest
1 Someone who is bold is brave and not afraid.
2 Bold writing is dark like **this** and easy to see.

bolt noun plural bolts
1 a piece of metal that you slide across to lock a door
2 A bolt is a thick metal pin that looks like a screw with a blunt end. You screw a bolt into a nut to fasten something.

bolt verb bolts, bolting, bolted
1 When you bolt a door or window, you lock it with a bolt. *Remember to bolt the back door.*
2 If you bolt, you run away suddenly. *There was a sudden crash of thunder which made all the horses bolt.*

a b c d e f g h i j k l m n o p q r s t u v w x y z

A
B
C
D
E
F
G
H
I
J
K
L
M
N
O
P
Q
R
S
T
U
V
W
X
Y
Z

bomb noun *plural* bombs
a weapon that explodes and hurts people or damages things

bone noun *plural* bones
Your bones are the hard white parts inside your body. Your skeleton is made of bones.

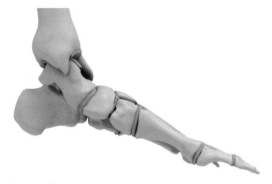

bonfire noun *plural* bonfires
a large fire that you make outside, especially to burn rubbish

bonnet noun *plural* bonnets
the part of a car that covers the engine

book noun *plural* books
A set of pages that are joined together inside a cover. You can read a book.

book verb books, booking, booked
When you book something, you arrange for it to be reserved for you. *Dad's booked seats for the cinema tonight.*

boot noun *plural* boots
1 a type of shoe that also covers your ankle and part of your leg

2 the part of a car that you carry luggage in

border noun *plural* borders
1 the place where two countries meet *You need a passport to cross the border.*
2 a narrow strip along the edge of something *On the table was a white tablecloth with a blue border.*

bore verb bores, boring, bored
1 If something bores you, you find it dull and not interesting. *These silly games bore me to death!*
2 If you bore a hole in something, you make a hole.
3 past tense of bear **verb**

born adjective
When a baby is born, it comes out of its mother's body and starts to live.

borrow verb borrows, borrowing, borrowed
When you borrow something, you take it and use it for a while and then give it back. *Can I borrow your pen?*

boss noun *plural* bosses (informal)
the person who is in charge

both determiner, pronoun
the two of them *Hold the camera in both hands.*

bother verb bothers, bothering, bothered
1 If something bothers you, it worries you or annoys you. *Does this loud piano music bother you?*
2 If you do not bother to do something, you do not do it because it would take too much effort. *Joe never bothers to answer his text messages.*

bottle noun *plural* bottles
a tall glass or plastic container that you keep liquids in

bottom noun *plural* bottoms
The bottom of something is the lowest part of it. *The others waited for us at the bottom of the hill.*

bought verb past tense of buy

boulder noun *plural* boulders
(say **bole**-der)
a large rock

bounce verb bounces, bouncing, bounced
When something bounces, it springs back into the air when it hits something hard.

bound verb bounds, bounding, bounded
When you bound, you run and jump. *Babe bounded up the hill.* — Dick King-Smith, *The Sheep Pig*

bound adjective
If something is bound to happen, it will definitely happen. *We've got the best team, so we're bound to win.*

bound verb past tense of bind

boundary noun *plural* boundaries
a line that marks the edge of a piece of land

bow noun *plural* bows
(rhymes with *go*)
1 a knot with large loops *She tied the ribbon into a bow.*
2 a weapon that you use for shooting arrows *The men were armed with bows and arrows.*

bow verb bows, bowing, bowed
(rhymes with *cow*)
When you bow, you bend forwards to show respect to someone or to thank people for clapping.

bowl verb bowls, bowling, bowled
When you bowl in a game of cricket, you throw the ball for someone else to hit.

box noun *plural* boxes
a container with straight sides, made of cardboard or plastic

box verb boxes, boxing, boxed
When people box, they fight by hitting each other with their fists.

boy noun *plural* boys
a male child

bracelet noun *plural* bracelets
a piece of jewellery that you wear round your wrist

bracket noun *plural* brackets
Brackets are marks like these ( ) that you use in writing.

Braille noun
Braille is a way of writing that uses a pattern of raised dots on paper. Blind people can read Braille by touching the dots with their fingers.

a
b
c
d
e
f
g
h
i
j
k
l
m
n
o
p
q
r
s
t
u
v
w
x
y
z

A
B
C
D
E
F
G
H
I
J
K
L
M
N
O
P
Q
R
S
T
U
V
W
X
Y
Z

brain noun *plural* brains

Your brain is the part inside your head that controls your body and allows you to think and remember things.

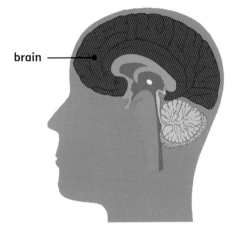

brain

brainy adjective brainier, brainiest

Someone who is brainy is very clever. *Samir is the brainy one in our family.*

brake noun *plural* brakes

the part of a car or bicycle that makes it slow down and stop

branch noun *plural* branches

a part that grows out from the trunk of a tree

brass noun

Brass is a yellow metal.

brave adjective braver, bravest

Someone who is brave is willing to do dangerous things. *I knew I had to be brave and try to rescue my friends.*

bread noun

a food that is made from flour and water, and baked in the oven

breadth noun

The breadth of something is how wide it is. *We measured the length and breadth of the field.*

break verb breaks, breaking, broke, broken

1 If you break something, you smash it into several pieces.
2 If you break something, you damage it so that it no longer works. *Someone's broken my MP3 player.*
3 If you break a law or a promise, you do something that goes against it. *You should never break a promise.*
4 If something breaks down, it stops working. *Our bus broke down on the motorway.*

break noun *plural* breaks

1 a gap in something *We managed to escape through a break in the hedge.*
2 a short rest *We'll have a short break before we continue.*

breakfast noun *plural* breakfasts

the first meal of the day, which you eat in the morning

breast noun *plural* breasts

1 A woman's breasts are the parts on the front of her body that can produce milk to feed a baby.
2 The breast on a chicken or other bird is its chest.

breath noun *plural* breaths

the air that you take into your body and then blow out again *I took a deep breath and dived into the water.*

breathe verb breathes, breathing, breathed

When you breathe, you take air into your lungs through your nose or mouth and then blow it out again.

breed noun *plural* breeds

a particular type of animal *Poodles are my favourite breed of dog.*

breeze noun *plural* breezes
a gentle wind

brick noun *plural* bricks
A brick is a small block made from baked clay. People use bricks for building houses.

bride noun *plural* brides
a woman who is getting married

bridegroom noun *plural* bridegrooms
a man who is getting married

bridesmaid noun *plural* bridesmaids
a girl or woman who walks behind the bride at her wedding

bridge noun *plural* bridges
something that is built over a river, railway, or road so that people can go across it

brief adjective briefer, briefest
Something that is brief is short and does not last very long. *We only had time for a brief visit.*

briefcase noun *plural* briefcases
a small case that you carry books and papers in

bright adjective brighter, brightest
1 A bright light shines with a lot of light.
2 A bright colour is strong and not dull. *Alice was wearing a bright red T-shirt.*
3 A bright day is sunny. *It was a lovely, bright, sunny day.*

4 Someone who is bright is clever and learns things quickly.
brightly adverb If something shines brightly, it has a lot of light. *The sun shone brightly.*
brightness noun when something is bright *They saw the blinding brightness of the sun.*

brilliant adjective
1 Someone who is brilliant is very clever, or very good at something. *Adam's a brilliant footballer.*
2 Something that is brilliant is very good. *We saw a brilliant film yesterday.*

brim noun *plural* brims
1 the edge round the top of a container *Her cup was filled to the brim.*
2 the part of a hat that sticks out round the bottom edge

bring verb brings, bringing, brought
1 If you bring something with you, you carry it with you. *Don't forget to bring your swimming costume.*
2 If you bring someone with you, they come with you. *Can I bring a friend with me?*

brittle adjective
Something that is brittle is hard and dry and will break easily.

broad adjective broader, broadest
Something that is broad is wide. *At the bottom of the field was a broad river.*

broadcast verb broadcasts, broadcasting, broadcast
To broadcast something means to send it out as a television or radio programme. *The match will be broadcast live on television.*

broke, broken verb past tense of break

brooch noun *plural* brooches (say broach)
a piece of jewellery that you pin to your clothes

a
b
c
d
e
f
g
h
i
j
k
l
m
n
o
p
q
r
s
t
u
v
w
x
y
z

25

A B C D E F G H I J K L M N O P Q R S T U V W X Y Z

broom noun *plural* **brooms**
a brush with a long handle that you use for sweeping floors

brother noun *plural* **brothers**
Your brother is a boy who has the same parents as you.

brought verb past tense of **bring**

brown adjective
1 Something that is brown is the colour of soil.

BROWN

2 Brown bread is made with the whole wheat grain, not just the white part.

bruise noun *plural* **bruises** (say **brooze**)
a dark mark on your skin that you get when you have been hit

brush noun *plural* **brushes**
A brush is an object with short, stiff hairs on the end of a handle. You use a brush for cleaning things, and you also use a brush for painting.

brush verb **brushes, brushing, brushed**
When you brush something, you clean it using a brush.

bubble noun *plural* **bubbles**
Bubbles are small balls of air or gas inside a liquid, for example like the ones you find in fizzy drinks.

bubble verb **bubbles, bubbling, bubbled**
When a liquid bubbles, it makes bubbles.

bucket noun *plural* **buckets**
a container with a handle that you use for carrying water

buckle noun *plural* **buckles**
the part of a belt that you use to fasten the two ends together

bud noun *plural* **buds**
a small lump on a plant that will later open into a flower or leaf

Buddhist noun *plural* **Buddhists**
someone who follows the **Buddhist** religion and follows the teachings of the Buddha

bug noun *plural* **bugs**
1 an insect
2 a germ that gets into your body and makes you ill
3 a problem in a computer program that makes it go wrong

build verb **builds, building, built**
When you build something, you make it by joining or fixing different parts together. *It took nearly three years to build this bridge.*

builder noun *plural* **builders**
A builder is someone who builds houses and other buildings.

building noun *plural* **buildings**
a structure like a house, school, shop, or church

bulb noun *plural* **bulbs**
1 the part of an electric lamp that gives out light
2 A bulb is a part of a plant that grows under the ground and looks like an onion.

bulge verb **bulges, bulging, bulged**
If something bulges, it sticks out because it is so full. *His pockets were bulging with sweets.*

bull noun *plural* **bulls**
a male cow, elephant, or whale

bulldozer noun *plural* **bulldozers**
a heavy machine that moves earth and makes land flat

bullet noun *plural* **bullets**
a small piece of metal that is fired from a gun

bully verb **bullies, bullying, bullied**
To bully someone means to hurt them or be unkind to them.

bully noun *plural* **bullies**
someone who hurts other people or is unkind to them

bump verb **bumps, bumping, bumped**
If you bump something, you knock it or hit it. *I bumped my head on the shelf.*

bump noun *plural* **bumps**
1 the noise that something makes when it falls to the ground *The book fell to the ground with a bump.*
2 a small lump on your skin that you get when you have knocked it

bumper noun *plural* **bumpers**
A bumper is a bar along the front or back of a car. The bumper protects the car if it hits something.

bun noun *plural* **buns**
1 a small, round cake
2 a round piece of bread

bunch noun *plural* **bunches**
a group of things that are tied together *What a lovely bunch of flowers!*

bundle noun *plural* **bundles**
a group of things that are tied together *She was carrying a bundle of old clothes.*

bungalow noun *plural* **bungalows**
a house without any upstairs rooms

bunk noun *plural* **bunks**
a bed that has another bed above or below it *Can I sleep in the top bunk?*

burger noun *plural* **burgers**
a piece of minced meat that has been made into a round, flat cake and cooked

burglar noun *plural* **burglars**
someone who goes into a building and steals things

burn verb **burns, burning, burned, burnt**
1 When something burns, it catches fire.
2 If you burn something, you damage it or destroy it using fire or heat. *We burnt all our rubbish on a bonfire.*
3 If you burn yourself, you hurt your skin with fire or heat. *Be careful you don't burn in the hot sun.*

a
b
c
d
e
f
g
h
i
j
k
l
m
n
o
p
q
r
s
t
u
v
w
x
y
z

burrow noun *plural* **burrows**
a hole in the ground that an animal lives in

burst verb **bursts, bursting, burst**
if something bursts, it suddenly breaks open
Don't blow the balloons up too much or they'll burst.

bury verb **buries, burying, buried**
(rhymes with *merry*)
1 When you bury something, you put it in a hole in the ground and cover it over.
2 When a dead person is buried, their body is put into the ground.

bus noun *plural* **buses**
a vehicle that a lot of people can travel in

bush noun *plural* **bushes**
a plant that looks like a small tree

business noun *plural* **businesses**
(say **bizz**-niss)
1 When people do business, they buy and sell things.
2 a shop or company that makes or sells things *My uncle runs his own business making sports equipment.*

busy adjective **busier, busiest**
1 If you are busy, you have a lot of things to do.
2 A busy place has a lot of people and traffic in it.

but conjunction
however *We wanted to play outside, but we couldn't because it was raining.*

butcher noun *plural* **butchers**
someone who cuts up meat and sells it in a shop

butter noun
Butter is a yellow food that is made from milk.

butterfly noun *plural* **butterflies**
an insect with large colourful wings

button noun *plural* **buttons**
1 a small round thing that you use to fasten clothes by pushing it through a small hole in the clothes

2 a part of a machine that you press to switch it on or off

buy verb **buys, buying, bought**
When you buy something, you get it by giving someone money for it.

buzz verb **buzzes, buzzing, buzzed**
When something buzzes, it makes a sound like a bee.

by preposition
1 near *You can leave your shoes by the front door.*
2 travelling in *We're going by train.*

A B C D E F G H I J K L M N O P Q R S T U V W X Y Z

Cc

cab noun *plural* cabs
1 a taxi
2 the part at the front of a lorry, bus, or train where the driver sits

cabbage noun *plural* cabbages
a round, green vegetable with a lot of leaves that are wrapped tightly round each other

cabin noun *plural* cabins
1 a room for passengers in a ship or an aeroplane
2 a small hut

cable noun *plural* cables
1 strong, thick wire or rope
2 A cable is a bundle of wires that are held together in a plastic covering. They carry electricity or television signals.

cactus noun *plural* cacti
A cactus is a plant with a thick, green stem that has no leaves but is covered in prickles.

cafe noun *plural* cafes (say **kaff**-ay)
a place where you can buy a drink or food and sit down to eat or drink it

cage noun *plural* cages
a box or small room with bars across it for keeping animals or birds in

cake noun *plural* cakes
a sweet food that you make with flour, fat, eggs, and sugar and bake in the oven

calculate verb calculates, calculating, calculated
When you calculate an amount, you do a sum and work out how many or how much it is. *If a bar of chocolate has five rows of three blocks, how many blocks are there?*

$$5 \times 3 = ?$$

calculator noun *plural* calculators
a machine that you use to do sums

calendar noun *plural* calendars
A calendar is a list of all the days, weeks, and months in a year. You can write on a calendar things that you are going to do each day.

calf noun *plural* calves
1 a young cow, elephant, or whale
2 Your calf is the back part of your leg between your knee and your ankle.

call verb calls, calling, called
1 When you call to someone, you speak loudly so that they can hear you. *'Look out!' he called.*
2 When you call someone, you tell them to come to you. *Mum called us in for tea.*
3 When you call someone a name, you give them that name. *We decided to call the puppy Patch.*
4 When you call someone, you telephone them. *I'll call you later.*

a
b
c
d
e
f
g
h
i
j
k
l
m
n
o
p
q
r
s
t
u
v
w
x
y
z

29

calm adjective calmer, calmest
1 If the sea or the weather is calm, it is still and not stormy. *It was a lovely calm day.*
2 If you are calm, you are quiet and not noisy or excited. *He told everyone to stay calm and not panic.*

camel noun plural camels
A camel is a big animal with one or two humps on its back.

camera noun plural cameras
a machine that you use for taking photographs

camouflage verb camouflages, camouflaging, camouflaged
If something is camouflaged, it is hidden because it looks very like the things around it.

camp noun plural camps
a place where people stay for a short time in tents or small huts

camp verb camps, camping, camped
When you camp, you sleep in a tent.

can noun plural cans
a tin with food or drink in

can verb could
If you can do something, you are able to do it. *Can you swim?*

canal noun plural canals
a river that people have made for boats to travel on

cancel verb cancels, cancelling, cancelled
When you cancel something that was arranged, you say that it will not happen. *The chess club was cancelled this week because the teacher was ill.*

candle noun plural candles
A candle is a stick of wax with string through the centre. You light the string and it burns slowly to give you light.

cane noun plural canes
a long, thin stick made of wood

cannot verb
can not *I cannot understand what you are saying.*

canoe noun plural canoes (say ka-**noo**)
a light, narrow boat that you sit in and paddle along

can't verb
can not *I can't read your writing.*

canvas noun
a type of strong cloth that is used for making tents and sails

cap noun plural caps
1 a soft hat with a stiff part that sticks out at the front, over your eyes
2 a lid for a bottle or other container

capable adjective
If you are capable of doing something, you can do it. *You're capable of much better work than this.*

capacity noun *plural* capacities
The capacity of a container is the amount that it can hold.

capital noun *plural* capitals
A country's capital is its most important city. *London is the capital of England.*

capital letter noun
plural capital letters
Capital letters are the big letters you put at the beginning of names and sentences. A, B, C, D, and so on are capital letters.

captain noun *plural* captains
1 The captain of a ship or aeroplane is the person in charge of it.
2 The captain of a team is the person in charge of it, who tells the others what to do.

caption noun *plural* captions
words that are printed next to a picture and tell you what the picture is about

capture verb captures, capturing, captured
To capture someone means to catch them. *My grandfather was captured by enemy soldiers during the war.*

car noun *plural* cars
something that you can drive along in on roads

caravan noun *plural* caravans
a small house on wheels that can be pulled from place to place

carbon noun
Carbon is the substance that is found in soot and coal.

carbon footprint noun
Your carbon footprint is the effect that the carbon that is released from something has on the environment. *You have to work out the size of your family's carbon footprint and find ways to reduce it.*

card noun *plural* cards
1 Card is thick, stiff paper.
2 A card is a piece of card with a picture and a message on it. You send cards to people at special times like their birthday or Christmas.
3 Cards are small pieces of card with numbers or pictures on them, that you use to play games.

cardboard noun
very thick, strong paper

cardigan noun *plural* cardigans
a knitted jumper that has buttons down the front

care noun *plural* cares
1 If you take care when you are doing something, you do it carefully.
2 If you take care of someone, you look after them.

care verb cares, caring, cared
1 If you care about something, it is important to you. *I don't care where I sit.*
2 If you care for someone, you look after them.

careful adjective
If you are careful, you make sure that you do things safely and well so that you do not have an accident
carefully adverb If you do something carefully, you make sure that you do it safely and well so that you do not have an accident. *He picked the eggs up carefully.*

a
b
c
d
e
f
g
h
i
j
k
l
m
n
o
p
q
r
s
t
u
v
w
x
y
z

A B C D E F G H I J K L M N O P Q R S T U V W X Y Z

careless adjective

If you are careless, you are not careful and so you make mistakes or have an accident.

caretaker noun plural caretakers

someone whose job is to look after a building

carnival noun plural carnivals

A carnival is a large party that takes place in the streets.

carpenter noun plural carpenters

someone whose job is to make things out of wood

carpet noun plural carpets

a thick, soft material that is put on a floor to cover it

carriage noun plural carriages

1 The carriages on a train are the parts where people sit.
2 something that is pulled by horses for people to travel in

carrot noun plural carrots

a long, thin, orange vegetable

carry verb carries, carrying, carried

1 When you carry something, you hold it in your hands or arms and take it somewhere.

2 If you carry on doing something, you keep doing it. *I called to Rosie, but she carried on walking.*

cart noun plural carts

A cart is a wooden vehicle that you can put things in to take them somewhere.

carton noun plural cartons

a small plastic or cardboard box in which food or drink is sold

cartoon noun plural cartoons

1 a funny drawing that makes people laugh

2 a film that has drawings instead of real people

cartwheel noun plural cartwheels

When you do a cartwheel, you put your hands on the ground and swing your legs into the air in a circle.

carve verb carves, carving, carved

1 When you carve something, you make it by cutting wood or stone into the right shape.
2 When you carve meat, you cut slices from it.

case noun plural cases

1 a box for keeping things in
2 a suitcase

cash noun

money

cast verb casts, casting, cast

1 To cast something means to throw it.
2 To cast a spell on someone means to say a spell that will affect them.

castle noun *plural* castles
a large, strong building with thick, stone walls

cat noun *plural* cats
A cat is a furry animal that people often keep as a pet. Lions, tigers, and leopards are large, wild cats.

catalogue noun *plural* catalogues
a list of all the things that you can buy from a place, sometimes with pictures of the things

catch verb catches, catching, caught
1 If you catch something that is moving through the air, you get hold of it. *Try to catch the ball.*
2 To catch someone means to find them and take them prisoner. *The police finally caught the bank robbers.*
3 If you catch an illness, you get it.
4 When you catch a bus or train, you get on it.

caterpillar noun *plural* caterpillars
a small animal that looks like a worm and will turn into a butterfly or moth

cathedral noun *plural* cathedrals
a big, important church

cattle noun
cows and bulls

caught verb past tense of catch

cause noun *plural* causes
The cause of something is the thing that makes it happen. *We don't know the cause of the explosion yet.*

cause verb causes, causing, caused
To cause something to happen means to make it happen. *The wind caused the door to slam.*

cautious adjective (say **kor**-shuss)
If you are cautious, you are very careful not to do anything that might be dangerous.

cave noun *plural* caves
a big hole in the rock under the ground or inside a mountain

CD noun *plural* CDs
A CD is a round, flat disc on which music or computer information can be stored. CD is short for **compact disc**.

CD-ROM noun *plural* CD-ROMs
A CD-ROM is a round, flat disc on which computer information is stored. CD-ROM is short for **compact disc read-only memory**.

ceiling noun *plural* ceilings
(say **see**-ling)
the part of a room above your head

celebrate verb celebrates, celebrating, celebrated
When you celebrate, you do something special because it is an important day *Hindus and Sikhs celebrate Diwali in October or November.*
celebration noun A celebration is when you do something special on an important day. *Everyone joined in the celebration.*

a
b
c
d
e
f
g
h
i
j
k
l
m
n
o
p
q
r
s
t
u
v
w
x
y
z

33

celebrity noun *plural* celebrities
a famous person

cell noun *plural* cells
1 a small room in which a prisoner is kept in a prison
2 (in science) Cells are the tiny parts that all living things are made of.

cellar noun *plural* cellars
a room underneath a building

Celsius adjective (say **sell**-see-us)
We can measure temperature in degrees Celsius. Water boils at 100 degrees Celsius.

cement noun
the substance that builders use to hold bricks together

cemetery noun *plural* cemeteries
a place where dead people are buried

centigrade adjective
We can measure temperature in degrees centigrade. Water boils at 100 degrees centigrade.

centimetre noun *plural* centimetres
We can measure length in centimetres. There are 100 centimetres in one metre.

centre noun *plural* centres
1 The centre of something is the part in the middle of it. *There was a large table in the centre of the room.*
2 a place where you go to do certain things *Have you been to the new sports centre yet?*

century noun *plural* centuries
a hundred years

cereal noun *plural* cereals
1 Cereals are plants such as wheat and corn that are grown by farmers for their seeds.
2 A breakfast cereal is a food that you eat at breakfast. Cereals are often made from wheat, oats, or rice, and you eat them with milk.

ceremony noun *plural* ceremonies
A ceremony is an event at which something important is announced to people. There is usually a ceremony when people get married, or when someone has died.

certain adjective
If you are certain about something, you are sure that it is true. *Are you certain it was Jessica that you saw?*

certificate noun *plural* certificates
a piece of paper that says you have achieved something

chain noun *plural* chains
a metal rope that is made of a line of metal rings fastened together

chair noun *plural* chairs
a seat for one person to sit on

chalk noun *plural* chalks
1 a type of soft white rock *We could see the white chalk cliffs in the distance.*
2 a white or coloured stick that you use for writing on a blackboard

champion noun *plural* **champions**
the person who has won a game or competition and shown that they are the best

chance noun *plural* **chances**
1 A chance to do something is a time when it is possible for you to do it. *This is our last chance to escape.*
2 When something happens by chance, it just happens, with no one planning or organizing it.

change verb **changes, changing, changed**
1 When you change something, you make it different. *If you don't like your first design, you can always change it.*
2 When something changes, it becomes different. *Caterpillars change into butterflies or moths.*
3 When you change something, you get rid of it, and get a different one instead.

change noun
1 Change is the money you get back when you give too much money to pay for something.
2 *plural* **changes** When there is a change, something becomes different.

channel noun *plural* **channels**
1 a narrow area of sea
2 a television station

chaos noun (say **kay**-oss)
When there is chaos, everything is very confused and no one knows what is happening.

chapter noun *plural* **chapters**
one part of a book

character noun *plural* **characters**
1 a person in a story *Who is your favourite character in the book?*
2 Your character is the sort of person you are. *The twins look the same, but they have very different characters.*

charge noun *plural* **charges**
A charge is the amount of money that you have to pay for something.

charge verb **charges, charging, charged**
1 If you charge money for something, you ask for money.
2 If you charge at someone, you rush at them suddenly. *I was worried the bull might charge at us.*
in charge If you are in charge of something, you have the job of organizing it or looking after it.

charity noun *plural* **charities**
an organization that raises money and uses it to help people who are poor or need help

charm noun *plural* **charms**
1 If someone has charm, they are pleasant and polite and so people like them.
2 a magic spell
3 a small ornament that you wear to bring good luck

chart noun *plural* **charts**
1 a big map
2 a sheet of paper that has rows of numbers or dates on it
the charts a list of the pop songs that are most popular each week

chase verb **chases, chasing, chased**
To chase someone means to run after them and try to catch them.

chat verb chats, chatting, chatted
When people chat, they talk in a friendly way.

chatroom noun plural chatrooms
a place on the Internet where people can have a conversation by sending messages to each other

chatter verb chatters, chattering, chattered
1 If you chatter, you talk a lot about things that are not very important.
2 When your teeth chatter, they bang together because you are cold. *He stood there so long that his teeth would have been chattering with cold if they had not been chattering with fear.* — C. S. Lewis, *The Lion, the Witch and the Wardrobe*

cheap adjective cheaper, cheapest
Something that is cheap does not cost very much money.
cheaply adverb If something is sold cheaply then it does not cost very much money. *They're selling everything really cheaply in the sale.*

cheat verb cheats, cheating, cheated
If you cheat in a game or test, you break the rules so that you can do well.
cheat noun plural cheats
someone who cheats in a game or test

check verb checks, checking, checked
If you check something, you look at it carefully to make sure that it is right.

cheek noun plural cheeks
1 Your cheeks are the sides of your face.
2 Cheek is talking or behaving in a rude way towards someone.

cheeky adjective cheekier, cheekiest
If you are cheeky, you are rude to someone and do not show that you respect them.

cheer verb cheers, cheering, cheered
When you cheer, you shout to show that you are pleased.

cheerful adjective
If you are cheerful, you are happy.

cheese noun plural cheeses
a type of food that is made from milk and has a strong, salty taste

chemist noun plural chemists
someone who makes or sells medicines

chemistry noun
the subject in which you study the substances that things are made of and how these substances behave, for example when they are mixed together

cherry noun plural cherries
a small, round, red fruit with a stone in the middle

chess noun
a game in which two people move special pieces across a black and white board

chest noun plural chests
1 a big, strong box
2 Your chest is the front part of your body between your neck and your waist.

chew verb chews, chewing, chewed
When you chew food, you keep biting on it in your mouth before you swallow it.

chick noun plural chicks
a baby bird

chicken noun *plural* **chickens**
a bird that is kept on farms for its meat and eggs

chickenpox noun
an illness that gives you red itchy spots on your body

chief noun *plural* **chiefs**
a leader who is in charge of other people

child noun *plural* **children**
1 a young boy or girl
2 Someone's child is their son or daughter.

childhood noun *plural* **childhoods**
the time when you are a child

childish adjective
Someone who is childish behaves in a silly way, like a young child

chilly adjective **chillier, chilliest**
If you are chilly, you are slightly cold. If the weather is chilly, it is quite cold.

chime verb **chimes, chiming, chimed**
When a clock or bell chimes, it makes a ringing sound.

chimney noun *plural* **chimneys**
a tall pipe that takes smoke away from a fire inside a building

chimpanzee noun
plural **chimpanzees**
A chimpanzee is an African ape. Chimpanzees look like large monkeys and have long arms and no tail.

chin noun *plural* **chins**
Your chin is the part at the bottom of your face, under your mouth.

chip noun *plural* **chips**
1 Chips are small pieces of fried potato.
2 If there is a chip in something, a small piece of it has broken off.

3 A computer chip is the small electronic part inside it that makes it work.

chip verb **chips, chipping, chipped**
If you chip something, you break a small piece off it.

chocolate noun *plural* **chocolates**
a sweet food that is made from cocoa and sugar

choice noun *plural* **choices**
1 When you make a choice, you choose something. *There were lots of bikes to choose from, and I think I made a good choice.*
2 If there is a choice, there are several different things to choose from. *There's a choice of vanilla, chocolate, or strawberry.*

choir noun *plural* **choirs** (say **kwire**)
a group of people who sing together

choke verb **chokes, choking, choked**
When you choke, you cannot breathe properly.

choose verb **chooses, choosing, chose, chosen**
When you choose something, you decide that it is the one you want.

chop verb **chops, chopping, chopped**
When you chop something, you cut it with a knife or axe.

chop noun *plural* **chops**
a thick slice of pork or lamb with a bone still attached to it

chorus noun *plural* **choruses**
(**ch-** in this word sounds like **k-**)
The chorus is the part of a song or poem that you repeat after each verse.

chorus verb **choruses, chorusing, chorused** (**ch-** in this word sounds like **k-**)
To chorus a word means to all say it at the same time.

a
b
c
d
e
f
g
h
i
j
k
l
m
n
o
p
q
r
s
t
u
v
w
x
y
z

chose, chosen verb
past tense of **choose**

Christian noun *plural* Christians
(**ch-** in this word sounds like **k-**)
someone who follows the **Christian** religion and believes in Jesus Christ

Christmas noun *plural* Christmases
(**ch-** in this word sounds like **k-**)
25 December, when Christians celebrate the birth of Jesus Christ

chrysalis noun *plural* chrysalises
(say **kriss**-a-liss)
the hard cover that a caterpillar makes round itself before it changes into a butterfly or moth

chuckle verb chuckles, chuckling, chuckled
When you chuckle, you laugh quietly to yourself.

church noun *plural* churches
a building where Christians pray and worship

cinema noun *plural* cinemas
a place where people go to watch films

circle noun *plural* circles
a round shape like a ring or a wheel

circle verb circles, circling, circled
To circle means to go round in a circle. *Birds circled around above us.*

circumference noun
plural circumferences
The circumference of a circle is how much it measures round its edge.

circus noun *plural* circuses
a show in which clowns, acrobats, and sometimes animals perform in a large tent

city noun *plural* cities
a big town

claim verb claims, claiming, claimed
1 When you claim something, you say that you want it because it is yours.
2 If you claim that something is true, you say that it is true.

class noun *plural* classes
a group of children who learn things together

classify verb classifies, classifying, classified
When you classify things, you arrange them into different groups depending on what they are like.

classroom noun *plural* classrooms
a room where children have lessons

claw noun *plural* claws
An animal's claws are its sharp nails.

clay noun
Clay is a type of sticky mud that becomes very hard when it dries out. Clay is used for making pots and pottery.

clean adjective cleaner, cleanest
Something that is clean has no dirt on it.

clean verb cleans, cleaning, cleaned
To clean something means to take the dirt off it so that it is clean.

clear adjective clearer, clearest
1 If water or glass is clear, it is not dirty and you can see through it.
2 If a picture or sound is clear, you can see it or hear it easily. *Please speak in a nice, clear voice.*
3 If something is clear, you can understand it. *All this mess has to be tidied up. Is that clear?*
4 If a place is clear, there is nothing blocking it or getting in the way.

clear verb clears, clearing, cleared
To clear a place means to get rid of things that are in the way. *I helped clear the table after dinner.*

clearly adverb If you can see something clearly there is nothing blocking it or getting in the way. *I could see his face quite clearly.*

clench verb clenches, clenching, clenched
When you clench your teeth or fists, you close them tightly.

clever adjective cleverer, cleverest
Someone who is clever learns things quickly and easily.

click verb clicks, clicking, clicked
1 When something clicks, it makes a short sound like the sound a light switch makes.
2 (in ICT) When you click on something on a computer, you move the cursor so that it is on that thing and then you press the button on the mouse.

cliff noun plural cliffs
a steep hill made of rock next to the sea

climate noun plural climates
The climate that a place has is the sort of weather that it has. *India has a very hot climate.*

climb verb climbs, climbing, climbed
1 To climb means to go upwards. *She climbed the stairs slowly.*
2 When you climb, you use your hands and feet to move over things. *They climbed over the rocks.*

cling verb clings, clinging, clung
When you cling to something, you hold on to it very tightly.

clinic noun plural clinics
a place where you can go to see a doctor or nurse

clip noun plural clips
a fastener that you use for keeping things in place

a
b
c
d
e
f
g
h
i
j
k
l
m
n
o
p
q
r
s
t
u
v
w
x
y
z

clip verb clips, clipping, clipped
To clip something means to cut it with scissors or shears.

cloak noun plural cloaks
a piece of clothing that you wrap around your shoulders and fasten round your neck

cloakroom noun plural cloakrooms
the room where you can hang your coat

clock noun plural clocks
a machine that shows you the time

clockwise adverb
If something moves clockwise, it moves round in a circle in the same direction as the hands of a clock.

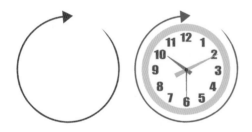

clockwork adjective
A clockwork toy is worked by a spring which you have to wind up.

close adjective closer, closest
(rhymes with *dose*)
1 If you are close to something, you are near it. *Don't get too close to the fire.*
2 If you take a close look at something, or keep a close watch on something, you do it very carefully.

close verb closes, closing, closed
(rhymes with *doze*)
1 To close something means to shut it. *Please can you close the door after you?*
2 When a shop closes, it is no longer open and people cannot go there. *The shop closes at half past five.*
closely adverb If you move closely to something you are near it. *She followed the boys closely as they crossed the road.*

closed adjective
If something is closed, it is not open.

cloth noun
material for making things like clothes and curtains

clothes, clothing noun
the things that you wear to cover your body

cloud noun plural clouds
Clouds are the large grey or white things that sometimes float high in the sky.
cloudy adjective If a sky is cloudy there are lots of clouds. *It was a dull cloudy day.*

clown noun plural clowns
someone in a circus who wears funny clothes and make-up and does silly things to make people laugh

club noun plural clubs
1 a group of people who get together because they are interested in doing the same thing
2 a thick stick that is used as a weapon

clue noun *plural* **clues**
something that helps you to find the answer to a puzzle

clump noun *plural* **clumps**
A clump of trees or bushes is a group of them growing close together.

clumsy adjective **clumsier, clumsiest**
If you are clumsy, you are not careful and so are likely to knock things over or drop things.

clutch verb **clutches, clutching, clutched**
When you clutch something, you hold on to it very tightly. *I staggered to my bedroom and lay on my bed, clutching my tummy.* — Jacqueline Wilson, *Best Friends*

clutter noun
a lot of things in an untidy mess

coach noun *plural* **coaches**
1 a bus that takes people on long journeys
2 The coaches on a train are the carriages where people sit.
3 someone who trains people in a sport

coal noun
Coal is a type of hard, black rock that people burn on fires. Coal is found under the ground.

coarse adjective **coarser, coarsest**
Something that is coarse is rough or hard. *His clothes were made of coarse cloth.*

coast noun *plural* **coasts**
the land that is right next to the sea
We went to the coast last Sunday.

coat noun *plural* **coats**
1 a piece of clothing with sleeves that you wear on top of other clothes to keep warm
2 An animal's coat is the hair or fur that covers its body.
3 A coat of paint is a layer of paint.

cobweb noun *plural* **cobwebs**
a thin, sticky net that a spider spins to catch insects

cockerel noun *plural* **cockerels**
a male chicken

cocoa noun
Cocoa is a brown powder that tastes of chocolate. It is used for making hot chocolate drinks and also for making chocolate cakes and biscuits.

coconut noun *plural* **coconuts**
A coconut is a big, round, hard nut that grows on palm trees. It is brown and hairy on the outside and it has sweet, white flesh inside that you can eat.

cocoon noun *plural* **cocoons**
a covering that some insects spin from silky threads to protect themselves while they are changing into their adult form

cod noun *plural* **cod**
a sea fish that you can eat

code noun *plural* **codes**
a set of signs or letters that you use for sending messages secretly

a b **c** d e f g h i j k l m n o p q r s t u v w x y z

A B **C** D E F G H I J K L M N O P Q R S T U V W X Y Z

coffee noun *plural* coffees
a hot drink that is made by adding hot water to roasted coffee beans that have been ground into a powder

coil verb coils, coiling, coiled
To coil something means to wind it round and round in the shape of a lot of circles.

coin noun *plural* coins
a piece of metal money

cold adjective colder, coldest
1 Something that is cold is not hot. *The sea was really cold!*
2 Someone who is cold is not friendly.

cold noun *plural* colds
an illness that makes you sneeze and gives you a runny nose

collage noun *plural* collages
(say **coll**-arj)
a picture that you make by gluing small pieces of paper and material

collapse verb collapses, collapsing, collapsed
1 If something collapses, it falls down. *Buildings collapsed after the earthquake.*
2 If someone collapses, they fall over because they are ill.

collar noun *plural* collars
1 The collar on a piece of clothing is the part that goes round your neck.
2 a thin band of leather or material that goes round an animal's neck

collect verb collects, collecting, collected
1 If you collect things, you get them and keep them together.
2 When you collect someone, you go to a place and get them. *Mum collected us from school as usual.*
collection adjective A set of things that someone has collected is a collection.

collective noun noun
plural collective nouns (in grammar)
A collective noun is a noun that is the name of a group of things, people, or animals. *Flock* and *herd* are collective nouns.

college noun *plural* colleges
a place where you can go to study after you have left school.

colon noun *plural* colons
a mark like this : that you use in writing

colour noun *plural* colours
Red, green, blue, and yellow are different colours.

column noun *plural* columns
1 a thick stone post that supports or decorates a building
2 a line of numbers or words one below the other

comb noun *plural* combs
A comb is a strip of plastic or metal with a row of thin teeth along it. You use a comb to make your hair neat and tidy.

combine verb combines, combining, combined
When you combine things, you join or mix them together.

come verb comes, coming, came, come
1 To come to a place means to move towards it. *Do you want to come to my house after school?*
2 When something comes, it arrives in a place. *Has the letter come yet?*

comedy noun *plural* comedies
a play, film, or TV programme that is funny and makes you laugh

comet noun *plural* comets
an object that moves around the sun and looks like a bright star with a tail

comfort verb comforts, comforting, comforted
When you comfort someone, you are kind to them and try to make them feel better when they are hurt or upset.

comfortable adjective
1 If something is comfortable, it is pleasant to use or to wear and does not hurt you at all. *The bed was large and very comfortable.*
2 If you are comfortable, you are relaxed and are not in any pain.
comfortably adverb If you are sitting comfortably, you are relaxed and not in pain.

comic adjective
Something that is comic is funny and makes you laugh.

comic noun *plural* comics
1 a magazine for children that has stories told in pictures

2 a person who does funny things to make people laugh

comma noun *plural* commas
a mark like this , that you use in writing

command verb commands, commanding, commanded
If you command someone to do something, you tell them to do it.

common adjective commoner, commonest
Something that is common is normal and ordinary.

common noun noun *plural* common nouns (in grammar)
A common noun is a noun that is the name of a thing. For example, *hat, dog,* and *teacher* are all common nouns.

common sense noun
If you have common sense, you are usually sensible and make the right decisions about what to do and how to behave.

commotion noun
When there is a commotion, people are making a noise and moving about all at once.

communicate verb communicates, communicating, communicated
When people communicate, they talk or write to each other.

compact disc noun
plural compact discs
a CD, a round, flat disc on which music or computer information can be stored

company noun *plural* companies
1 A company is a group of people who make and sell things, or do things together.
2 If you have company, you are not alone.

comparative adjective (in grammar)
The comparative form of an adjective is the part that means more, for example *bigger* is the comparative form of *big*.

a b c d e f g h i j k l m n o p q r s t u v w x y z

A
B
C
D
E
F
G
H
I
J
K
L
M
N
O
P
Q
R
S
T
U
V
W
X
Y
Z

compare verb compares, comparing, compared
When you compare things, you try to see how they are the same and how they are different.

compass noun *plural* compasses
1 an instrument with a needle that always points north

2 A compass is an instrument that you use for drawing circles. It is also called **a pair of compasses**.

competition noun
plural competitions
a game or race that people take part in and try to win

complain verb complains, complaining, complained
If you complain, you say that you are not happy about something or do not like something. *'You didn't wait for me,' she complained.*

complete adjective
1 Something that is complete has all its parts and has nothing missing. *Is the jigsaw complete, or are there some bits missing?*
2 If something is complete, it is finished. *After three days the work was complete.*
3 Complete means in every way. *Winning the game was a complete surprise.*
completely adverb totally *The building was completely destroyed.*

complicated adjective
Something that is complicated is difficult to understand or do.

compound noun *plural* compounds
(in grammar)
a word that is made up of two words joined together, *bedroom* and *blackboard* are compounds

computer noun *plural* computers
A computer is a machine which can store information and do calculations. You can also play games on computers.

concave adjective
Something that is concave curves inwards.

conceal verb conceals, concealing, concealed (say kon-**seel**)
To conceal something means to hide it.

concentrate verb concentrates, concentrating, concentrated
When you concentrate, you think hard about the thing you are doing. *I'm trying to concentrate on my work!*

concern verb concerns, concerning, concerned
If something concerns you, it is important to you and you should be interested in it. If something does not concern you, it is nothing to do with you.

concerned adjective
If you are concerned about something, you are worried about it.

concert noun *plural* concerts
a show in which people play music for other people to listen to *We're giving a concert at the end of this term.*

concrete noun
a mixture of cement and sand used for making buildings and paths

condition noun *plural* conditions
1 The condition something is in is how new or clean it is, and how well it works. If it is in good condition, it looks new and works properly. If it is in bad condition, it is old or dirty, or does not work properly.
2 The conditions in which a plant or animal lives are everything in the world around it, for example how hot or cold it is, or how much rain there is. *Very few plants will grow in these dry conditions.*
3 A condition is something you must do before you can do or have something else. *You can go to the fair on condition that you're home by eight o'clock.*

conductor noun *plural* conductors
1 someone who stands in front of an orchestra and controls the way the musicians play
2 something that conducts electricity or heat

cone noun *plural* cones
1 a shape that is round at one end and goes in to a point at the other end

2 a hard, brown fruit that grows on pine trees and fir trees

confess verb confesses, confessing, confessed
If you confess, you admit that you have done something wrong.

confident adjective
If you are confident, you are not nervous or afraid.

confuse verb confuses, confusing, confused
1 If something confuses you, you cannot understand it.
2 If you confuse things, you get them muddled up in your mind.

congratulate verb congratulates, congratulating, congratulated
If you congratulate someone, you tell them that you are pleased that something special has happened to them.

conjunction noun
plural conjunctions (in grammar)
a word that you use to join two parts of a sentence together, *and* and *but* are conjunctions

connect verb connects, connecting, connected
To connect things means to join them together. *You need to connect the printer to your computer.*

connective noun *plural* connectives
(in grammar)
a word or phrase that you use to join different sentences or parts of sentences, *however, and*, and *meanwhile* are connectives

conquer verb conquers, conquering, conquered
To conquer people means to beat them in a battle or war.

conscious adjective (say **kon**-shuss)
When you are conscious, you are awake and able to understand what is happening around you. *He slowly became conscious again after the operation.*

conservation noun

taking good care of the world's air, water, plants, and animals *If we all use less paper it will help with conservation of the rainforest.*

consider verb considers, considering, considered

When you consider something, you think about it carefully.

consonant noun *plural* consonants

Consonants are all the letters of the alphabet except a, e, i, o, and u, which are vowels.

constant adjective

Something that is constant goes on all the time.

construct verb constructs, constructing, constructed

To construct something means to build it.

consume verb consumes, consuming, consumed

1 to eat or drink something *All the food was quickly consumed.*
2 to use something *We must reduce the amount of energy that we consume.*

contain verb contains, containing, contained

To contain something means to have it inside.

container noun *plural* containers

A container is anything that you can put other things into. Buckets, cups, bags, boxes, and jars are all containers.

contents noun

The contents of something are the things that are inside it.

contest noun *plural* contests

a competition

continent noun *plural* continents

A continent is one of the seven very large areas of land in the world. Asia, Europe, and Africa are all continents.

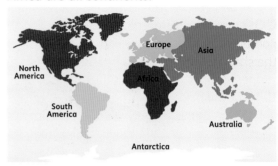

continue verb continues, continuing, continued

If you continue doing something, you go on doing it. *Miss Hardcastle opened the window and then continued talking.*

continuous adjective

Something that is continuous goes on happening and never stops. *The factory machines made a continuous humming noise.*

contraction noun *plural* contractions

A contraction is a short form of one or more words. *Haven't is a contraction of have not.*

contradict verb contradicts, contradicting, contradicted

If you contradict someone, you say that what they have said is wrong.

control noun *plural* controls

The controls are the switches and buttons that you use to make a machine work.

control verb controls, controlling, controlled

When you control something, you make it do what you want it to do. *You use these levers to control the model aeroplane in the air.*

convenient adjective

If something is convenient, you can reach it and use it easily.

conversation noun
plural **conversations**
When people have a conversation, they talk to each other.

convex adjective
Something that is convex curves outwards in the shape of a ball.

convince verb **convinces, convincing, convinced**
If you convince someone about something, you make them believe it.

cook verb **cooks, cooking, cooked**
When you cook food, you prepare it and heat it so that it is ready to eat.

cook noun *plural* **cooks**
someone whose job is to cook

cookie noun
a kind of small, crisp cake

cool adjective **cooler, coolest**
Something that is cool is slightly cold. *I'd love a cool drink.*

coordinates noun
two numbers or letters which tell you exactly where a point is on a grid or map

cope verb **copes, coping, coped**
If you can cope with something, you can manage to do it.

copper noun
a shiny, brown metal

copy verb **copies, copying, copied**
1 When you copy something, you write it down or draw it in the same way as it has already been written or drawn. *She copied the poem in her best writing.*
2 (in ICT) When you copy something from one file to another file on a computer, you move it to the second file but do not delete it from the first file.
3 When you copy someone, you do exactly the same as them.

copy noun *plural* **copies**
something that is made to look exactly like something else

coral noun
a type of rock that is made in the sea from the bodies of tiny creatures

cord noun *plural* **cords**
a thin rope

core noun *plural* **cores**
The core of an apple or pear is the hard part in the middle of it.

cork noun *plural* **corks**
something that is pushed into the top of a bottle of wine to close it

corn noun
the seeds of plants such as wheat, which we use as food

corner noun *plural* **corners**
1 the place where two edges meet *He was sitting by himself in the corner of the room.*
2 the place where two streets meet

a b c d e f g h i j k l m n o p q r s t u v w x y z

correct adjective
Something that is correct is right and has no mistakes. *All my answers were correct.*

correct verb corrects, correcting, corrected
When you correct something, you find the mistakes in it and put them right.
correction **noun** When you make a correction, you change a mistake and put it right. *I had to make a few corrections to my work.*
correctly **adverb** When you do something correctly, you do it right. *You answered all the questions correctly.*

corridor noun plural corridors
a passage in a building with rooms leading off it

cost verb costs, costing, cost
The amount that something costs is the amount you have to pay to buy it. *How much did your new bike cost?*

costume noun plural costumes
clothes that you wear for acting in a play

cosy adjective cosier, cosiest
A cosy place is warm and comfortable.

cot noun plural cots
a bed with sides for a baby

cottage noun plural cottages
a small house in the country

cotton noun
1 thread that you use for sewing
2 a type of cloth that is used for making clothes

cough verb coughs, coughing, coughed
(rhymes with *off*)
When you cough, you make a rough sound in your throat and push air out through your mouth.

could verb past tense of can verb

council noun plural councils
a group of people who are chosen to discuss things and make decisions for everyone

count verb counts, counting, counted
1 When you count things, you use numbers to say how many there are. *I counted the books.*
2 When you count, you say numbers in order. *Can you count to 1000?*

counter noun plural counters
1 the table where you pay for things in a shop
2 a small, round piece of plastic that you use for playing some games

country noun plural countries
1 A country is a land with its own people and laws. England, Australia, and China are all countries.
2 The country is land that is not in a town.

couple noun plural couples
1 two people who are married or going out with each other
2 A couple of things means two of them.

coupon noun plural coupons
a special piece of paper which you can use to pay for something

courage noun
the feeling you have when you are not afraid, and you dare to do something difficult or dangerous
courageous adjective If someone is courageous or if they do something courageous, they do not feel afraid of something that is dangerous or difficult.

course noun *plural* courses
1 The course of an aeroplane or a ship is the direction it travels in.
2 a set of lessons
3 a piece of ground where people play golf or run races

court noun *plural* courts
1 a piece of ground that is marked out so that people can play a game such as tennis
2 a building where people decide whether someone is guilty of committing a crime
3 The court of a king or queen is the place where they live and rule the country.

cousin noun *plural* cousins
Your cousin is a child of your aunt or uncle.

cover verb covers, covering, covered
When you cover something, you put something else over it. *She covered him with a blanket.*

cover noun *plural* covers
a piece of material which goes over or round something

cow noun *plural* cows
a large animal that is kept on farms for its milk and meat

coward noun *plural* cowards
someone who is afraid when they ought to be brave

cowboy noun *plural* cowboys
a man who looks after the cattle on large farms in America

crab noun *plural* crabs
A crab is an animal with a hard shell on its back, which lives in the sea. Crabs have ten legs and large, powerful claws for catching food.

crack noun *plural* cracks
1 a thin line on something where it has nearly broken
2 a sudden loud noise *We heard a crack of thunder.*

crack verb cracks, cracking, cracked
1 When you crack something, you break it so that it has lines on it but does not break into pieces. *Be careful not to crack the glass.*
2 When something cracks, it makes a sharp noise like the noise a dry twig makes when you break it.

cradle noun *plural* cradles
a bed with sides for a young baby

crane noun *plural* cranes
a large machine for lifting heavy things

a b **c** d e f g h i j k l m n o p q r s t u v w x y z

A B **C** D E F G H I J K L M N O P Q R S T U V W X Y Z

crash noun *plural* crashes
1 an accident in which a car, lorry, train, or plane hits something
2 the noise of something falling or crashing

crash verb crashes, crashing, crashed
1 If something crashes, it bumps into something else and makes a loud noise.
2 (in ICT) If a computer crashes, it stops working suddenly.

crate noun *plural* crates
a large box

crawl verb crawls, crawling, crawled
1 When you crawl, you move along on your hands and knees. *We crawled through the tunnel.*
2 When a car or train crawls along, it moves very slowly.

crayon noun *plural* crayons
a coloured pencil

crazy adjective crazier, craziest
Someone who is crazy does very silly or strange things. Something that is crazy is very silly or strange.

creak verb creaks, creaking, creaked
If something creaks, it makes a rough, squeaking noise.

cream noun
Cream is a thick white liquid that is taken from milk. You eat cream with fruit and other sweet foods.

crease verb creases, creasing, creased
When you crease something, you make untidy lines in it by pressing on it.

create verb creates, creating, created
(say kree-**ate**)
When you create something new, you make it.

creature noun *plural* creatures
any animal

creep verb creeps, creeping, crept
1 When you creep, you move along with your body very close to the ground. *Mr Fox crept up the dark tunnel to the mouth of his hole.*
— Roald Dahl, *Fantastic Mr Fox*
2 When you creep, you walk very quietly and secretly. *We crept away and nobody saw us.*

creep noun *plural* creeps
1 a nasty person
2 If something gives you the creeps, it frightens you.

crescent noun *plural* crescents
a curved shape, like the shape of a new moon

crew noun *plural* crews
a group of people who work together on a boat or aeroplane

cricket noun
1 a game in which two teams hit a ball with a bat and try to score runs by running between two wickets
2 an insect that makes a shrill chirping sound

cried verb past tense of cry

crime noun *plural* crimes
something bad that a person does, which is against the law

criminal noun *plural* criminals
someone who has done something bad that is against the law

crisp adjective crisper, crispest
1 Food that is crisp is dry and breaks easily.
2 Fruit that is crisp is firm and fresh.

crisp noun plural crisps
Crisps are thin, crisp slices of fried potato that you eat as a snack.

criticize verb criticizes, criticizing, criticized (say **krit**-iss-ize)
If you criticize someone, you say that they have done something wrong.

crocodile noun plural crocodiles
A crocodile is a large animal that lives in rivers in some hot countries. Crocodiles are reptiles, and have short legs, a long body, and sharp teeth.

crooked adjective
Something that is crooked is not straight.

crop noun plural crops
a type of plant which farmers grow as food

cross adjective crosser, crossest
If you are cross, you are angry.

cross noun plural crosses
a mark like x or +

cross verb crosses, crossing, crossed
1 When you cross a road or a river, you go across it. *How are we going to cross the river with no boat?*
2 When you cross your arms or legs, you put one over the other.
3 When you cross out writing, you draw a line through it.

crossing noun plural crossings
a place where you can cross the road safely

crow noun plural crows
a big, black bird

crowd noun plural crowds
a large number of people *There were crowds of people in the streets.*

crown noun plural crowns
a special hat made of silver or gold which a king or queen wears

cruel adjective crueller, cruellest
If you are cruel to someone, you hurt them or are very unkind to them.

crumb noun plural crumbs
Crumbs are very small pieces of bread or cake.

crumble verb crumbles, crumbling, crumbled
When something crumbles, it breaks into a lot of small pieces. *The old buildings were beginning to crumble.*

crumple verb crumples, crumpling, crumpled
When you crumple something, you make it very creased. *My clothes were all crumpled in the bottom of my bag.*

crunch verb crunches, crunching, crunched
When you crunch food, you eat it by breaking it noisily with your teeth.

crush verb crushes, crushing, crushed
When you crush something, you squash it by pressing it hard. *Mind you don't crush the flowers.*

a b **c** d e f g h i j k l m n o p q r s t u v w x y z

51

crust noun *plural* crusts
The hard part around the outside of bread.

cry verb cries, crying, cried
1 When you cry, tears come out of your eyes.
2 When you cry, you shout something. *'Look out!' she cried.*

crystal noun *plural* crystals
1 Crystal is a type of mineral that is found in rock. It is hard and clear like glass.
2 a small, hard, shiny piece of something *Crystals of ice had formed on the window.*

cub noun *plural* cubs
a young bear, lion, tiger, fox, or wolf

cube noun *plural* cubes
A cube is a square shape like the shape of a dice. Cubes have six square sides that are all the same size.

cuckoo noun *plural* cuckoos
a bird that lays its eggs in other birds' nests

cucumber noun *plural* cucumbers
a long, green vegetable that you eat raw in salads

cuddle verb cuddles, cuddling, cuddled
When you cuddle someone, you put your arms round them to show that you love them.

cunning adjective
Someone who is cunning is clever and very good at getting what they want.

cup noun *plural* cups
1 a container with a handle, which you use for drinking from
2 a silver cup that is given as a prize to the winner of a competition

cupboard noun *plural* cupboards
a piece of furniture with doors on the front, which you use for keeping things in

cure verb cures, curing, cured
To cure someone means to make them better after they have been ill.

curious adjective (say **kure**-ee-uss)
1 If you are curious about something, you want to know more about it.
2 Something that is curious is strange or unusual.

curl noun *plural* curls
a piece of hair that is curved, not straight

currant noun *plural* currants
a small dried grape

current noun *plural* currents
A current of water, air, or electricity is an amount of it that is moving in one direction.

curriculum noun *plural* curriculums, curricula
all the subjects that you study at school

curry noun *plural* curries
meat or vegetables in a spicy sauce

A B C D E F G H I J K L M N O P Q R S T U V W X Y Z

cursor noun *plural* **cursors**
the mark which shows your position on a computer screen *Move the cursor to the end of the line.*

curtain noun *plural* **curtains**
a piece of cloth that you can pull in front of a window to cover it

curve noun *plural* **curves**
a line that is bent smoothly like the letter C
curved **adjective** When something is curved, it is bent smoothly like the letter C. *Draw a curved line.*

cushion noun *plural* **cushions**
a soft object that you put on a chair to sit on or lean against

custom noun *plural* **customs**
If something is a custom, you do it because people have done it in that way for a long time. *Each country has its own customs.*

customer noun *plural* **customers**
someone who buys something in a shop

cut verb **cuts, cutting, cut**
1 If you cut yourself, you break a part of your skin on something sharp. *He fell over and cut his knee.*
2 When you cut something, you use a knife or scissors to break it into pieces.

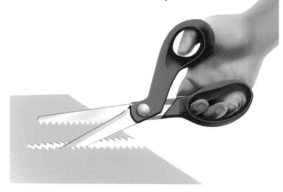

3 (in ICT) When you cut something on a computer, you delete it.

cut noun *plural* **cuts**
If you have a cut on your skin, your skin has been broken by something sharp.

cutlery noun
knives, forks, and spoons

cyber- **prefix**
Words that begin with cyber have something to do with the Internet. *I checked my emails at the cybercafe.*

cycle verb **cycles, cycling, cycled**
(say **sye**-kul)
When you cycle, you ride a bicycle.

cylinder noun *plural* **cylinders**
(say **sil**-in-der)
a shape that looks like a tube with flat, round ends

cymbals noun (say **sim**-bals)
two round pieces of metal that you bang together when you are playing music

a
b
c
d
e
f
g
h
i
j
k
l
m
n
o
p
q
r
s
t
u
v
w
x
y
z

A
B
C
D
E
F
G
H
I
J
K
L
M
N
O
P
Q
R
S
T
U
V
W
X
Y
Z

Dd

dad, daddy noun *plural* dads, daddies
Your dad is your father.

daffodil noun *plural* daffodils
a yellow flower that grows in the spring

daily adverb
If something happens daily, it happens every day.

dairy noun *plural* dairies
a place where people make cheese, butter, and yogurt from milk

daisy noun *plural* daisies
a small flower with white petals and a yellow centre

dam noun *plural* dams
a wall that is built across a river to hold water back

damage verb damages, damaging, damaged
To damage something means to break it or spoil it. *Mind you don't damage any of the paintings.*

damp adjective damper, dampest
Something that is damp is slightly wet.

dance verb dances, dancing, danced
When you dance, you move in time to music.
dance noun *plural* dances
1 When you do a dance, you move about in time to music.
2 A dance is a party where people dance.

danger noun *plural* dangers
When there is danger, there is the chance that something horrible might happen and someone might get hurt.

dangerous adjective
Something that is dangerous might kill or hurt you. *Parachuting is quite a dangerous sport.*

dare verb dares, daring, dared
1 If you dare to do something, you are brave enough to do it.
2 If you dare someone to do something, you tell them to do it to show how brave they are.

dark adjective darker, darkest
1 If a place is dark, there is no light in it. *The streets outside were very dark.*
2 Something that is dark is nearly black in colour.

dart noun *plural* darts
a small arrow that you throw at a board in a game called **darts**
dart verb darts, darting, darted
To dart means to move quickly and suddenly. *He darted behind a bush.*

dash verb dashes, dashing, dashed
To dash means to run or move very quickly. *I dashed into the house.*
dash noun *plural* dashes
1 When you make a dash, you run or move quickly.
2 a long mark like this — that you use in writing

data noun (say **day**-ta)
information about something

database noun *plural* databases
a store of information that is kept on a computer

date noun *plural* dates
1 If you say what the date is, you say what day of the month and what year it is.
2 If you have a date with someone, you have arranged to go out with them.
3 a sweet, brown fruit that grows on a palm tree

daughter noun *plural* daughters
Someone's daughter is their female child.

dawdle verb dawdles, dawdling, dawdled
If you dawdle, you walk very slowly.

dawn noun
the time of day when the sun rises and it becomes light

day noun *plural* days
1 a period of twenty-four hours *We'll be leaving in five days.*
2 the part of the day when it is light *The days are shorter in winter.*

dazzle verb dazzles, dazzling, dazzled
If a bright light dazzles you, you cannot see anything because it is shining in your eyes.

dead adjective
Someone who is dead is not alive.

deaf adjective deafer, deafest
Someone who is deaf cannot hear.

deal verb deals, dealing, dealt
1 When you deal out cards, you give them to each person at the beginning of a game.
2 When you deal with something, you do the work that needs to be done on it.

dear adjective dearer, dearest
1 If someone is dear to you, you love them a lot.
2 Something you write before someone's name at the start of a letter.
3 Something that is dear costs a lot of money.

death noun *plural* deaths
Death is the time when someone dies.

decay verb decays, decaying, decayed
When something decays, it goes bad and rots.

deceive verb deceives, deceiving, deceived (say de-**seeve**)
When you deceive someone, you make them believe something that is not true.

December noun
the twelfth and last month of the year

decide verb decides, deciding, decided
When you decide to do something, you choose to do it.

decimal adjective
A decimal system counts in tens.

decimal noun *plural* decimals
(in mathematics)
a number that has tenths shown as numbers after a dot, for example 2.5

decision noun *plural* decisions
When you make a decision, you decide what you are going to do.

a
b
c
d
e
f
g
h
i
j
k
l
m
n
o
p
q
r
s
t
u
v
w
x
y
z

deck noun *plural* decks
a floor in a ship or bus

decorate verb decorates, decorating, decorated
1 When you decorate something, you make it look nice or pretty. *We decorated the whole house with coloured lights.*
2 When you decorate a room, you put paint or wallpaper on the walls.

decrease verb decreases, decreasing, decreased
When something decreases, it becomes less. *The temperature decreases at night.*

deep adjective deeper, deepest
Something that is deep goes down a long way from the top. *Be careful, the water's quite deep.*
deeply adverb If you breath deeply, you take a lot of air into your lungs. *He swallowed and breathed deeply.*

deer noun *plural* deer
A deer is an animal that eats grass and can run fast. Male deer have long horns called antlers.

defeat verb defeats, defeating, defeated
If you defeat someone, you beat them in a game or battle.

defend verb defends, defending, defended
To defend a place means to keep it safe and stop people from attacking it.

definite adjective
Something that is definite is certain. *Is it definite that you can come?*
definitely adverb You say that you will definitely do something if you are certain that you will. *I'll definitely be there tomorrow.*

definition noun *plural* definitions
a sentence that explains what a word means

degree noun *plural* degrees
We can measure how hot or cold something is in degrees. You can write the number of degrees using the sign °. *The temperature could be over 30°C today.*

delay verb delays, delaying, delayed
1 If you are delayed, something makes you late. *The train was delayed by heavy snow.*
2 If you delay something, you put off doing it until later. *We'll delay giving the prizes until everyone is here.*

delete verb deletes, deleting, deleted
When you delete something that you have written, you rub it out or remove it.

deliberate adjective
If something is deliberate, someone has done it on purpose.
deliberately adverb You say that you have done something deliberately when it has been done on purpose. *He pushed me over deliberately!*

delicate adjective
Something that is delicate will break easily.

delicious adjective (say de-**lish**-uss)
Something that is delicious tastes very nice.

delight verb delights, delighting, delighted
If something delights you, it makes you feel very happy. *My mum said I could have a day off school, which delighted me.*

A
B
C
D
E
F
G
H
I
J
K
L
M
N
O
P
Q
R
S
T
U
V
W
X
Y
Z

deliver verb delivers, delivering, delivered
When you deliver something, you take it to someone's house.

demand verb demands, demanding, demanded
If you demand something, you ask for it very strongly. *He demanded his money back.*

demonstrate verb demonstrates, demonstrating, demonstrated
If you demonstrate something to someone, you show them how to do it. *I will now demonstrate how the machine works.*

demonstration noun
plural demonstrations
1 If you give someone a demonstration of something, you show them how to do it.
2 When there is a demonstration, a lot of people march through the streets to show that they are angry about something.

den noun *plural* dens
1 a place where a wild animal lives
2 a secret place where you can hide

dense adjective denser, densest
Something that is dense is thick. *We couldn't see because of the dense fog.*

dent verb dents, denting, dented
If you dent something, you bang it and make a hollow in it.

dentist noun *plural* dentists
someone who looks after people's teeth

deny verb denies, denying, denied
If you deny something, you say that it is not true. *She denied breaking the cup.*

depart verb departs, departing, departed
To depart means to leave a place. *The train departs from Platform 1.*

depend verb depends, depending, depended
If you depend on someone, you need them to help you. *The young lions depend on their mother for food.*

depth noun *plural* depths
The depth of something is how deep it is. *We measured the depth of the water.*

descend verb descends, descending, descended (say de-**send**)
To descend means to go down.

describe verb describes, describing, described
When you describe something, you talk about it and say what it is like.
description noun When you give a description of something, you say what it is like. *Can you give me a description of the thief?*

desert noun *plural* deserts
dry land where very few plants can grow

a b c **d** e f g h i j k l m n o p q r s t u v w x y z

A B C **D** E F G H I J K L M N O P Q R S T U V W X Y Z

deserted adjective
A place that is deserted is empty, with no one in it.

deserve verb deserves, deserving, deserved
If you deserve a punishment or reward, you should get it. *He was so brave he deserves a medal.*

design verb designs, designing, designed
When you design something, you plan it and draw a picture of it.

desk noun plural desks
a table where you can read, write, and keep books

desktop adjective plural desktops
You use desktop to describe a computer which you keep on top of a desk or table all the time.

dessert noun plural desserts
sweet food that you eat at the end of a meal

destroy verb destroys, destroying, destroyed
To destroy something means to break it or spoil it so badly that you cannot use it again.

detail noun plural details
one small part of something, or one small piece of information about it *Jessica could remember every detail about the house.*

detective noun plural detectives
someone who looks at clues and tries to find out who committed a crime

determined adjective
If you are determined to do something, you have made up your mind that you want to do it. *We are determined to win.*

develop verb develops, developing, developed
When something develops, it changes and grows. *Seeds develop into plants.*

dew noun
tiny drops of water that form on the ground during the night

diagonal adjective
A diagonal line goes from one corner of something to the opposite corner.

diagram noun plural diagrams
a picture that shows what something is like or explains how it works

dial noun plural dials
a circle with numbers round it, like on a clock

dial verb dials, dialling, dialled
When you dial a number, you call that number on a telephone. *He dialled 999 and asked for an ambulance.*

dialogue noun plural dialogues
a conversation in a book, play, or film

diameter noun plural diameters
The diameter of a circle is the distance across the centre of it.

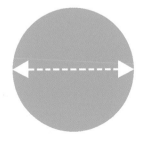

diamond noun plural diamonds
1 a very hard jewel that looks like clear glass
2 a shape that looks like a square standing on one of its corners

diary noun plural diaries
a book where you write down the things that you do each day

dice noun plural dice
A dice is a small cube with each side marked with a different number of dots. You use dice in some games.

dictionary noun plural dictionaries
a book that explains what words mean and shows you how to spell them

did verb past tense of do

die verb dies, dying, died
When someone dies, they stop living.

diet noun plural diets
1 Your diet is the kind of food that you eat. *You should try to eat a healthy diet.*
2 If you go on a diet, you eat less food because you want to become thinner.

difference noun plural differences
1 A difference between things is a way in which they are different. *We had to look for five differences between the two pictures.*
2 (in mathematics) The difference between two numbers is the number you get when you take one away from the other. *The difference between five and three is two.*

different adjective
If things or people are different, they are not the same.

difficult adjective
Something that is difficult is not easy. *I find maths quite difficult.*

dig verb digs, digging, dug
When you dig, you move soil away and make a hole in the ground.

digest verb digests, digesting, digested
(say dye-**jest**)
When you digest food, your stomach breaks it down and changes it so that your body can use it.

digit noun plural digits (in mathematics)
one of the numbers between 0 and 9

digital adjective
1 A digital watch or clock shows the time with numbers, rather than with hands.

2 A digital camera or television uses a special kind of electronic signal to make pictures.

dim adjective dimmer, dimmest
A dim light or a dim place is not very bright. *Violet looked around the dim and messy room.* — Lemony Snicket, *The Bad Beginning*

A
B
C
D
E
F
G
H
I
J
K
L
M
N
O
P
Q
R
S
T
U
V
W
X
Y
Z

din noun
a very loud, annoying noise

dinghy noun *plural* dinghies
a small sailing boat

dining room noun
plural dining rooms
a room where people have their meals

dinner noun *plural* dinners
the main meal of the day

dinosaur noun *plural* dinosaurs
an animal like a huge lizard that lived
millions of years ago

dip verb dips, dipping, dipped
When you dip something into liquid, you put
it in and leave it there for only a short time.
I dipped my toe into the water.

direct adjective
If you go somewhere in a direct way, you go
straight there, without going anywhere else
first. *We got on the direct train to London.*

direct verb directs, directing, directed
1 If you direct someone to a place, you
explain to them how to get there. *Can you
direct me to the station?*
2 The person who directs a play or film
organizes it and tells everyone what they
should do.

direction noun *plural* directions
The direction you are going in is the way you
are going.

dirt noun
dust or mud

dirty adjective dirtier, dirtiest
Something that is dirty has mud or dirt on it.

disabled adjective
Someone who is disabled finds it hard to do
some things because a part of their body
does not work properly.

disagree verb disagrees, disagreeing,
disagreed
If you disagree with someone, you think that
they are wrong.

disappear verb disappears,
disappearing, disappeared
When something disappears, it goes away
and you cannot see it any more.

disappoint verb disappoints,
disappointing, disappointed
If something disappoints you, you feel sad
because it is not as good as you thought it
would be.

disapprove verb disapproves,
disapproving, disapproved
If you disapprove of something, you do not
like it and do not think that it is right.

disaster noun *plural* disasters
something very bad that happens

disc, disk noun *plural* discs, disks
1 any round, flat object
2 A disc is a round, flat piece of plastic that
has music or computer information on it.
This is also called a **compact disc.**

disco noun *plural* discos
a party where you dance to pop music

discover verb discovers, discovering, discovered
When you discover something, you find it, or find out about it.

discuss verb discusses, discussing, discussed
When people discuss something, they talk about it.

disease noun plural diseases
an illness

disguise noun plural disguises
special clothes that you wear so that you will look different and people will not recognize you

disgust verb disgusts, disgusting, disgusted
If something disgusts you, it is horrible and you hate it.

dish noun plural dishes
1 a container in which food is served
2 food that has been prepared and cooked in a particular way

dishonest adjective
Someone who is dishonest is not honest and does not tell the truth. *We thought he was very dishonest when we realized that he'd lied about the money.*

dislike verb dislikes, disliking, disliked
If you dislike something, you do not like it.

dismiss verb dismisses, dismissing, dismissed
To dismiss someone means to send them away. *Miss Watkins asked me a few questions, then she dismissed me.*

display noun plural displays
a show or exhibition *We made a display of our paintings.*

dissolve verb dissolves, dissolving, dissolved
When something dissolves in water, it mixes with the water so that you can not see it.

distance noun plural distances
The distance between two places is the amount of space between them. *We measured the distance between the two buildings.*

distant adjective
Something that is distant is far away.

district noun plural districts
part of a town, city, or country

disturb verb disturbs, disturbing, disturbed
1 If you disturb someone, you interrupt them and stop them from doing something. *I'm working, so please don't disturb me.*
2 If something disturbs you, it makes you feel worried.

ditch noun plural ditches
a long, narrow hole in the ground

dive verb dives, diving, dived
If you dive into water, you jump in head first.

diver noun plural divers
A diver is someone who dives into water and swims around under the water, wearing special breathing equipment.

a
b
c
d
e
f
g
h
i
j
k
l
m
n
o
p
q
r
s
t
u
v
w
x
y
z

divide verb divides, dividing, divided
1 When you divide things, you share them out. *Divide the sweets equally between you.*
2 When you divide something, you split it into smaller parts. *The cake was divided into eight pieces.*
3 (in mathematics) When you divide numbers, you find out how many times one number goes into another. *Six divided by two is three, 6 ÷ 2 = 3.*

divisible adjective (in mathematics)
If one number is divisible by another, it can be divided by that number without leaving a remainder. *Ten is divisible by two.*

divorce verb plural divorces, divorcing, divorced
When two people divorce, they end their marriage.

Diwali noun
Diwali is an important Hindu festival at which lamps are lit. It is held in October or November.

dizzy adjective dizzier, dizziest
If you feel dizzy, you feel as if everything is spinning round you.

do verb does, doing, did, done
When you do something, you carry out that action. *She did a little dance in the middle of the room.*

doctor noun plural doctors
someone whose job is to give people medicines and treatment when they are ill

document noun plural documents
1 an important piece of paper with official information on it *Your passport is a very important document.*
2 (in ICT) a piece of work that you write and store on a computer

does verb a tense of do

dog noun plural dogs
A dog is an animal people often keep as a pet. Dogs can bark, and you can train them to obey you.

doll noun plural dolls
a toy in the shape of a baby or person

dollar noun plural dollars
A dollar is a unit of money. Dollars are used in the United States of America, Australia, and some other countries.

dolphin noun plural dolphins
A dolphin is a large animal that swims like a fish and lives in the sea. Dolphins are mammals, and breathe air.

dome noun plural domes
a round roof that is shaped like the top half of a ball

done verb past tense of do

donkey noun plural donkeys
an animal that looks like a small horse with long ears

don't verb
do not *Don't be silly!*

door noun plural doors
something that you can open and go through to get into a place

dose noun plural doses
A dose of medicine is the amount that you have to take.

dot noun *plural* dots
a small spot that looks like a full stop

double adjective
Something that is double the size of something else is twice as big.

double verb doubles, doubling, doubled
If you double an amount, you make it twice as big.

doubt noun *plural* doubts
(rhymes with *out*)
If you have doubts about something, you are not sure about it.

doubt verb doubts, doubting, doubted
(rhymes with *out*)
If you doubt something, you do not believe it. *I doubt that we'll hear from him again.*

dove noun *plural* doves
a bird that looks like a small pigeon

down noun
very soft feathers

download verb downloads, downloading, downloaded (in ICT)
When you download information, you copy it from the Internet onto your computer.

doze verb dozes, dozing, dozed
If you are dozing, you are nearly asleep. If you doze off, you fall asleep.

dozen noun *plural* dozens
a set of twelve *I bought a dozen eggs.*

draft noun *plural* drafts
a first copy of a piece of work, which you do not do very neatly

drag verb drags, dragging, dragged
When you drag something heavy, you pull it along the ground.

dragon noun *plural* dragons
a large monster with wings, in a story

dragonfly noun *plural* dragonflies
a large insect with a brightly coloured body that lives near water

drain noun *plural* drains
a pipe that carries water away under the ground

drain verb drains, draining, drained
When water drains away, it flows away.

drama noun
acting in a play or story

dramatic adjective
Something that is dramatic is very exciting.

drank verb past tense of drink

draught noun *plural* draughts (say *draft*)
1 cold air that blows into a room
2 Draughts are round pieces of wood or plastic that you move across a board when you are playing a game called **draughts**.

draw verb draws, drawing, drew, drawn
1 When you draw a picture, you make a picture with a pen, pencil, or crayon.
2 When you draw curtains, you open them or close them.
3 When two people draw in a game, they have the same score at the end of the game. *We drew 1–1.*

drawer noun *plural* drawers
a part of a piece of furniture that you can pull out and use for keeping things in

a
b
c
d
e
f
g
h
i
j
k
l
m
n
o
p
q
r
s
t
u
v
w
x
y
z

drawing noun *plural* drawings
a picture that someone has drawn

dreadful adjective
Something that is dreadful is very bad.

dream noun *plural* dreams
1 things that you seem to see when you are asleep
2 something that you would like very much
My dream is to become a pop singer.

dream verb dreams, dreaming, dreamed, dreamt
1 When you dream, you seem to see things in your head when you are asleep.
2 If you dream about something, you think about it because you would like to do it.
He had always dreamt of being an Olympic champion.

dress noun *plural* dresses
A dress is a piece of clothing that a woman or girl wears. It has a skirt, and also covers the top half of her body.

dress verb dresses, dressing, dressed
When you dress, you put on clothes. You can also say that you **get dressed.**

drew verb past tense of draw

dribble verb dribbles, dribbling, dribbled
1 If you dribble, water comes out of your mouth. Babies often dribble.
2 When you dribble with a ball, you kick it as you run along, so that it stays close to your feet.

drift verb drifts, drifting, drifted
If something drifts along, it is carried along gently by water or air. *The empty boat drifted along on the sea.*

drill noun *plural* drills
a tool that you use for making holes

drink verb drinks, drinking, drank, drunk
When you drink, you swallow liquid.

drink noun *plural* drinks
a liquid that you take into your mouth and swallow

drip verb drips, dripping, dripped
When water drips, it falls in small drops.

drive verb drives, driving, drove, driven
1 When you drive, you control a car, bus, train, or lorry. *You can learn to drive when you're seventeen.*
2 When you drive animals, you make them move along. *We drove the cows into the field.*

drizzle noun
very light rain

drop noun *plural* drops
A drop of water is a very small amount of it. *I felt a few drops of rain on my face.*

drop verb drops, dropping, dropped
If you drop something, you do not hold it tightly enough and it falls out of your hands.

drought noun *plural* droughts
(rhymes with *out*)
a time when there is very little rain and the ground becomes very dry

drove verb past tense of drive

drown verb drowns, drowning, drowned
If you drown, you die because you are under water and cannot breathe.

drug noun plural drugs
1 a medicine that can help you feel better if you are ill or in pain
2 A drug is a substance that some people take for pleasure because it changes the way they feel or behave. This type of drug is against the law and dangerous.

drum noun plural drums
a hollow musical instrument that you bang with a stick or with your hands

drunk verb past tense of drink

dry adjective drier, driest
Something that is dry is not wet or damp.

duck noun plural ducks
a bird that lives near water and swims on the water

duck verb ducks, ducking, ducked
If you duck, you bend down quickly so that something will not hit you.

due adjective
The time that something is due is the time you expect it to arrive. *The train is due at two o'clock.*

dug verb past tense of dig

dull adjective duller, dullest
1 A dull colour is not very bright.
2 Something that is dull is boring and not interesting.

dungeon noun plural dungeons
a prison underneath a castle

during preposition
while something else is going on *I fell asleep during the film.*

dusk noun
the dim light at the end of the day, just before it gets dark

dust noun
dry dirt that is like powder

dustbin noun plural dustbins
a large container that you use for putting rubbish in

duty noun plural duties
If it is your duty to do something, you have to do it.

duvet noun plural duvets
(say **doo**-vay)
a thick, warm cover for a bed

DVD noun plural DVDs
A DVD is a round, flat disc on which music, pictures, or film can be stored. DVD is short for **digital versatile disc.**

dye verb dyes, dyeing, dyed
When you dye something, you change its colour by putting it in a special coloured liquid.

dying verb a tense of die

dyslexic adjective (say dis-**lex**-ic)
Someone who is dyslexic finds it difficult to learn to read and write because their brain muddles up letters and words.

a b c **d** e f g h i j k l m n o p q r s t u v w x y z

A B C D **E** F G H I J K L M N O P Q R S T U V W X Y Z

Ee

each determiner
every *She gave each child a present.*

eager adjective
If you are eager to do something, you are very keen to do it.

eagle noun *plural* eagles
An eagle is a large bird that hunts and eats small animals. Eagles live in mountain areas.

ear noun *plural* ears
Your ears are the parts of your body that you use for hearing.

early adjective earlier, earliest
1 If you are early, you arrive before people are expecting you. *We were ten minutes early.*
2 When it is early in the day, it is in the morning, not the afternoon or evening. *I got up very early this morning.*

earn verb earns, earning, earned
When you earn money, you get it by working for it.

earphone noun *plural* earphones
Earphones are small speakers that you wear in your ears so that you can listen to music from a music player.

earring noun *plural* earrings
Earrings are jewellery that you wear in your ears.

earth noun
1 the planet that we all live on
2 the soil in which plants grow

earthquake noun *plural* earthquakes
When there is an earthquake, the ground suddenly shakes. Strong earthquakes can destroy buildings.

east noun
East is the direction where the sun rises in the morning. E stands for east on a compass.

Easter noun
the day when Christians celebrate Jesus Christ coming back from the dead

easy adverb easier, easiest
If something is easy, you can do it or understand it without any trouble. *Do you find maths easy?*
easily adverb If you do something easily, you do it without any trouble. *I managed to do all my homework quite easily.*

eat verb eats, eating, ate, eaten
When you eat, you put food in your mouth and swallow it.

e-book noun *plural* e-books
An e-book is a book which is published as an electronic file or on the Internet. You can read an e-book on a small computer called an **e-book reader**. *I have over 20 e-books on my e-book reader.*

echo noun *plural* **echoes** (say **ek**-oh)
When you hear an echo, you hear a sound again as it bounces back off something solid. You often hear echoes in caves and tunnels.

eclipse noun *plural* **eclipses**
When there is an eclipse of the sun, the moon moves in front of it and hides it for a short time. When there is an eclipse of the moon, the moon passes behind the earth and is hidden from the sun for a short time.

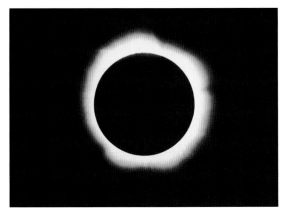

edge noun *plural* **edges**
The edge of something is the part along the end or side of it.

edit verb **edits, editing, edited**
1 When you edit something that you have written, you check it and change some parts so that it is better.
2 When people edit a film or television programme, they choose the parts that they want to keep and take some parts out.

educate verb **educates, educating, educated**
To educate someone means to teach them things they need to know like reading and writing. *A teacher's job is to educate children.*

effect noun *plural* **effects**
If something has an effect, it makes something else happen. *Some chemicals have a harmful effect on the environment.*

effort noun *plural* **efforts**
If you put effort into something, you work hard to do it.

egg noun *plural* **eggs**
An egg is an oval object with a thin shell. Eggs are laid by birds, snakes, and insects. We can cook and eat hens' eggs.

Eid noun *plural* **Eid**
a Muslim festival that marks the end of Ramadan

eight noun *plural* **eights**
the number 8

eighteen noun
the number 18

eighty noun
the number 80

elastic noun
a strip of material that can stretch and then go back to its usual size

elbow noun *plural* **elbows**
Your elbow is the joint in the middle of your arm, where your arm can bend.

elect verb **elects, electing, elected**
When people elect someone, they choose them by voting for them.

electricity noun
Electricity is the power or energy that is used to give light and heat and to work machines.
electric, electrical **adjective** An electric or electrical machine is worked by electricity.

a
b
c
d
e
f
g
h
i
j
k
l
m
n
o
p
q
r
s
t
u
v
w
x
y
z

electronic adjective
An electronic machine uses electrical signals to control the way it works. Televisions, computers, and automatic washing machines have electronic systems inside them.

elephant noun *plural* elephants
a very big, grey animal with tusks and a very long nose called a trunk

eleven noun
the number 11

else adverb
different *Let's do something else today.*

email noun *plural* emails
a message that you send from your computer to someone else's computer

embarrass verb embarrasses, embarrassing, embarrassed
If something embarrasses you, it makes you feel shy, nervous, or ashamed.

emerald noun *plural* emeralds
a green jewel or precious stone

emerge verb emerges, emerging, emerged
When something emerges, it comes out of a place and you can see it. *Five minutes later the dog emerged from the tent.*

emergency noun *plural* emergencies
When there is an emergency, something very dangerous suddenly happens and people must act quickly so that no one gets hurt. *Call the doctor, it's an emergency.*

emotion noun *plural* emotions
Your emotions are your feelings.

employ verb employs, employing, employed
To employ someone means to pay them to work for you.

empty adjective
Something that is empty has nothing in it. *I looked in the box, but it was empty.*

empty verb empties, emptying, emptied
When you empty something, you take everything out of it. *He emptied his pocket.*

enchanted adjective
Something that is enchanted is under a magic spell.

encourage verb encourages, encouraging, encouraged
When you encourage someone, you tell them to do something and make them feel brave enough to do it. *Everyone encouraged me to try again.*

A B C D **E** F G H I J K L M N O P Q R S T U V W X Y Z

encyclopedia noun

plural **encyclopedias**
(say en-sye-clo-**pee**-dee-a)
a book that gives you information about a lot of different things

end noun *plural* ends

The end of something is the place or time where it stops.

end verb ends, ending, ended

When something ends, it stops.

enemy noun *plural* enemies

1 someone who wants to hurt you
2 the people fighting against you

energetic adjective

If you are energetic, you have a lot of energy and run round a lot. *I wasn't feeling very energetic.*

energy noun

1 If you have energy, you feel strong and fit.
2 Energy is the power that comes from coal, electricity, and gas. Energy makes machines work and gives us heat and light.

engine noun *plural* engines

a machine that can make things move

engineer noun *plural* engineers

someone who makes machines, or plans the building of roads and bridges

enjoy verb enjoys, enjoying, enjoyed

If you enjoy something, you like doing it or watching it.
enjoyable adjective If something is enjoyable, you like doing it or watching it. *We had a very enjoyable day.*

enormous adjective

Something that is enormous is very big. *One of the crocodiles was enormous. The other was not so big.* — Roald Dahl, *The Enormous Crocodile*

enough adjective

If you have enough of something, you have as much as you need. *I haven't got enough money to buy an ice cream.*

enter verb enters, entering, entered

1 When you enter a place, you go into it. *I knocked on the door and entered the room.*
2 If you enter a race or competition, you take part in it.

entertain verb entertains, entertaining, entertained

To entertain people means to do things that they enjoy watching, or things that make them laugh. *There were singers and dancers there to entertain the guests.*

enthusiastic adjective

If you are enthusiastic about something, you are very keen on it and want to do it.

entrance noun *plural* entrances

the way into a place

envelope noun *plural* envelopes

a paper cover that you put a letter in before you send it

envious adjective (say en-vee-uss)

If you feel envious, you want something that someone else has. *I was so envious of Salim when he got a ticket for the Cup Final.*

environment noun

plural **environments**
the world we live in, especially the plants, animals, and things around us *Planting more trees will improve our environment.*

a
b
c
d
e
f
g
h
i
j
k
l
m
n
o
p
q
r
s
t
u
v
w
x
y
z

A B C D **E** F G H I J K L M N O P Q R S T U V W X Y Z

envy noun
the feeling you have when you would like to have something that someone else has

episode noun *plural* episodes
one programme in a radio or TV serial

equal adjective
If two things are equal, they are the same size or worth the same amount. *Divide the mixture into two equal amounts.*
equally adverb If you do something equally, you do it in the same way or in the same amount. *We shared the money equally between us.*

equator noun
The equator is an imaginary line round the middle of the earth. Countries near the equator are very hot.

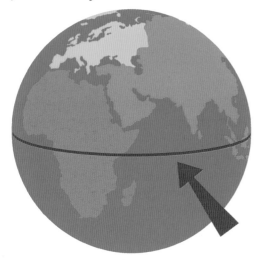

equipment noun
the things that you need for doing something

error noun *plural* errors
a mistake

erupt verb erupts, erupting, erupted
When a volcano erupts, hot, liquid rock comes up out of it.

escape verb escapes, escaping, escaped
If you escape, you get away from a place and become free. *How are we going to escape from here?*

especially adverb
more than anything else *I love fruit, especially apples.*

essential adjective
very important or absolutely necessary

estimate verb estimates, estimating, estimated
When you estimate an amount, you guess how much it will be. *Can you estimate how long it would take to walk twenty kilometres?*

e-ticket noun
An e-ticket is a ticket that you buy on the Internet and which is sent to you as an email. You can use an e-ticket to travel on a train or plane instead of a printed ticket.
I had an e-ticket for my flight, so I didn't need to check in at the airport.

EU noun
The EU is an organization of countries that work together.

euro noun *plural* euros
A euro is a unit of money. Euros are used in Germany, France, and some other countries.

evaporate verb evaporates, evaporating, evaporated
When water evaporates, it changes into a gas and so disappears.

even adjective
1 Something that is even is smooth and level. *You need an even surface to work on.*
2 Amounts that are even are equal.
3 (in mathematics) An even number is a number that you can divide by two. 4, 6, and 8 are even numbers.

evening noun *plural* **evenings**
the time at the end of the day before people go to bed

event noun *plural* **events**
something important that happens

eventually adverb
in the end   *We got home eventually.*

ever adverb
at any time   *Have you ever been to America?*
for ever always

evergreen noun *plural* **evergreens**
a tree that keeps its green leaves all year

every determiner
each   *I go swimming every week.*

everybody, everyone pronoun
every person   *Everybody cheered when he scored the winning goal.*

everything pronoun
all things

everywhere adverb
in all places   *I've looked everywhere but I can't find my phone.*

evidence noun
anything that proves that something is true, or that something happened

evil adjective
Something that is evil is wicked.

ewe noun *plural* **ewes** (say **you**)
a female sheep

exact adjective
completely right or accurate   *Show me the exact spot where you were standing.*
exactly adverb You use exactly before an amount or a number of something to say that it is completely right or accurate.   *I had exactly 24p in my pocket.*

exaggerate verb **exaggerates, exaggerating, exaggerated**
If you exaggerate, you say that something is bigger or better than it really is.

exam, examination noun
plural **exams, examinations**
an important test

examine verb **examines, examining, examined**
When you examine something, you look at it very carefully.

example noun *plural* **examples**
1 one thing that shows what all the others are like   *Can you show me an example of your handwriting?*
2 Someone who sets an example behaves well and shows other people how they should behave.

excellent adjective
Something that is excellent is very good.

except preposition
apart from   *Everyone got a prize except me.*

exchange verb **exchanges, exchanging, exchanged**
If you exchange something, you give it to someone and get something else in return.

excite verb **excites, exciting, excited**
If something excites you, it makes you feel happy, interested, and keen to do something.

excitement noun
Excitement is when you feel happy and keen to do something.   *He was jumping up and down with excitement.*
exciting adjective Something is exciting when you are happy and keen to do it.   *It was very exciting seeing so many animals in the wild.*

exclaim verb exclaims, exclaiming, exclaimed
When you exclaim, you shout something suddenly because you are surprised or excited.

exclamation noun
plural exclamations
An exclamation is something you say or shout which shows that you are very happy, angry, or surprised, for example, *Oh, dear!* In writing, you use an exclamation mark after an exclamation.

exclamation mark noun
plural exclamation marks
An exclamation mark is a mark like this ! that you use in writing. You put an exclamation mark after words to show that they have been shouted.

excuse noun plural excuses
(rhymes with *goose*)
a reason you give to try to explain why you have done wrong so that you will not get into trouble

excuse verb excuses, excusing, excused
(rhymes with *choose*)
1 If you excuse someone, you forgive them. *I'm sorry for interrupting you. Please excuse me.*
2 If you are excused from doing something, you do not have to do it. *I was excused from swimming because I had a cold.*

exercise noun plural exercises
1 When you do exercise, you run around or move your body to make your body healthy and strong.
2 a piece of work that you do to make yourself better at something

exhausted adjective
If you are exhausted, you are very tired.

exhibition noun plural exhibitions
a collection of things that are put on show so that people can come to see them

exist verb exists, existing, existed
Things that exist are real, not imaginary. *Do you think that aliens exist?*

exit noun plural exits
the way out of a place

expand verb expands, expanding, expanded
When something expands, it gets bigger. *A balloon expands when you blow air into it.*

expect verb expects, expecting, expected
If you expect that something will happen, you think that it will happen.

expensive adjective
Something that is expensive costs a lot of money.

experience noun plural experiences
1 If you have experience of something, you have done it before and so know what it is like.
2 An experience is something very good or bad that happens to you. *Going to Disneyland was a wonderful experience.*

experiment noun plural experiments
a test that you do to find out whether an idea works

expert noun *plural* experts
someone who does something very well or knows a lot about something

explain verb explains, explaining, explained
When you explain something, you talk about it so that other people understand it. *Max explained to us how the machine worked.*

explode verb explodes, exploding, exploded
When something explodes, it bursts or blows up with a loud bang.

explore verb explores, exploring, explored
When you explore a place, you look around it carefully to find out what it is like. *Let's explore the castle.*

explosion noun *plural* explosions
a loud bang that is made when something bursts or blows up

express verb expresses, expressing, expressed
When you express your ideas or feelings, you talk about them or show them to other people.

expression noun *plural* expressions
1 Your expression is the look on your face. *He had a really sad expression on his face.*

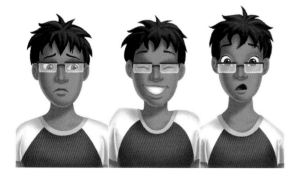

2 An expression is a word or phrase.

extinct adjective
Animals that are extinct no longer exist because they are all dead.

extra adjective
Something extra is something more than you would usually have or do. *Bring some extra clothes in case it gets cold.*

extraordinary adjective
Something that is extraordinary is very unusual. *An extraordinary sight met their eyes.*

extreme adjective
1 Extreme means very great. *No plants can grow in the extreme heat of the desert.*
2 The extreme part of a place is the part that is furthest away.

eye noun *plural* eyes
1 Your eyes are the parts of your body that you use for seeing.

side view of an eye

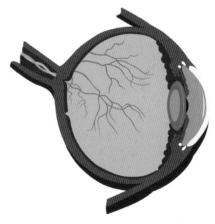

2 the small hole in the top of a needle

eyesight noun
Your eyesight is your ability to see.

a
b
c
d
e
f
g
h
i
j
k
l
m
n
o
p
q
r
s
t
u
v
w
x
y
z

73

Ff

fable noun *plural* fables
A fable is a story that teaches you something, for example one that teaches you not to be selfish or greedy.

face noun *plural* faces
1 Your face is the front part of your head, which has your eyes, nose, and mouth on it.
2 The face of a clock or watch is the front part of it, which shows the time.

face verb faces, facing, faced
The direction that you are facing is the direction in which you are looking.

fact noun *plural* facts
something that we know is true

factor noun *plural* factors
(in mathematics)
a number that will divide exactly into another number without leaving a remainder. *Three is a factor of nine.*

factory noun *plural* factories
a large building where people make things with machines

fade verb fades, fading, faded
1 When a colour or light fades, it becomes less bright.
2 When a sound fades, it becomes less loud.

fail verb fails, failing, failed
If you fail a test, you do not pass it.

failure noun *plural* failures
1 someone who has failed a test, or has not managed to do something very well
2 something that does not work well or is not successful

faint adjective fainter, faintest
1 A faint sound is not very loud and you cannot hear it very well.
2 A faint colour, mark, or light is not very bright or clear.
3 If you feel faint, you feel dizzy

faint verb faints, fainting, fainted
If you faint, you feel dizzy and become unconscious for a short time.

fair adjective fairer, fairest
1 Something that is fair treats everyone in the same way so that everyone is equal. *It's not fair if my brother gets more money than me.*
2 Fair hair is light in colour.

fair noun *plural* fairs
a place with a lot of rides and stalls, where you can go to enjoy yourself by going on the rides and trying to win things at the stalls

fairy noun *plural* fairies
a small, magical person in a story

fairy tale noun *plural* fairy tales
a story for young children in which magic things happen

faithful adjective
If you are faithful to someone, you always help them and support them.

fake noun *plural* fakes
something that has been made to look like a valuable thing, but is not real

fall verb falls, falling, fell, fallen
1 To fall means to drop down towards the ground. *Be careful you don't fall!*
2 When you fall asleep, you start sleeping.

false adjective
Something that is false is not true or real. *He gave a false name to the police.*

familiar adjective
If something is familiar to you, you recognize it or know about it.

family noun *plural* families
1 Your family is all the people who are related to you, for example your parents, brothers and sisters, aunts and uncles.
2 A family of animals or plants is a group of them that are closely related.

famine noun *plural* famines
If there is a famine, there is not enough food for people.

famous adjective
Someone or something famous is very well known. *A lot of people dream about being rich and famous.*

fan noun *plural* fans
1 a machine that blows air about to cool a place
2 something that you hold in your hand and wave in front of your face to cool your face

3 someone who supports a famous person or a sports team *Are you a football fan?*

fantastic adjective
Something that is fantastic is wonderful.

fantasy noun *plural* fantasies
A fantasy is something that is magical and cannot happen in real life. *I like reading fantasy stories.*

far adverb farther, further, farthest, furthest
Something that is far away is a long way away.

fare noun *plural* fares
the amount of money that you have to pay to travel on a train, bus, boat, or aeroplane

farm noun *plural* farms
a piece of land where someone grows crops and keeps animals for food
farmer noun A farmer is someone who has a farm.

fascinate verb fascinates, fascinating, fascinated
If something fascinates you, you are very interested in it.

fashion noun *plural* fashions
A fashion is a style of clothes that is popular for a short time. Clothes that are **in fashion** are popular now. Clothes that are **out of fashion** are not popular.

fashionable adjective
Clothes that are fashionable are in fashion and popular now.

fast adjective faster, fastest
1 Something that is fast moves quickly.
2 If a clock or watch is fast, it shows a time that is later than the right time. *My watch is ten minutes fast.*

fast verb fasts, fasting, fasted
When you fast, you do not eat any food for a period of time.

a
b
c
d
e
f
g
h
i
j
k
l
m
n
o
p
q
r
s
t
u
v
w
x
y
z

75

A B C D E **F** G H I J K L M N O P Q R S T U V W X Y Z

fasten verb fastens, fastening, fastened
1 When you fasten something, you close it or do it up. *Don't forget to fasten your seat belt.*
2 If you fasten two things together, you tie or join them together.

fat noun
1 the white, greasy part of meat
2 a substance such as butter or margarine used in cooking

fat adjective fatter, fattest
Someone who is fat has a big, round body. *The ticket collector was a little fat man.*

father noun plural fathers
Your father is your male parent.

fault noun plural faults
1 If there is a fault in something, there is something wrong with it. *I think there is a fault in the computer program.*
2 If something is your fault, you made it happen.

favour noun plural favours
If you do someone a favour, you do something for them. *Please do me a favour and post those letters for me.*

favourite adjective
Your favourite thing is the one that you like the most.

fax noun plural faxes
a copy of a letter or a picture that you send to someone using a machine called a **fax machine**

fear noun plural fears
the feeling you get when you are frightened because you think something bad is going to happen

fear verb fears, fearing, feared
If you fear something, you are afraid of it. *Don't worry. You have nothing to fear.*

feast noun plural feasts
a special big meal for a lot of people

feather noun plural feathers
A bird's feathers are the light, soft things that it has all over its body.

feature noun plural features
an article in a newspaper or magazine

February noun
the second month of the year

fed verb past tense of feed

feed verb feeds, feeding, fed
To feed a person or an animal means to give them food.

feel verb feels, feeling, felt
1 When you feel something, you touch it to find out what it is like.
2 When you feel an emotion such as anger, fear, or happiness, you have that emotion.

feeling noun plural feelings
something that you feel inside yourself, like anger or love

feet noun plural of foot

felt verb past tense of feel

female adjective
A female animal or person can become a mother.

feminine adjective
Something that is feminine looks as if it is suitable for girls and women, not boys or men.

fence noun *plural* **fences**
A fence is a kind of wall made from wood or wire. Fences are put round gardens and fields.

ferocious adjective (say fer-**oh**-shuss)
A ferocious animal is fierce and dangerous.

ferry noun *plural* **ferries**
a boat that takes people across a river or short stretch of water

festival noun *plural* **festivals**
a special time when people celebrate something

fetch verb **fetches, fetching, fetched**
When you fetch something, you go and get it. *'Fetch the ball!'*

fete noun *plural* **fetes** (say **fate**)
an event outside with games and competitions, and a lot of stalls selling different things

fever noun *plural* **fevers**
If you have a fever, you have a high temperature and your body feels very hot.

few determiner, pronoun
A few means a small number. *There were only a few people there.*

fewer adjective
not as many *We scored fewer goals than the other team, so we lost the match.*

fibre noun *plural* **fibres**
1 a thin thread
2 a substance in some foods which we need to help our body digest things properly

fiction noun
books and stories that are made up and are not true

fidget verb **fidgets, fidgeting, fidgeted**
When you fidget, you keep moving about because you are bored or nervous. *Noah was very nervous and he couldn't stop fidgeting.*

field noun *plural* **fields**
a piece of ground with crops or grass growing on it

fierce adjective **fiercer, fiercest**
A fierce animal is dangerous because it might bite you or attack you.

fifteen noun
the number 15

fifty noun
the number 50

fight verb **fights, fighting, fought**
When people fight, they hit each other or attack each other.

figure noun *plural* **figures**
1 a number, such as 1, 2, or 3
2 Your figure is the shape of your body. *In art, we were asked to draw people with different types of figures.*

file noun *plural* **files**
1 a book or box that you keep pieces of paper in
2 (in ICT) an amount of information that is stored together on a computer
3 a tool that you rub against things to make them smooth
4 If people walk in single file, they walk in a line, with one person behind the other.

a
b
c
d
e
f
g
h
i
j
k
l
m
n
o
p
q
r
s
t
u
v
w
x
y
z

A
B
C
D
E
F
G
H
I
J
K
L
M
N
O
P
Q
R
S
T
U
V
W
X
Y
Z

fill verb fills, filling, filled
1 When you fill something, you put so much in it that it is full. *We filled our bottles with water from the stream.*
2 If food fills you up, it makes you feel full.

film noun plural films
1 a roll of plastic you put in some cameras for taking photographs
2 a moving picture that you watch on a screen at the cinema or on television

filthy adjective filthier, filthiest
Something that is filthy is very dirty.

fin noun plural fins
The fins on a fish are the parts on its sides that it uses to help it swim.

final adjective
The final thing is the one that comes last. *This will be the final song in our concert.*

find verb finds, finding, found
When you find something, you see it. *I found 50p on the ground.*

fine adjective finer, finest
1 Something that is fine is thin and light. *I've got very fine hair.*
2 If the weather is fine, it is sunny.
3 If you feel fine, you feel well and happy.

fine noun plural fines
an amount of money that you have to pay because you have done something wrong

finger noun plural fingers
Your fingers are the parts of your body on the ends of your hands.

finish verb finishes, finishing, finished
1 When you finish something, you come to the end of it. *Have you finished your maths yet?*
2 When something finishes, it ends. *What time does the film finish?*

fir noun plural firs
a tall tree that has cones, and long, thin leaves shaped like needles

fire noun plural fires
1 When there is a fire, something is burning.
2 A fire is a machine that gives out heat.

fire verb fires, firing, fired
When you fire a gun, you make it shoot.

fire engine noun plural fire engines
a large truck that carries firefighters and the equipment that they need to put out fires

firefighter noun plural firefighters
a person whose job is to put out fires

firework noun plural fireworks
something that explodes with coloured lights and loud bangs

firm adjective firmer, firmest
1 Something that is firm is hard and does not move easily when you pull it or press on it.
2 Someone who is firm is quite strict and will not change their mind.
firmly adverb If you do or say something firmly you do it or say it strictly. *'We stay together,' I said firmly.*

first adjective
The first thing is the one that comes before all the others. *A is the first letter of the alphabet.*

first aid noun
help that you give to a person who is hurt, before a doctor comes

first person noun (in grammar)
When you use the first person, you use the words *I* and *me* to write about yourself in a story.

fish noun plural fishes, fish
A fish is an animal that swims and lives in water. Fish have fins to help them swim and scales on their bodies.

fish verb fishes, fishing, fished
When you fish, you try to catch fish.

fisherman noun plural fishermen
a person who catches fish

fist noun plural fists
When you make a fist, you close your hand tightly.

fit adjective fitter, fittest
1 If you are fit, your body is healthy and strong. *Swimming helps to keep you fit.*
2 If something is fit to use or eat, it is good enough. *This food is not fit to eat!*

fit verb fits, fitting, fitted
1 If something fits you, it is the right size for you to wear.
2 If something fits into a place, it is the right size to go there.

five noun plural fives
the number 5

fix verb fixes, fixing, fixed
1 When you fix one thing onto another, you join it on firmly. *My dad fixed the lamp onto my bike for me.*
2 When you fix something, you mend it.

fizzy adjective fizzier, fizziest
A fizzy drink has a lot of tiny bubbles of gas in it.

flag noun plural flags
a piece of cloth with a special design on, which is fixed to a pole *Do you know the colour of the United Nations flag?*

flake noun plural flakes
a small piece of something *A few flakes of snow were beginning to fall.*

flame noun plural flames
Flames are the orange, pointed parts that come up out of a fire.

a b c d e **f** g h i j k l m n o p q r s t u v w x y z

flap noun *plural* flaps
a part of something that hangs down and can move about

flap verb flaps, flapping, flapped
When something flaps, it moves up and down or from side to side. *The huge bird flapped its wings and flew off.*

flash noun *plural* flashes
a sudden bright light

flash verb flashes, flashing, flashed
When a light flashes, it shines brightly and then stops shining again. *The lights flashed on and off.*

flask noun *plural* flasks
a container that keeps hot drinks hot and cold drinks cold

flat adjective flatter, flattest
1 Something that is flat is smooth and level, and has no bumps on it. *You need a nice flat surface for rollerblading.*
2 A flat battery has no more power in it.
3 A flat tyre or ball does not have enough air in it.

flat noun *plural* flats
a set of rooms that you can live in inside a large building

flavour noun *plural* flavours
The flavour of something is the taste that it has when you eat it or drink it.

flea noun *plural* fleas
a small jumping insect that lives on larger animals and sucks their blood

fleece noun *plural* fleeces
1 A sheep's fleece is the wool on its body.
2 A fleece is a type of warm coat or jacket made of thick material.

flesh noun
Your flesh is the soft part of your body between your bones and your skin.

flew verb past tense of **fly** verb

flick verb flicks, flicking, flicked
When you flick something, you knock it with your finger so that it flies through the air. *He rolled the paper into a little ball and flicked it into the air.*

flight noun *plural* flights
1 a journey in an aeroplane *Our flight leaves at ten o'clock.*
2 A flight of stairs is a set of stairs.

flip verb flips, flipping, flipped
When you flip something over, you turn it over quickly.

flipper noun *plural* flippers
1 The flippers on a seal or a penguin are the parts on the sides of its body that it uses for swimming.
2 Flippers are large, flat shoes that you wear on your feet to help you swim.

float verb floats, floating, floated
When something floats, it does not sink but stays on the surface of water.

flock noun *plural* flocks
A flock of sheep or birds is a large group of them.

flood noun *plural* floods
When there is a flood, a lot of water spreads over the land.

flood verb floods, flooding, flooded
When a river floods, it becomes too full and spills out over the land.

floor noun *plural* floors
1 The floor in a building is the part that you walk on.
2 A floor in a tall building is one of the levels in it.

flop verb flops, flopping, flopped
1 If you flop down, you sit or lie down suddenly because you are very tired.
2 If something flops, it hangs and moves about loosely. *My hair kept flopping into my eyes.*

flour noun
Flour is a powder that is made from crushed wheat. You use flour for making bread, pastry, and cakes.

flow verb flows, flowing, flowed
When water flows, it moves along like a river.

flow chart noun *plural* flow charts
a diagram that shows the different stages of how something happens

flower noun *plural* flowers
the brightly coloured part of a plant

flown verb past tense of **fly** verb

flu noun
Flu is an illness that gives you a bad cold and makes you ache all over and feel very hot. Flu is short for **influenza**.

fluid noun *plural* fluids (say **floo**-id)
a liquid

flute noun *plural* flutes
a musical instrument which you hold sideways across your mouth and play by blowing across a hole in it

flutter verb flutters, fluttering, fluttered
When something flutters, it flaps gently.

fly noun *plural* flies
a small insect with wings

fly verb flies, flying, flew, flown
When something flies, it moves along through the air.

foal noun *plural* foals
a young horse

foam noun
1 a thick mass of small bubbles on the top of a liquid
2 a soft, light substance that is used inside chairs and cushions to make them soft to sit on

focus verb focuses, focusing, focused
When you focus a camera or telescope, you move the controls so that you get a clear picture.

fog noun
When there is fog, there is thick cloud just above the ground, which makes it difficult to see.

a b c d e **f** g h i j k l m n o p q r s t u v w x y z

A B C D E **F** G H I J K L M N O P Q R S T U V W X Y Z

fold verb folds, folding, folded

When you fold something, you bend one part of it over another part. *She folded the letter and put it in her bag.*

folder noun plural folders

1 a thin cardboard case that you keep pieces of paper in
2 a place where you keep several files together on a computer

follow verb follows, following, followed

1 If you follow someone, you go after them. *I felt sure that someone was following me.*
2 If you follow a road or path, you go along it. *Follow this path until you come to a river.*
3 If you follow instructions, you do what they tell you to do.

fond adjective fonder, fondest

If you are fond of something, you like it a lot. If you are fond of someone, you like them a lot.

font noun plural fonts

a set of letters in a particular style and size that you can use on a computer

food noun plural foods

anything that you eat to help you grow and be healthy

food chain noun plural food chains

(in science)

A food chain is a set of plants and animals that are linked because each one eats the one below it on the chain. For example, grass is eaten by a rabbit, then a rabbit is eaten by a fox.

foot noun plural feet

1 Your feet are the parts of your body that you stand on.
2 We can measure length in feet. One foot is about 30 centimetres.

football noun

1 a game in which two teams try to score goals by kicking a ball into a net
2 a ball that you use for playing football

for preposition

1 If something is for a person, you are going to give it to that person. *I've bought a present for you.*
2 If you say what something is for, you are saying how you use it. *You need a sharp knife for cutting bread.*

forbid verb forbids, forbidding, forbade, forbidden

To forbid someone to do something means to tell them that they must not do it. If something is forbidden, you are not allowed to do it.

force noun plural forces

1 If you use force to do something, you use your strength.
2 (in science) A force is something that pushes or pulls an object.
3 A police force is all the police who work together in one town or area.

force verb forces, forcing, forced

1 If you force someone to do something, you make them do it. *You can't force me to help you!*
2 If you force something open, you use your strength to open it.

forecast noun plural forecasts

When you give a forecast, you say what you think is going to happen.

forehead noun plural foreheads

Your forehead is the part of your head that is above your eyes.

foreign adjective

Things that are foreign come from other countries or are to do with other countries. *My brother speaks four foreign languages.*

forest noun plural forests

an area of land where a lot of trees grow close together

forget verb forgets, forgetting, forgot, forgotten

If you forget something, you do not remember it. *I forgot to do my homework.*

forgive verb forgives, forgiving, forgave, forgiven

If you forgive someone, you stop being angry with them.

fork noun plural forks

1 A fork is a tool with three sharp points called prongs. You use a fork for eating food, and you use a large fork for digging in the ground.
2 A fork in a road is a place where the road splits, and two roads go off in different directions.

form noun plural forms

1 a piece of paper that has writing on it and spaces where you must fill in your name and other information
2 a class in a school
3 a type *A bicycle is a form of transport.*

form verb forms, forming, formed

When something forms, it is made. *These rocks formed millions of years ago.*

formal adjective

1 Formal events or clothes are very smart and not relaxed.
2 Formal language is language that you write down, not language you use when you are talking to friends.

fortnight noun plural fortnights

A fortnight is two weeks.

fortress noun plural fortresses

A large building or group of buildings that is made strong against attack.

fortunate adjective

If you are fortunate, you are lucky. *I know I'm very fortunate to have such good friends.*

a
b
c
d
e
f
g
h
i
j
k
l
m
n
o
p
q
r
s
t
u
v
w
x
y
z

fortune noun *plural* **fortunes**
A fortune is a very large amount of money.

forty noun
the number 40

forwards, forward
1 towards the place that is in front of you
The train moved slowly forwards.
2 If you are looking forward to something, you are excited because it is going to happen.

fossil noun *plural* **fossils**
part of a dead plant or animal that has been in the ground for millions of years and has gradually turned to stone

fought verb past tense of **fight**

found verb past tense of **find**

fountain noun *plural* **fountains**
a jet of water that shoots up into the air

four noun *plural* **fours**
the number 4

fourteen noun
the number 14

fox noun *plural* **foxes**
a wild animal that looks like a dog and has red fur and a long, furry tail

fraction noun *plural* **fractions**
(in mathematics)
A fraction is a number that is not a whole number, $\frac{1}{3}$, $\frac{1}{2}$, and $\frac{3}{4}$ are fractions.

fracture noun *plural* **fractures**
a place where a bone is cracked or broken

fragile adjective (say **fraj**-ile)
Something that is fragile will break easily if you drop it.

fragment noun *plural* **fragments**
a small piece that has broken off something
There were a few fragments of glass on the ground.

frame noun *plural* **frames**
1 the part round the outside of a picture or a pair of glasses
2 the part that supports an object

freckle noun *plural* **freckles**
Freckles are the small brown spots that some people have on their skin, especially when they have been in the sun.

free adjective **freer, freest**
1 If you are free, you can go where you want and do what you want to do. *After five days locked in that room I was finally free.*
2 If something is free, you do not have to pay for it. *Entry to the museum is free.*

free verb **frees, freeing, freed**
To free someone means to let them go after they have been locked up.

freeze verb freezes, freezing, froze, frozen

1 When something freezes, it becomes very cold and hard and changes into ice. *The lake froze over last winter.*
2 If you are freezing or frozen, you are very cold.

freezer noun plural freezers

a large, very cold container in which you can store frozen food for a long time

frequent adjective

Something that is frequent happens quite often.

fresh adjective fresher, freshest

1 Something that is fresh is clean and new. *I went home and changed into some fresh clothes.*
2 Fresh food has been made or picked only a short time ago.
3 Fresh air is clean and cool.
4 Fresh water is not salty.
5 If you feel fresh, you do not feel tired.

friction noun (in science)

the force which is produced when one thing rubs against another

Friday noun plural Fridays

the day after Thursday

fridge noun plural fridges

A fridge is a large cool container that you keep food in so that it does not go bad. Fridge is short for **refrigerator**.

friend noun plural friends

Your friends are the people you like and know well.
friendly adjective If you are friendly, you like people and are nice to them. *Everyone is very friendly.*
friendship noun being friends with someone *Her friendship means a lot me.*

fright noun plural frights

a sudden feeling of fear *The face at the window gave me a bit of a fright.*
frightening adjective If something is frightening, it makes you suddenly feel fear. *It looks dark and mysterious and a bit frightening.*

frighten verb frightens, frightening, frightened

If something frightens you, it makes you feel scared. *I'm sorry, I didn't mean to frighten you.*

fringe noun plural fringes

short hair that hangs down over your forehead

frog noun plural frogs

A frog is a small animal with a smooth, wet skin and long back legs. Frogs live near water and can jump by using their strong back legs.

from preposition

1 When you go away from a place, you leave that place. *We flew from London to Paris.*
2 If a present is from a person, that person gave it to you. *I got a lovely present from my aunt.*

front noun plural fronts

The front of something is the part that faces forwards. *We sat at the front of the bus.*

a b c d e **f** g h i j k l m n o p q r s t u v w x y z

frost noun *plural* frosts
ice that looks like powder and covers the ground when the weather is cold

frown verb frowns, frowning, frowned
When you frown, you have lines on your forehead because you are angry or worried.

froze, frozen verb
past tenses of freeze

frozen adjective
Something that is frozen has turned to ice. *We skated on the frozen pond.*

fruit noun *plural* fruits, fruit
A fruit is the part of a plant which contains seeds. A lot of fruits taste sweet and are good to eat. Apples, oranges, and bananas are all types of fruit.

fry verb fries, frying, fried
When you fry food, you cook it in hot fat.

fuel noun *plural* fuels (say **fyoo**-el)
anything that people burn to give heat or power

full adjective fuller, fullest
If something is full, it has as much inside it as it can hold. *The room was full of people.*

full stop noun *plural* full stops
a dot like this **.** which you put at the end of every sentence

fun noun
When you have fun, you enjoy yourself.

funeral noun *plural* funerals
the ceremony that takes place when a dead person is buried or burned

funnel noun *plural* funnels
a chimney on a ship or steam engine

funny adjective funnier, funniest
1 Something that is funny makes you laugh or smile.
2 Something that is funny is strange or surprising. *There was a funny smell in the classroom.*

fur noun *plural* furs
the soft hair that covers some animals

furious adjective
If you are furious, you are very angry.
furiously adverb If you do or say something furiously, you do it or say it because you are very angry. *'I don't care!' he shouted furiously.*

furniture noun
things such as beds and tables that you need inside a house

further adverb a tense of far

fuss verb fusses, fussing, fussed
If you fuss about something, you worry about it too much.

future noun
The future is the time that will come.

fuzzy adjective fuzzier, fuzziest
A picture or sound that is fuzzy is not very clear.

Gg

gain verb gains, gaining, gained
If you gain something, you get something good or useful. *I got the answer right and gained two points for my team.*

galaxy noun *plural* galaxies
A galaxy is a large group of stars and planets. The Milky Way is a galaxy.

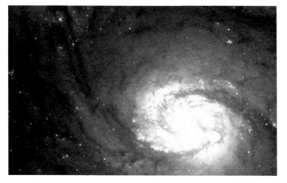

gale noun *plural* gales
a very strong wind

gallery noun *plural* galleries
a building or large room where there are paintings on the walls for people to look at

gallon noun *plural* gallons
We can measure liquids in gallons. A gallon is about $4\frac{1}{2}$ litres.

gallop verb gallops, galloping, galloped
When a horse gallops, it runs as fast as it can.

game noun *plural* games
something that you play for fun

gang noun *plural* gangs
a group of people who spend time together and do things together

gaol noun *plural* gaols (say **jail**)
Gaol is another spelling of jail.

gap noun *plural* gaps
a hole, or an empty space between two things

garage noun *plural* garages
1 a building in which people keep a car, motorbike, or bus
2 a place that sells petrol and mends cars

garden noun *plural* gardens
a piece of ground where people grow flowers, fruit, or vegetables

garlic noun
a plant like an onion with a very strong smell and taste

gas noun *plural* gases
A gas is any substance that is like air, and is not a solid or a liquid. We can burn some types of gas to give heat to cook with or heat our homes.

gasp verb gasps, gasping, gasped
When you gasp, you breathe in quickly and noisily because you are surprised, or because you have been running. *'I can't run any further,' he gasped.*

gate noun *plural* gates
a door in a wall or fence

gather verb gathers, gathering, gathered
1 When people gather, they come together. *A crowd gathered to watch the fight.*
2 When you gather things, you collect them and bring them together. *I need to gather some information for my project.*

gave verb past tense of give

gaze verb gazes, gazing, gazed
If you gaze at something, you look at it for a long time.

general adjective
1 Something that is general includes most people. *There was general agreement that something had to be done.*
2 Something that is general does not go into details. *We had a general discussion about what life was like in Roman times.*

generally adverb
usually *It is generally very cold here in the winter.*

generous adjective
Someone who is generous is kind and always ready to give or share the things that they have.

genre noun *plural* genres (say **jahn**-ra)
A genre is one type of writing. Poetry, adventure stories, and fairy tales are examples of different genres.

gentle adjective gentler, gentlest
If you are gentle, you touch something in a kind, careful way and are not rough. *I gave Sarah a gentle nudge.*
gently adverb If you do or say something gently, you do it or say it in a careful way, and are not rough. *She very gently put the baby bird back in the nest.*

gentleman noun *plural* gentlemen
a polite name for a man

genuine adjective (say **jen**-yoo-in)
Something that is genuine is real. *Do you think this is genuine gold?*

geography noun (say jee-**og**-ra-fee)
the subject in which you learn about the earth, with its mountains, rivers, countries, and the people who live in them

germ noun *plural* germs
A germ is a tiny living thing, that is too small to see. Germs sometimes make you ill if they get inside your body.

get verb gets, getting, got
1 When you get something, you receive it, buy it, or earn it, and it becomes yours. *What did you get for your birthday?*
2 To get means to become. *Are you getting tired yet?*

ghost noun *plural* ghosts
the shape of a dead person that some people think they can see

giant noun *plural* giants
a very big person, especially in stories

gift noun *plural* gifts
a present

gigantic adjective
Something that is gigantic is very big. *He lifted the tree with one of his gigantic arms.*

giggle verb giggles, giggling, giggled
If you giggle, you laugh in a silly way.

gill noun *plural* gills
The gills on a fish are the parts on its sides that it breathes through.

ginger noun
a spice with a strong, hot taste
ginger adjective
Ginger hair is a reddish-orange colour.

giraffe noun *plural* giraffes
A giraffe is a very tall African animal with a very long neck. Giraffes are the tallest animals in the world.

girl noun *plural* girls
a female child

give verb gives, giving, gave, given
If you give something to someone, you let them have it.

glad adjective
If you are glad about something, you are happy about it.

glance verb glances, glancing, glanced
If you glance at something, you look at it quickly.

glare verb glares, glaring, glared
1 If you glare at someone, you look at them angrily. *Mr Dempster glared at the two boys.*
2 If a light glares, it shines with a very bright light that hurts your eyes.

glass noun plural glasses
1 the hard, clear substance that windows are made of
2 a cup made of glass, which you drink out of

glasses noun
two round pieces of glass in a frame, which some people wear over their eyes to help them to see better

gleam verb gleams, gleaming, gleamed
If something gleams, it shines. *The cat's eyes gleamed in the dark.*

glide verb glides, gliding, glided
When something glides along, it moves along very smoothly. *The skaters glided over the ice.*

glider noun plural gliders
a type of aeroplane without an engine

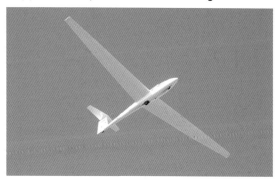

glimpse verb glimpses, glimpsing, glimpsed
If you glimpse something, you see it for only a few seconds. *I glimpsed an animal in the bushes.*

glitter verb glitters, glittering, glittered
If something glitters, it shines and sparkles brightly.

gloat verb gloats, gloating, gloated
If you gloat, you show that you are pleased because you have done well and someone else has done badly.

global warming noun
the process by which the earth is gradually getting warmer because of pollution in the atmosphere

globe noun plural globes
a ball with the map of the whole world on it

gloomy adjective gloomier, gloomiest
1 A gloomy place is dark.
2 If you feel gloomy, you feel sad.

glossary noun plural glossaries
a list at the back of a book, which explains the meanings of difficult words that are used in the book

glossy adjective glossier, glossiest
Something that is glossy is smooth and shiny.

a
b
c
d
e
f
g
h
i
j
k
l
m
n
o
p
q
r
s
t
u
v
w
x
y
z

glove noun *plural* gloves
A glove is something that you wear on your hands in cold weather. Gloves have separate parts for your thumb and each finger.

glow verb glows, glowing, glowed
1 If something glows, it shines with a warm, gentle light.
2 When your cheeks glow, they are pink because you are cold or have been running around.

glue noun *plural* glues
a sticky substance that you use for sticking things together

gnarled adjective
(**gn-** in this word sounds like **n-**)
Something that is gnarled is bent and twisted because it is very old. *We sat on a gnarled, old tree trunk.*

gnaw verb gnaws, gnawing, gnawed
(**gn-** in this word sounds like **n-**)
When an animal gnaws on something, it keeps biting it. *The dog was outside, gnawing on a bone.*

gnome noun *plural* gnomes
(**gn-** in this word sounds like **n-**)
a small, ugly fairy in stories

go verb goes, going, went, gone
1 When you go somewhere, you move or travel so that you are there. *Where are you going?*
2 If a machine is going, it is working.
3 To go means to become. *Clay goes hard when you bake it.*

goal noun *plural* goals
1 the net where you must kick or throw the ball to score a point in a game such as football or netball
2 something that you want to achieve

goat noun *plural* goats
an animal with horns that is kept on farms for its milk

god noun *plural* gods
a person or thing that people worship

goggles noun
special thick glasses that you wear to protect your eyes, for example when you are swimming

go-kart noun *plural* go-karts
a type of small car that people use for racing

gold noun
a shiny, yellow metal that is very valuable

golf noun
Golf is a game that you play by hitting small, white balls with sticks called **golf clubs**. You have to hit the balls into holes in the ground.

gone verb past tense of go

good adjective better, best
1 Something that is good is nice, pleasant, or enjoyable. *Have you had a good day at school?*
2 Someone who is good is kind and honest. *You have been a very good friend to me.*
3 When you are good, you behave well and do not do anything naughty. *Be good for your aunt and uncle.*

A B C D E F **G** H I J K L M N O P Q R S T U V W X Y Z

4 If you are good at something, you can do it well.

goodbye interjection
the word you say to someone when you are leaving them

goods noun
Goods are things that people buy and sell.

goose noun *plural* geese
A goose is a large bird that is kept on farms for its meat and eggs. A male goose is called a **gander**.

gorilla noun *plural* gorillas
A gorilla is an African animal like a very large monkey with long arms and no tail. A gorilla is a type of ape.

got verb past tense of get

government noun
plural governments
The government is the group of people who are in charge of a country.

grab verb grabs, grabbing, grabbed
If you grab something, you take hold of it quickly or roughly. *The thief grabbed my purse and ran off.*

graceful adjective
Someone who is graceful moves in a smooth, gentle way. *She is a very graceful dancer.*

gradual adjective
Something that is gradual happens slowly, bit by bit, not all at once.
gradually adverb If something happens gradually, it happens slowly. *I was gradually beginning to feel better.*

graffiti noun (say gra-**fee**-tee)
writing and pictures that people have scribbled or scratched onto walls

grain noun *plural* grains
1 Grain is the seeds of plants like corn and wheat.
2 A grain of salt or sand is one tiny bit of it.

gram noun *plural* grams
We can measure weight in grams. There are 1000 grams in one kilogram.

grammar noun
Grammar is all the rules of a language, which tell us how to put the words together correctly.

grand adjective grander, grandest
Something that is grand is very big and important.

grandchild noun *plural* grandchildren
Someone's grandchild is a child of their son or daughter. A grandchild can also be called a **granddaughter**, or a **grandson**.

grandparent noun
plural grandparents
Your grandparents are the parents of your father or mother. You can also call your grandparents your **grandmother** and **grandfather**. A grandmother is often called **grandma** or **granny**. A grandfather is often called **grandpa** or **granddad**.

grape noun *plural* grapes
a small, soft green or purple fruit that grows in bunches

A B C D E F **G** H I J K L M N O P Q R S T U V W X Y Z

grapefruit noun *plural* **grapefruits**
a large, sour-tasting fruit that has thick yellow skin

graph noun *plural* **graphs**
a diagram that shows information about something *We drew a graph showing the drinks we like.*

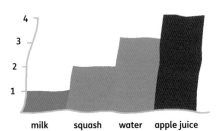

grasp verb **grasps, grasping, grasped**
If you grasp something, you get hold of it and hold it tightly. *She grasped my arm to stop herself from falling.*

grass noun *plural* **grasses**
a green plant that covers the ground and is used for lawns and parks

grasshopper noun
plural **grasshoppers**
an insect that has long back legs and can jump a long way

grate verb **grates, grating, grated**
When you grate food, you cut it into very small pieces by rubbing it against a rough tool.

grateful adjective
If you are grateful for something, you are glad that you have it. *We are very grateful for all your help.*

grave noun *plural* **graves**
a place where a dead person is buried in the ground

grave adjective **graver, gravest**
Something that is grave is very serious and worrying.

gravel noun
tiny stones that are used to make paths
Her feet crunched over the gravel.

gravity noun (in science)
the force that pulls things towards the earth

graze verb **grazes, grazing, grazed**
1 If you graze a part of your body, you hurt it by scraping it against something and making it bleed. *I fell over and grazed my knee.*
2 When animals graze, they eat grass. *The sheep were grazing in the field.*

grease noun
a thick, oily substance

great adjective **greater, greatest**
1 Something that is great is very big and impressive.
2 A great person is very clever and important. *Van Gogh was a great artist.*
3 Something that is great is very good. *It's a great film!*

greedy adjective **greedier, greediest**
Someone who is greedy wants more food or money than they need.

green adjective
Something that is green is the colour of grass.

greengrocer noun
plural **greengrocers**
someone who sells fruit and vegetables in a shop

greenhouse noun *plural* **greenhouses**
a glass building that people use for growing plants in

greet verb **greets, greeting, greeted**
When you greet someone, you welcome them and say hello to them.

grew verb past tense of **grow**

grey adjective (rhymes with *day*)
Something that is grey is the colour of the sky on a cloudy day.

GREY

grid noun *plural* **grids**
a pattern of straight lines that cross over each other to make squares

grill verb **grills, grilling, grilled**
When you grill food, you cook it on metal bars either under or over heat. *We grilled some sausages for tea.*

grin verb **grins, grinning, grinned**
When you grin, you smile in a cheerful way.

grind verb **grinds, grinding, ground**
When you grind something, you crush it into tiny bits. *The wheat is taken to the mill and ground into flour.*

grip verb **grips, gripping, gripped**
When you grip something, you hold on to it tightly.

groan verb **groans, groaning, groaned**
When you groan, you make a low sound because you are in pain or are disappointed about something.

grocery noun *plural* **groceries**
a shop that sells tea, sugar, jam, and other kinds of food

groove noun *plural* **grooves**
a long, narrow cut in something

ground noun *plural* **grounds**
1 The ground is the earth.
2 A sports ground is a piece of land that people play sport on.

ground verb past tense of **grind**

group noun *plural* **groups**
1 a number of people, animals, or things that are together or belong together
There was a group of children standing by the ice cream stall.
2 a number of people who play music together

grow verb **grows, growing, grew, grown**
1 To grow means to become bigger. *My aunt always says, 'My! Haven't you grown!'*
2 When you grow plants, you put them in the ground and look after them.

3 To grow means to become. *Everyone was beginning to grow tired.*

a b c d e f **g** h i j k l m n o p q r s t u v w x y z

A B C D E F **G** H I J K L M N O P Q R S T U V W X Y Z

growl verb growls, growling, growled
When an animal growls, it makes a deep, angry sound in its throat.

grown-up noun plural grown-ups
a man or woman who is not a child any more

growth noun
the way in which something grows and gets bigger *We measured the growth of the plants.*

grub noun plural grubs
1 an animal that looks like a small worm and will become an insect when it is an adult
2 (informal) food

grumble verb grumbles, grumbling, grumbled
If you grumble about something, you complain about it.

grunt verb grunts, grunting, grunted
When a pig grunts, it makes a rough sound.

guarantee noun plural guarantees
(**gu-** in this word sounds like **g-**)
a promise that something you have bought will be mended or replaced free if it goes wrong

guard verb guards, guarding, guarded
1 When you guard a place, you watch it to keep it safe from other people. *The dog was guarding the house.*
2 When you guard a person, you watch them to keep them safe or to stop them from escaping.

guard noun plural guards
someone who protects a place or watches a person to keep them safe or stop them from escaping

guess verb guesses, guessing, guessed
When you guess, you say what you think the answer to a question is when you do not really know. *Can you guess what I've got in my pocket?*

guest noun plural guests
a person who is invited to a party or is invited to stay in someone else's home for a short time

guide noun plural guides
1 a person who shows you around a place
2 a book that gives you information about something

guide verb guides, guiding, guided
If you guide someone to a place, you lead them or take them there.

guilty adjective guiltier, guiltiest
1 If you are guilty, you have done something wrong. *The prisoner was found guilty of murder.*
2 If you feel guilty, you feel bad because you have done something wrong.

guitar noun plural guitars
A guitar is a musical instrument with strings across it. You hold a guitar in front of your body and play it by pulling on the strings with your fingers.

gulf noun plural gulfs
an area of the sea that stretches a long way into the land

gulp verb gulps, gulping, gulped
When you gulp food or drink, you swallow it very quickly.

gum noun *plural* **gums**
1 Your gums are the hard pink parts of your mouth that are around your teeth.
2 Gum is a sweet that you chew but do not swallow.

gun noun *plural* **guns**
a weapon that fires bullets from a metal tube

gurdwara noun *plural* **gurdwaras**
a Sikh temple

guru noun *plural* **gurus**
a Hindu religious leader

gust noun *plural* **gusts**
A gust of wind is a sudden rush of wind.

gutter noun *plural* **gutters**
1 a place at the side of a road where water collects and flows away when it rains
2 a pipe that goes along the edge of a roof and collects water from the roof when it rains

gym noun *plural* **gyms** (say **jim**)
A gym is a large room with special equipment in for doing exercises. A gym is also called a **gymnasium**.

gymnastics noun
special exercises that you do to make your body strong and to show how well you can bend, stretch, and twist your body

Hh

habit noun *plural* **habits**
If something that you do is a habit, you do it without thinking, because you have done it so often before.

habitat noun *plural* **habitats**
The habitat of an animal or plant is the place where it usually lives or grows.

had verb past tense of **have**

hail noun
small pieces of ice that fall from the sky like rain

hair noun *plural* **hairs**
Your hair is the long, soft stuff that grows on your head. An animal's hair is the soft stuff that grows all over its body.

hairdresser noun *plural* **hairdressers**
someone who cuts people's hair

hairy adjective **hairier, hairiest**
Something that is hairy is covered with hair. A person who is hairy has a lot of hair on their body.

a b c d e f **g h** i j k l m n o p q r s t u v w x y z

95

A
B
C
D
E
F
G
H
I
J
K
L
M
N
O
P
Q
R
S
T
U
V
W
X
Y
Z

Hajj noun

The Hajj is the journey to Mecca that all Muslims try to make at least once in their lives.

half noun *plural* halves

One half of something is one of two equal parts that the thing is divided into. It can also be written as $\frac{1}{2}$.

halfway adverb

in the middle *I'll meet you halfway between my house and your house.*

hall noun *plural* halls

1 the part of a house that is just inside the front door
2 a very big room
3 a large, important building

Hallowe'en noun

31 October, when you dress up, often as ghosts or witches

halve verb halves, halving, halved

To halve something means to cut it into two equal parts.

ham noun

meat from a pig's leg that has been salted or smoked

hammer noun *plural* hammers

a heavy tool that you use for hitting nails

hand noun *plural* hands

Your hands are the parts of your body at the ends of your arms.

handbag noun *plural* handbags

a small bag in which women carry money and other things

handkerchief noun

plural handkerchiefs
a piece of material you use for blowing your nose

handle noun *plural* handles

the part of something that you hold in your hand

handle verb handles, handling, handled

When you handle something, you pick it up and hold it in your hands. *You have to handle the young animals very gently.*

handsome adjective

A handsome man or boy is attractive to look at.

handwriting noun

Your handwriting is the way in which you write.

handy adjective handier, handiest

Something that is handy is useful and easy to use.

hang verb hangs, hanging, hung

When you hang something up, you put it on a hook or nail.

hanger noun *plural* hangers

a piece of wood or metal that you hang clothes on

Hanukkah noun (say **hah**-noo-ka)

the Jewish festival of lights, which lasts for eight days and begins in December

happen verb happens, happening, happened

1 When something happens, it takes place. *When did the accident happen?*
2 If you happen to do something, you do it by chance, without planning to do it.

happy **adjective** happier, happiest
When you are happy, you feel pleased and you are enjoying yourself.
happiness noun Happiness is when you are pleased and are enjoying yourself. *She was crying tears of happiness.*

harbour **noun** *plural* harbours
a place where people can tie up boats and leave them

hard **adjective** harder, hardest
1 Something that is hard is not soft. *In winter the ground is often hard and frozen.*
2 Something that is hard is difficult. *The last maths test was really hard.*

hard **adverb**
When you work hard, you work a lot and with a lot of effort.

hard disk **noun** *plural* hard disks
the part inside a computer where information is stored

hardly **adverb**
If you can hardly do something, you can only just do it. *I was so tired that I could hardly walk.*

hardware **noun**
1 tools, nails, and other things made of metal
2 (in ICT) A computer's hardware is the parts that you can see, and the parts inside that make it work. The **software** is the programs you put into it.

hare **noun** *plural* hares
A hare is an animal that looks like a big rabbit with very long ears. Hares have strong back legs and can run very fast.

harm **verb** harms, harming, harmed
To harm something means to damage it or spoil it in some way. To harm someone means to hurt them.

harness **noun** *plural* harnesses
1 a set of straps that you wear round your body to keep you safe. *You must wear a safety harness when you are rock climbing.*
2 a set of straps that you put over a horse's head and round its neck so that you can control it

harsh **adjective** harsher, harshest
1 Something that is harsh is not soft or gentle. *His violin made a harsh sound.*
2 Someone who is harsh is very strict and sometimes unkind. *The new headmistress is very harsh.*

harvest **noun** *plural* harvests
the time when farmers gather in the crops that they have grown

hat **noun** *plural* hats
something that you wear on your head

hatch **verb** hatches, hatching, hatched
When a baby bird or animal hatches, it comes out of an egg and is born.

hate **verb** hates, hating, hated
If you hate something, you do not like it at all. If you hate someone, you do not like them at all.

a
b
c
d
e
f
g
h
i
j
k
l
m
n
o
p
q
r
s
t
u
v
w
x
y
z

A B C D E F G **H** I J K L M N O P Q R S T U V W X Y Z

haul verb hauls, hauling, hauled
(rhymes with *ball*)
To haul something means to pull it along.
They hauled the boat out of the river.

haunted adjective
A haunted place is one where people believe
there are ghosts.

have verb has, having, had
1 If you have something, you own it. *I don't
have a computer at home.*
2 If you have an illness, you are suffering
from it. *I think you may have chickenpox.*
3 If you have to do something, you must do
it. *We have to tidy up before mum gets back!*

hay noun
dry grass that people use to feed animals

he pronoun
You use **he** when you are talking about a
man, boy, or male animal. *He feels sick.
He asked me to his house for tea.*

head noun *plural* heads
1 Your head is the part at the top of your
body that contains your brain, eyes, and
mouth.
2 The head is the person in charge of
something.

headache noun *plural* headaches
If you have a headache, your head hurts.

heading noun *plural* headings
words you write as a title at the top of a
piece of writing

headlight noun *plural* headlights
The headlights on a car are the lights that
you use at night so that you can see where
you are going.

headline noun *plural* headlines
the words in large print at the top of a piece
of writing in a newspaper

headphones noun
a set of small speakers that you wear over
your ears so that you can listen to music
from a music player

headquarters noun
the place where an organization is based,
and where the people in charge of it work

headteacher noun
plural headteachers
A headteacher is the person in charge of all
the teachers and children in a school.
A headteacher is also called a **headmaster**
or **headmistress**.

heal verb heals, healing, healed
When a cut or broken bone heals, it gets
better. *It usually takes about six weeks for a
broken bone to heal.*

health noun
Your health is how well you are.

healthy adjective healthier, healthiest
1 When you are healthy, you are not ill.
2 Things that are healthy are good for you
and keep you fit and well.

heap noun *plural* heaps
an untidy pile of things

hear verb hears, hearing, heard
When you hear something, you notice it
through your ears.

hearing noun
Your hearing is your ability to hear things.

heart noun *plural* hearts
1 Your heart is the part of your body in your chest that pumps blood all round your body.

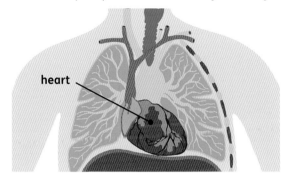

heart

2 A heart is a curved shape that looks like the shape of a heart and is used to represent love.

heat noun
the hot feeling you get from a fire or from the sun

heat verb heats, heating, heated
When you heat something, you make it warm or hot.

heaven noun
Heaven is the place where some people believe that a god lives. Some people believe that people go to heaven when they die.

heavy adjective heavier, heaviest
Something that is heavy weighs a lot and is hard to lift.
heavily adverb If you do something heavily, you do it with a lot of force. *We were breathing heavily through our noses.*

hedge noun *plural* hedges
a line of bushes that are growing very close together and make a sort of wall round a garden or field

hedgehog noun *plural* hedgehogs
a small animal that is covered with spines like sharp needles

heel noun *plural* heels
Your heel is the back part of your foot.

height noun *plural* heights
(rhymes with *bite*)
The height of something is how high it is. The height of a person is how tall they are.

held verb past tense of hold

helicopter noun *plural* helicopters
a flying machine with a big propeller that spins round on its roof

hello, hallo interjection
the word you say to someone when you meet them

helmet noun *plural* helmets
a strong hat that you wear to protect your head

help verb helps, helping, helped
1 When you help someone, you do something for them that makes things easier for them.
2 When you help yourself to something, you take it. *Please help yourselves to pizza.*
helpful adjective If you are helpful, you do something for someone that makes things easier for them. *Thank you, you've been very helpful.*

a
b
c
d
e
f
g
h
i
j
k
l
m
n
o
p
q
r
s
t
u
v
w
x
y
z

A
B
C
D
E
F
G
H
I
J
K
L
M
N
O
P
Q
R
S
T
U
V
W
X
Y
Z

helping noun plural helpings
A helping of food is an amount that you give to one person. *Can I have just a small helping please?*

helpless adjective
If you are helpless, you cannot look after yourself.

hemisphere noun
plural **hemispheres** (say **hem**-iss-fere) one half of the earth *Britain is in the northern hemisphere.*

hen noun plural hens
a bird that is kept on farms for the eggs that it lays

heptagon noun plural heptagons
a shape with seven straight sides

her determiner, pronoun
You use **her** when you are talking about a woman, girl, or female animal. *I can see her. He took the books from her.*

herb noun plural herbs
A herb is a plant that people add to food when they are cooking to make it taste nice. Parsley and mint are herbs.

herd noun plural herds
A herd of animals is a group of animals that live and feed together.

here adverb
in this place *Please wait here until I get back.*

hero noun plural heroes
1 a boy or man who has done something very brave
2 The hero of a story is the man or boy who is the main character.

heroine noun plural heroines
1 a girl or woman who has done something very brave
2 The heroine of a story is the woman or girl who is the main character.

hers pronoun
You use **hers** when you are talking about something that belongs to a woman, girl, or female animal. *The books is hers.*

hesitate verb hesitates, hesitating, hesitated
If you hesitate, you wait for a little while before you do something because you are not sure what you should do.

hexagon noun plural hexagons
a shape with six straight sides

hibernate verb hibernates, hibernating, hibernated
When animals hibernate, they spend the winter in a special kind of deep sleep. Bats, tortoises, and hedgehogs all hibernate.

hide verb hides, hiding, hid, hidden
1 When you hide, you go to a place where people cannot see you.
2 If you hide something, you put it in a secret place so that people cannot find it. *I hid the letter under my mattress.*

high adjective higher, highest
1 Something that is high is very tall. *There was a high wall around the garden.*
2 Something that is high up is a long way above the ground.
3 A high voice or sound is not deep or low.

hill noun plural hills
a bit of ground that is higher than the ground around it

him pronoun
You use **him** when you are talking about about a boy, man, or male animal. *Please give him the milk.*

Hindu noun plural Hindus
someone who follows the religion of **Hinduism**, which is an Indian religion with many gods

hinge noun plural hinges
A hinge is a piece of metal that is fixed to a door and to the wall. A hinge can move so that you can open and shut the door.

hint verb hints, hinting, hinted
When you hint, you suggest something without saying exactly what you mean.

hip noun plural hips
Your hips are the parts of your body where your legs join the rest of your body.

hippopotamus noun
plural hippopotamuses
A hippopotamus is a very large, heavy African animal that lives near water. It is sometimes called a **hippo** for short.

hire verb hires, hiring, hired
When you hire something, you pay to use it for a short time. *You can hire skates at the ice rink.*

his determiner, pronoun
You use **his** when you are talking about something that belongs to a man, boy, or male animal. *The car is his. That's his lunch.*

hiss verb hisses, hissing, hissed
When a snake hisses, it makes a long sss sound.

history noun
the subject in which you learn about things that happened in the past

hit verb hits, hitting, hit
To hit something means to bang against it. To hit someone means to knock them or slap them.

hive noun plural hives
A hive is a special box that bees live in. It is designed so that people can collect the honey that the bees make.

hoarse adjective
A hoarse voice sounds rough and deep.

hobby noun plural hobbies
something that you do for fun in your spare time

a
b
c
d
e
f
g
h
i
j
k
l
m
n
o
p
q
r
s
t
u
v
w
x
y
z

A
B
C
D
E
F
G
H
I
J
K
L
M
N
O
P
Q
R
S
T
U
V
W
X
Y
Z

hockey noun
a game in which two teams try to score goals by hitting a ball into a net with a special stick

hold verb holds, holding, held
1 When you hold something, you have it in your hands. *Please can I hold the puppy?*
2 The amount that something holds is the amount that you can put inside it. *This jug will hold one litre of water.*

hole noun plural holes
a gap or an empty space in something *I've got a hole in my sock.*

Holi noun (say hoe-li)
a Hindu festival that happens in the spring

holiday noun plural holidays
a time when you do not have to go to school or work

hollow adjective
Something that is hollow has an empty space inside it.

holy adjective holier, holiest
Something that is holy is special because it has something to do with a god or religion.

home noun plural homes
Your home is the place where you live.

home page noun plural home pages
the main page on a website, which you can look at by using the Internet

homework noun
school work that you do at home, in the evenings or at the weekend

honest adjective
Someone who is honest does not steal or cheat or tell lies.

honey noun
a sweet, sticky food that is made by bees

hood noun plural hoods
the part of a coat that you put over your head when it is cold or raining

hoof noun plural hoofs, hooves
An animal's hooves are the hard parts on its feet

hook noun plural hooks
a curved piece of metal that you use for hanging things on or catching things with

hoop noun plural hoops
a big wooden or plastic ring that you use in games

hoot verb hoots, hooting, hooted
To hoot means to make a sound like an owl or the horn of a car. *A van drove past and hooted at us.*

hop verb hops, hopping, hopped
1 When you hop, you jump on one foot.
2 When animals hop, they jump with two feet together.

hope verb hopes, hoping, hoped
If you hope that something will happen, you want it to happen. *I hope I get a new phone for my birthday.*

hopeful adjective
If you are hopeful, you think that something you want to happen will happen.
hopefully adverb If you do something hopefully you do it in a hopeful way, or you are hopeful that something will happen.

hopeless adjective

1 You say that something is hopeless when you think that it is never going to work. *I tried to open the door again, but it was hopeless.*
2 If you are hopeless at something, you are very bad at it. *He was hopeless at swimming.*

horizon noun

the line in the distance where the sky and the land or sea seem to meet *I can see a ship on the horizon.*

horizontal adjective

Something that is horizontal is flat and level.

horn noun *plural* horns

1 The horns on some animals are the hard, pointed parts that grow on their heads.
2 A horn is a musical instrument made of brass. You play it by blowing into it.
3 The horn on a car is the part that makes a loud noise to warn people when there is danger.

horrible adjective

Something that is horrible is very nasty or frightening. *The medicine tasted horrible.*

horror noun

a feeling of very great fear

horse noun *plural* horses

a big animal that people can ride on or use to pull carts

hospital noun *plural* hospitals

a place where people who are ill or hurt are looked after until they are better

hot adjective hotter, hottest

1 Something that is hot is very warm. *It was a lovely, hot summer's day.*
2 Hot food has a strong, spicy taste.

hotel noun *plural* hotels

a building where you can pay to stay the night and to have meals

hour noun *plural* hours

We measure time in hours. There are sixty minutes in one hour, and twenty-four hours in one day.

house noun *plural* houses

a building where people live

hover verb hovers, hovering, hovered

When something hovers in the air, it stays in one place in the air.

hovercraft noun hovercraft

a type of boat that travels on a cushion of air just above the surface of the water

how adverb

1 a word that you use to ask questions *How old are you?*
2 a word you use to explain the way something works or happens *He explained how a camera works.*

however adverb

1 no matter how much *You'll never catch him, however fast you run.*
2 in spite of this *We were losing 3–0 at half time. However, we still kept trying.*

howl verb howls, howling, howled

To howl means to make a long, high sound, like the sound of an animal crying or a strong wind blowing. *It was very dark, and the wind howled horribly around her. — L. Frank Baum, The Wizard of Oz*

a
b
c
d
e
f
g
h
i
j
k
l
m
n
o
p
q
r
s
t
u
v
w
x
y
z

A B C D E F G H I J K L M N O P Q R S T U V W X Y Z

hug verb hugs, hugging, hugged
When you hug someone, you hold them in your arms to show you love them.

huge adjective
Something that is huge is very big.

hum verb hums, humming, hummed
When you hum, you sing a tune with your lips closed.

human noun plural humans
A human is a man, woman, or child.
A human is also called a **human being**.

humour noun
1 If you have a sense of humour, you enjoy laughing at things.
2 If you are in a good humour, you are in a good mood.

hump noun plural humps
a round bump on a camel's back

hundred noun plural hundreds
the number 100

hung verb past tense of hang

hungry adjective hungrier, hungriest
If you are hungry, you feel that you need food.
hungrily adverb If you do something hungrily, you do it in a way that shows you are hungry.

hunt verb hunts, hunting, hunted
1 To hunt means to chase and kill animals for food or as a sport.
2 When you hunt for something, you look for it in a lot of different places.

hurricane noun plural hurricanes
a storm with a very strong wind

hurry verb hurries, hurrying, hurried
When you hurry, you walk or run quickly, or try to do something quickly.

hurt verb hurts, hurting, hurt
1 To hurt someone means to make them feel pain. *You shouldn't ever hurt animals.*
2 If a part of your body hurts, it feels sore.

husband noun plural husbands
A woman's husband is the man she is married to.

hut noun plural huts
a small building made of wood

hutch noun plural hutches
a small box or cage that you keep a pet rabbit in

hymn noun plural hymns
(sounds like him)
a Christian song that praises God

hyphen noun plural hyphens
(say **hye**-fen)
A hyphen is a mark like this - that you use in writing to join parts of words together. The word *grown-up* has a hyphen.

Ii

I pronoun
You use I when you are talking about yourself. *Can I have some milk? I think I'd like some milk.*

ice noun
water that has frozen hard

iceberg noun *plural* icebergs
a very big piece of ice floating in the sea

ice cream noun *plural* ice creams
a very cold, frozen food that is made from milk or cream and flavoured with sugar and fruit or chocolate

ice skate noun *plural* ice skates
Ice skates are special shoes with blades on the bottom, which you use for skating on ice.

icicle noun *plural* icicles
a thin, pointed piece of ice hanging down from a high place

icing noun
a sweet mixture that you spread over cakes to decorate them

ICT noun
ICT is the subject in which you study computers. It stands for information and communication technology.

icy adjective icier, iciest
1 Something that is icy is very cold.
2 When the road is icy, it is slippery because it is covered with ice.
3 If someone behaves or speaks in an icy way, they are very unfriendly.

idea noun *plural* ideas
1 When you have an idea, you think of something that you could do.
2 If you have an idea about something, you have a picture of it in your mind.

ideal adjective
Something that is ideal is perfect. *It was ideal weather for going to the beach.*

identical adjective
Things that are identical are exactly the same.

idle adjective idler, idlest
Someone who is idle is lazy.

idol noun *plural* idols
a famous person that a lot of people love

if conjunction, noun
1 You use **if** when you are talking about something that might happen. *If you go to the park, can you take your brother?*
2 You use **if** when you are talking about a choice between two things. *Do you know if you want to go to the park or not?*
3 **If** means on the condition that. *I'll take him to the park if we're allowed sweets.*

igloo noun *plural* igloos
a small, round house that is made of blocks of hard snow

a
b
c
d
e
f
g
h
i
j
k
l
m
n
o
p
q
r
s
t
u
v
w
x
y
z

ignore verb ignores, ignoring, ignored
If you ignore someone, you refuse to speak to them or take any notice of them. *I said hello to her, but she ignored me.*

ill adjective
If you are ill, you are not very well. *I feel too ill to go to school.*

illness noun *plural* illnesses
An illness is something that makes people ill. Measles, chickenpox, and colds are illnesses.

illustrate verb illustrates, illustrating, illustrated
To illustrate a book or story means to add pictures to it.

imaginary adjective
Something that is imaginary does not really exist, but is only in your mind or in a story. *Dragons are imaginary animals.*

imagine verb imagines, imagining, imagined
When you imagine something, you make a picture of it in your mind. *I closed my eyes and tried to imagine I was back at home.*

Imam noun *plural* Imams
a Muslim religious leader

imitate verb imitates, imitating, imitated
To imitate someone means to copy the way they speak or behave.

imitation noun *plural* imitations
something that has been made to look like something valuable

immediate adjective
Something that is immediate happens straight away.
immediately adverb If you do something immediately, you do it straight away. *Come here immediately!*

impatient adjective
Someone who is impatient gets bored and angry if they have to wait for something. *Don't be so impatient! It's your turn next.*

important adjective
1 If something is important, you must think about it carefully and seriously. *I've got an important message for you.*
2 An important person is special and well known.

impossible adjective
If something is impossible, no one can do it. *It's impossible to undo this knot.*

improve verb improves, improving, improved
1 To improve something means to make it better. *You need to improve your handwriting.*
2 When something improves, it gets better. *Your maths is improving.*

in preposition
1 inside *My pencil case is in my bag.*
2 wearing *I was still in my school uniform.*

inch noun *plural* inches
We can measure length in inches. One inch is about $2\frac{1}{2}$ centimetres.

include verb includes, including, included
If you include something you put it with other things and make it part of the set or group. If you include someone, you let them join a group.

A B C D E F G H **I** J K L M N O P Q R S T U V W X Y Z

increase verb increases, increasing, increased
When an amount increases, it gets bigger. *Our speed gradually increased to 70 miles per hour.*

index noun *plural* indexes
a list at the back of a book, which tells you what things are in the book and where to find them

indignant adjective
If you are indignant, you feel angry because someone has said or done something unfair.

individual adjective
Something that is individual is for just one person. *You can have group lessons or individual lessons.*

infant noun *plural* infants
a very young child

influence verb influences, influencing, influenced
If you influence someone, you change the way that they think or behave.

informal adjective
1 Informal events or clothes are relaxed and not too smart.
2 Informal language is language that you use when you are talking to friends, not language you would write down.

information noun
facts about something

infuriate verb infuriates, infuriating, infuriated (say in-**fyoor**-ee-ate)
If something infuriates you, it makes you very angry.

ingredient noun *plural* ingredients
Ingredients are the things that you mix together when you are cooking something.

inhabit verb inhabits, inhabiting, inhabited
To inhabit a place means to live in it.

initial noun *plural* initials
Your initials are the first letters of each of your names.

injection noun *plural* injections
When you have an injection, a doctor puts a needle into your arm to put medicine into your body.

injure verb injures, injuring, injured
To injure someone means to hurt them.

ink noun *plural* inks
the coloured liquid inside a pen, which comes out onto the paper when you write

inn noun *plural* inns
a small hotel

innocent adjective
If you are innocent, you have not done anything wrong.

insect noun *plural* insects
An insect is a small creature with six legs. Flies, ants, butterflies, and ladybirds are all different types of insect.

a
b
c
d
e
f
g
h
i
j
k
l
m
n
o
p
q
r
s
t
u
v
w
x
y
z

A
B
C
D
E
F
G
H
I
J
K
L
M
N
O
P
Q
R
S
T
U
V
W
X
Y
Z

insert verb inserts, inserting, inserted
1 When you insert something, you put it into a hole or a slot. *He inserted a coin into the slot.*
2 (in ICT) When you insert something into a computer document, you add it.

inside adverb, preposition
in something *Come inside, it's raining.*

insist verb insists, insisting, insisted
If you insist on something, you say very firmly that you want to do it. *He insisted on coming with us.*

inspect verb inspects, inspecting, inspected
When you inspect something, you look at it very carefully to check that it is all right.

instalment noun plural instalments
one part of a story that is told in parts

instant adjective
1 Something that is instant happens immediately.
2 Instant food is food that you can make very quickly.

instead adverb
in place of something else *They gave us water instead of lemonade.*

instrument noun plural instruments
1 something that you use for playing music *Violins and flutes are musical instruments.*
2 a tool or machine that you use for doing a job

insult verb insults, insulting, insulted
To insult someone means to upset them by saying rude or nasty things to them. *She insulted me by saying I was stupid.*

intelligent adjective
Someone who is intelligent is clever and can learn things quickly. *Klaus was a little older than twelve and wore glasses, which made him look intelligent.* — Lemony Snicket, *The Bad Beginning*

intend verb intends, intending, intended
If you intend to do something, you plan to do it.

intentional adjective
If something was intentional, you did it on purpose.

interactive adjective (in ICT)
An interactive computer program is one in which you can change and control things.

interactive whiteboard noun plural interactive whiteboards
An interactive whiteboard is a whiteboard that looks like a large computer screen and is connected to a computer. You can write on it using a special pen.

interest verb interests, interesting, interested
If something interests you, you think it is exciting and you want to see it or learn about it.
interesting adjective If something is interesting, you think it is exciting and want to see it or learn about it. *This is a really interesting book.*

interfere verb interferes, interfering, interfered
If you interfere, you get involved with something that has nothing to do with you.

interjection noun *plural* interjections (in grammar)
An interjection is a word that you say or shout on its own, not as part of a sentence. *Hello* and *hooray* are interjections.

international adjective
Something that is international involves people from different countries. *We're going to watch an international football match.*

Internet noun
a system that allows computers all over the world to get information and send messages to each other

interrupt verb interrupts, interrupting, interrupted
If you interrupt someone, you disturb them while they are talking or working, and make them stop.

interval noun *plural* intervals
a short break in the middle of a play or concert

interview verb interviews, interviewing, interviewed
To interview someone means to ask someone questions to find out what they are like, or what they think, or what they know.

into preposition
in *He threw a stone into the water.*

introduce verb introduces, introducing, introduced
When you introduce people, you bring them together and let them meet each other. *Salim and Sarah kindly introduced me to the professor.*

introduction noun
plural introductions
a short part at the beginning of a book or piece of music

invent verb invents, inventing, invented
If you invent something new, you are the first person to make it or think of it.

inverted commas noun
the marks like this ' ' or this " " that you use in writing to show what someone has said

investigate verb investigates, investigating, investigated
If you investigate something, you try to find out about it.

invisible adjective
If something is invisible, no one can see it.

invite verb invites, inviting, invited
When you invite someone, you ask them to come to your house or to go somewhere with you.

iron noun *plural* irons
1 a type of strong, heavy metal
2 An iron is an object that you use for making clothes smooth and flat. It has a flat piece of metal with a handle, and you heat it before you use it.

irritate verb irritates, irritating, irritated
To irritate someone means to make them feel annoyed.

Islam noun
the religion that Muslims follow

island noun *plural* islands
a piece of land with water all round it

a
b
c
d
e
f
g
h
i
j
k
l
m
n
o
p
q
r
s
t
u
v
w
x
y
z

ISP noun
ISP is short for **Internet Service Provider**, a company which connects you to the Internet.

it pronoun
You use **it** when you're talking about something that has already been mentioned. *It wasn't difficult.*

italics noun
sloping letters printed *like this*

itch verb itches, itching, itched
When your skin itches, it is uncomfortable and feels as if you need to scratch it.
itchy adjective If your skin is itchy, it is uncomfortable and feels as if you need to scratch it. *Insect bites are sometimes very itchy.*

item noun *plural* items
one thing in a list or group of things

its determiner
You use **its** when you're talking about something that belongs to something that has already been mentioned. *The horse threw back its head.*

it's
1 it is *It's raining.*
2 it has *It's been raining.*

jab verb jabs, jabbing, jabbed
When you jab something, you poke it roughly with your finger or with something sharp.

jacket noun *plural* jackets
a short coat

jagged adjective
Something that is jagged has a sharp, uneven edge. *We climbed over the jagged rocks.*

jail noun *plural* jails
a prison

jam noun *plural* jams
1 a thick, sweet, sticky food that is made by cooking fruit and sugar together
2 If there is a traffic jam, there are too many cars on the road and they cannot move forward.

jam verb jams, jamming, jammed
When something jams, it gets stuck and you cannot move it. *The back door keeps getting jammed.*

January noun
the first month of the year

jar noun *plural* jars
a glass container that food is kept in

jaw noun *plural* jaws
Your jaws are the bones that hold your teeth in place. You move your lower jaw to open your mouth.

jealous adjective
If you are jealous of someone, you are unhappy because they have something that you would like, or they can do something better than you can.

jeans noun
trousers that are made of strong cotton cloth

jelly noun *plural* jellies
a sweet food made from fruit and sugar that shakes when you move it

jellyfish noun jellyfish
A jellyfish is a sea animal that has a soft, clear body. Some types of jellyfish can sting you.

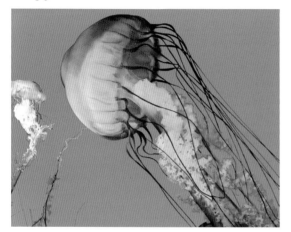

jerk verb jerks, jerking, jerked
When something jerks, it moves suddenly and roughly. *The bus jerked forward.*

jersey noun *plural* jerseys
a warm piece of clothing with long sleeves

jet noun *plural* jets
1 A jet of water is a thin stream that comes out of a small hole very quickly.
2 a fast aeroplane

jewel noun *plural* jewels
a beautiful and valuable stone

jewellery noun
Jewellery is jewels or ornaments such as necklaces, bracelets, earrings, and rings that people wear.

Jewish adjective
Someone who is Jewish follows the religion of **Judaism**.

jigsaw puzzle noun
plural jigsaw puzzles
a set of small pieces of cardboard or wood that fit together to make a picture

jingle verb jingles, jingling, jingled
When something jingles, it makes a light, ringing sound. *The keys jingled in my pocket as I walked along.*

jingle noun *plural* jingles
a short song or poem that is used to advertise something

job noun *plural* jobs
1 the work that someone does to earn money
2 something useful that you have to do

jog verb jogs, jogging, jogged
1 When you jog, you run slowly.
2 If you jog something, you knock it or bump it. *He jogged my elbow and I spilled my drink.*

a
b
c
d
e
f
g
h
i
j
k
l
m
n
o
p
q
r
s
t
u
v
w
x
y
z

A
B
C
D
E
F
G
H
I
J
K
L
M
N
O
P
Q
R
S
T
U
V
W
X
Y
Z

join verb joins, joining, joined
1 When you join things together, you fasten or tie them together.
2 When you join a club or group, you become a member of it. *I've joined a swimming club.*

joint noun *plural* joints
1 Your joints are the parts of your arms and legs that you can bend and turn. Your ankles, elbows, and hips are all joints.
2 a large piece of meat

joke noun *plural* jokes
something you say or do to make people laugh
joke verb jokes, joking, joked
When you joke, you say things to make people laugh.

jolt verb jolts, jolting, jolted
1 When something jolts, it moves with sudden and rough movements.
2 If you jolt something, you knock it or bump it.

journal noun *plural* journals
a diary in which someone writes about what they do each day

journalist noun *plural* journalists
someone who writes about the news in a newspaper

journey noun *plural* journeys
When you go on a journey, you travel somewhere.

joy noun
a feeling of great happiness

joystick noun *plural* joysticks
a lever that you move forwards, backwards, or sideways to control a computer game or a machine

Judaism noun
the religion that Jewish people follow

judge verb judges, judging, judged
When you judge something, you say how good or bad it is.

jug noun *plural* jugs
a container with a handle that you use for pouring out water and other liquids

juggle verb juggles, juggling, juggled
When you juggle, you keep throwing several balls or other things into the air and catching them again quickly.

juice noun *plural* juices
the liquid that is in fruit and vegetables

July noun
the seventh month of the year

jumble noun
A jumble of things is a lot of different things all mixed up together.

jump verb jumps, jumping, jumped
When you jump, you push yourself up into the air.

jumper noun *plural* jumpers
a warm piece of clothing with long sleeves which you wear on the top half of your body

junction noun *plural* junctions
a place where two roads or railway lines meet

June noun
the sixth month of the year

jungle noun *plural* jungles
a thick forest in a hot country

junior adjective
Junior means for young children. *I play football for a junior football team.*

junk noun
useless things that people do not want any more

just adverb
1 exactly *This game is just what I wanted.*
2 hardly *I only just caught the bus.*
3 recently *She has just left.*
4 only *I'll just brush my hair and then we can go.*

justice noun
fair treatment for everyone

Kk

kangaroo noun *plural* kangaroos
A kangaroo is an Australian animal that jumps along on its strong back legs. Female kangaroos have pouches in which they carry their babies.

keen adjective keener, keenest
1 If you are keen on something, you like it. *He's very keen on football.*
2 If you are keen to do something, you want to do it. *The children were keen to start exploring but they knew there would be plenty of time for that. — Alexander McCall-Smith, The Bubblegum Tree.*

keep verb keeps, keeping, kept
1 If you keep something, you have it for yourself and do not get rid of it or give it to anyone else.
2 When you keep something in a certain way, you make it stay that way. *I like to keep my hair short in the summer.*
3 If you keep doing something, you go on doing it. *Samir keeps teasing me!*
4 If you keep animals, you look after them.

kennel noun *plural* kennels
a little hut for a dog to sleep in

kept verb past tense of keep

kerb noun *plural* kerbs
the edge of a pavement, where you step down to go onto the road

ketchup noun
a type of thick, cold tomato sauce

kettle noun *plural* kettles
a container that you boil water in

a
b
c
d
e
f
g
h
i
j
k
l
m
n
o
p
q
r
s
t
u
v
w
x
y
z

113

A
B
C
D
E
F
G
H
I
J
K
L
M
N
O
P
Q
R
S
T
U
V
W
X
Y
Z

key noun *plural* keys
1 a piece of metal that is shaped so that it fits into a lock
2 The keys on a piano or computer keyboard are the parts that you press to make it work.

keyboard noun *plural* keyboards
The keyboard on a piano or computer is the set of keys that you press to make it work.

kick verb kicks, kicking, kicked
When you kick something, you hit it with your foot.

kid noun *plural* kids
1 a child
2 a young goat

kidnap verb kidnaps, kidnapping, kidnapped
To kidnap someone means to take them away and say that you will only let them go if someone pays you money.

kill verb kills, killing, killed
To kill a person or animal means to make them die.

kilogram noun *plural* kilograms
We can measure weight in kilograms. There are 1000 grams in one kilogram. A kilogram is also called a **kilo**.

kilometre noun *plural* kilometres
We can measure distance in kilometres. There are 1000 metres in one kilometre.

kilt noun *plural* kilts
A kilt is a kind of skirt. In Scotland, men sometimes wear kilts as part of their traditional costume.

kind noun *plural* kinds
a type *A terrier is a kind of dog.*

kind adjective kinder, kindest
Someone who is kind is friendly and nice to people. *It was very kind of you to help us.*

king noun *plural* kings
a man who rules a country

kingdom noun *plural* kingdoms
a land that is ruled by a king or queen

kiss verb kisses, kissing, kissed
When you kiss someone, you touch them with your lips because you like them or love them.

kit noun *plural* kits
1 the clothes and other things that you need to do a sport
2 a set of parts that you fit together to make something *I got a model aeroplane kit for my birthday.*

kitchen noun *plural* kitchens
the room in a house in which people prepare and cook food

kite noun *plural* kites
A kite is a light frame covered in cloth or paper. You hold a kite at the end of a long string and make it fly in the air.

kitten noun *plural* **kittens**
a young cat

kiwi fruit noun *plural* **kiwi fruits**
a fruit with a brown, hairy skin and green flesh

knee noun *plural* **knees**
Your knee is the part in the middle of your leg, where your leg can bend.

kneel verb **kneels, kneeling, kneeled**
When you kneel, you go down onto your knees.

knew verb past tense of **know**

knife noun *plural* **knives**
a tool with a long, sharp edge that you use for cutting things

knight noun *plural* **knights**
a man who wore armour and rode into battle on a horse, in the past

knit verb **knits, knitting, knitted**
When you knit, you make clothes out of wool by twisting the wool over a pair of long needles or using a machine.

knob noun *plural* **knobs**
1 a round handle on a door or drawer
2 a round button that you turn to make a machine work

knock verb **knocks, knocking, knocked**
When you knock something, you bang it or hit it.

knot noun *plural* **knots**
the twisted part where pieces of string or cloth have been tied together

know verb **knows, knowing, knew, known** (say **no**)
1 If you know something, you have learnt it and have it in your mind.
2 If you know someone, you have met them before and you recognize them.

knowledge noun (say **noll**-idge)
all the things that you know and understand

knuckle noun *plural* **knuckles**
Your knuckles are the parts where your fingers bend.

koala noun *plural* **koalas** (say koh-**ah**-la)
a furry Australian animal that lives in trees and looks like a small bear

Koran noun
the holy book of the religion of Islam

a
b
c
d
e
f
g
h
i
j
k
l
m
n
o
p
q
r
s
t
u
v
w
x
y
z

115

Ll

label noun *plural* labels
a piece of paper or cloth that is put on something to show what it is or tell you something about it

laboratory noun *plural* laboratories
a room in which people do experiments for science

lace noun *plural* laces
1 Lace is a type of thin, pretty material with a pattern of holes in it.
2 Laces are pieces of string that you use to tie up your shoes.

ladder noun *plural* ladders
A ladder is a tall frame that you can climb up. It has two long poles with short bars between them, which you climb up like steps.

lady noun *plural* ladies
1 a polite name for a woman
2 a title that is given to some important women

ladybird noun *plural* ladybirds
a red or yellow insect with black spots on its back

laid verb past tense of lay

lain verb past tense of lie **verb**

lake noun *plural* lakes
a large area of fresh water with land all around it

lamb noun *plural* lambs
a young sheep

lame adjective
A lame animal cannot walk properly because it has hurt one of its legs.

lamp noun *plural* lamps
A lamp is a light, especially one that you can hold or move around. The big lights in a street are called **street lamps**.

land noun *plural* lands
1 Land is the the dry part of the earth where there is no water.
2 A land is a country.

land verb lands, landing, landed
To land means to arrive on land again after being in the air. *What time will our plane land?*

landscape noun
The landscape is everything you can see when you look out over an area of land.

lane noun *plural* lanes
1 a narrow road
2 a strip of road that one line of traffic can drive along

language noun *plural* languages
Your language is the words that you use when you speak or write.

lantern noun *plural* lanterns
a candle inside a container

lap noun *plural* laps
1 Your lap is the flat part of your legs when you are sitting down.
2 A lap of a race course is once round it.
We had to do five laps of the race track.

A
B
C
D
E
F
G
H
I
J
K
L
M
N
O
P
Q
R
S
T
U
V
W
X
Y
Z

lap verb laps, lapping, lapped
1 When an animal laps, it drinks with its tongue.
2 When water laps, it moves gently backwards and forwards. *The waves lapped against the side of the boat.*

laptop noun plural laptops
a small computer that you can carry around with you and hold on your knees when you are sitting down

large adjective larger, largest
Something that is large is big. *On the table was a large wicker basket from which came mews and squeaks. — Jill Murphy, The Lost Witch*

larva noun
an animal that looks like a small worm and which will become an insect

laser noun plural lasers
A laser is a machine that makes a very narrow beam of strong light. Some lasers are used to cut metal, and some are used by doctors in operations.

last adjective
The last thing is the one that comes after all the others. *Z is the last letter of the alphabet.*

last verb lasts, lasting, lasted
If something lasts for a certain time, it goes on for that amount of time. *The film lasted two hours.*

late adjective later, latest
1 If you are late, you arrive after the time when people are expecting you. *The bus was ten minutes late.*
2 When it is late in the day, it is near the middle or end of the day, not the morning. *Hurry up, it's getting late.*

lately adverb
not very long ago

laugh verb laughs, laughing, laughed
When you laugh, you make sounds that show that you are happy or think something is funny.

launch verb launches, launching, launched
1 To launch a boat means to put it into water.
2 To launch a rocket or spaceship means to send it into space.

lava noun
very hot, liquid rock that comes out of a volcano

law noun plural laws
The law is all the rules that everyone in a country must obey.

lawn noun plural lawns
a piece of ground in a garden that is covered with short grass

lawyer noun plural lawyers
a person who has studied the law and who talks for people in a court of law

lay verb lays, laying, laid
1 When you lay something somewhere, you put it there. *We laid the map out on the table.*
2 When you lay a table, you put knives and forks on it so that it is ready for a meal.
3 When a bird lays an egg, it produces one.

layer noun plural layers
A layer of something is a covering of it on top of something else.

a
b
c
d
e
f
g
h
i
j
k
l
m
n
o
p
q
r
s
t
u
v
w
x
y
z

A
B
C
D
E
F
G
H
I
J
K
L
M
N
O
P
Q
R
S
T
U
V
W
X
Y
Z

lazy adjective lazier, laziest
Someone who is lazy does not want to work.

lead verb leads, leading, led
(rhymes with *seed*)
1 If you lead people, you go in front of them and take them somewhere. *He led us to the secret cave.*
2 If you lead people, you are in charge of them and tell them what to do.
3 If you are leading in a game or competition, you are winning.

lead noun *plural* leads (rhymes with *seed*)
1 a long strap that you fasten to a dog's collar so that you can keep hold of it and control it.
2 If you are in the lead, you are winning in a race or competition.

lead noun (rhymes with *bed*)
a type of heavy, grey metal

leaf noun *plural* leaves
The leaves on a plant are the green parts that grow at the ends of the stems and branches.

leaflet noun *plural* leaflets
a piece of paper that gives you information about something

leak verb leaks, leaking, leaked
If something is leaking, it has a hole or crack in it and liquid can get through. *My water bottle's leaking.*

lean verb leans, leaning, leaned, leant
1 If you lean forwards or backwards, you bend your body that way.
2 When you lean against something, you rest against it.

lean adjective leaner, leanest
Lean meat does not have any fat on it.

leap verb leaps, leaping, leaped, leapt
To leap means to jump.

leap year noun *plural* leap years
A leap year is a year which has 366 days instead of 365. Every four years is a leap year.

learn verb learns, learning, learned, learnt
1 When you learn about something, you find out about it. *We're learning about the Vikings in history.*
2 When you learn to do something, you find out how to do it.

least adverb
less than all the others *My mum wanted me to buy the least expensive trainers.*

leather noun
Leather is a strong material that is made from the skins of animals. Shoes and bags are often made of leather.

leave verb leaves, leaving, left
1 When you leave a place, you go away from it. *I leave home every morning at eight o'clock.*
2 When you leave something in a place, you let it stay there and do not take it away. *I'm sorry, I've left my homework at home.*

led verb past tense of lead

ledge noun *plural* ledges
a narrow shelf that sticks out from a wall

left verb past tense of leave

left adjective, adverb
The left side of something is the side that is opposite the right side. Most people write with their right hand, not their left hand. *She had a letter in her left hand. Turn left at the traffic lights.*

leg noun *plural* legs
1 Your legs are the parts of your body between your hips and your feet.
2 The legs on a table or chair are the parts that it stands on.

legend noun *plural* legends (say **lej**-end)
an old story that has been handed down from the past

leisure noun
Leisure time is time when you can do what you want because you do not have to work.

lemon noun *plural* lemons
a yellow fruit with a very sour taste

lemonade noun
a fizzy drink made from lemons, sugar, and water

lend verb lends, lending, lent
If you lend something to someone, you let them use it for a short time. *Can you lend me a pencil?*

length noun
The length of something is how long it is.

lens noun *plural* lenses
A lens is a curved piece of glass or plastic that makes things look bigger or smaller when you look through it. Glasses and telescopes all have lenses.

lent verb past tense of lend

less adjective, adverb
smaller in amount or not as much *Make less noise. It is less important.*

lesson noun *plural* lessons
1 a time when someone is teaching you *Maths is our first lesson this morning.*
2 something that you have to learn

let verb lets, letting, let
If you let someone do something, you allow them to do it. *Samir let me use his phone.*

letter noun *plural* letters
1 Letters are the signs that we use for writing words, such as A, B, or C.
2 A letter is a message that you write down and send to someone.

lettuce noun *plural* lettuces
a vegetable with green leaves that you eat in salads

level adjective
1 Something that is level is flat and smooth. *You need level ground to play tennis on.*
2 If you are level with someone, you are walking or running next to them.
3 If people are level in a game or competition, they have the same number of points.

level noun *plural* levels
If something is at a different level, it is higher or lower.

lever noun *plural* levers
a bar that you pull down to make a machine work

a
b
c
d
e
f
g
h
i
j
k
l
m
n
o
p
q
r
s
t
u
v
w
x
y
z

119

A
B
C
D
E
F
G
H
I
J
K
L
M
N
O
P
Q
R
S
T
U
V
W
X
Y
Z

liar noun *plural* liars
someone who tells lies

library noun *plural* libraries
a building or room where a lot of books are kept for people to use or borrow

lick verb licks, licking, licked
When you lick something, you move your tongue over it.

lid noun *plural* lids
a cover on the top of a box or jar

lie verb lies, lying, lied
When you lie, you say something that you know is not true.

lie noun *plural* lies
something you say that you know is not true

lie verb lies, lying, lay, lain
1 When you lie down, you rest with your body spread out on the ground or on a bed.
2 When something lies somewhere, it is there. *Thick snow lay on the ground.*

life noun *plural* lives
Your life is the time when you are alive.

lifeboat noun *plural* lifeboats
a boat that goes out to sea in bad weather to rescue people

lift verb lifts, lifting, lifted
When you lift something, you pick it up or move it upwards. *I lifted the lid of the box to see what was inside.*

lift noun *plural* lifts
1 a machine that takes people up and down inside a building
2 If someone gives you a lift, they take you somewhere in their car.

light noun *plural* lights
1 Light is brightness that comes from the sun, the stars, fires, and lamps.
2 A light is a lamp, bulb, or torch that gives out light.

light adjective lighter, lightest
1 Something that is light is not heavy. *My suitcase is quite light.*
2 A place that is light is not dark, but has plenty of light in it.
3 A light colour is pale and not very bright. *She was wearing a light blue top.*

light verb lights, lighting, lit
1 To light something means to put light in it so that you can see. *We used our torches to light the tunnel.*
2 To light a fire means to make it burn. *We tried to light the bonfire.*

lightly adverb If you do or say something lightly, you do it or say it carefully. *He touched her lightly on the arm.*

lighthouse noun *plural* lighthouses
a tower with a bright light that warns ships about rocks or other dangers

lightning noun
a bright flash of light that you see in the sky when there is a storm

like verb likes, liking, liked
If you like something, you think it is nice.
If you like someone, you think that they are nice.

like preposition
If one thing is like another, it is similar to it. *This tastes like roast lamb. I really like bananas and apples but I don't like oranges.*

likely adjective likelier, likeliest
If something is likely to happen, it will probably happen.

limb noun plural limbs
Your limbs are your arms and legs.

limerick noun plural limericks
a funny poem with five lines and a strong rhythm

limit noun plural limits
an amount or a point which people must not go past *You must not drive faster than the speed limit.*

limp verb limps, limping, limped
When you limp, you walk with uneven steps because you have hurt one of your legs or feet.

line noun plural lines
1 a long mark like this _____
2 a row of people or things *There was a long line of people waiting to get into the cinema.*
3 A railway line is the two metal rails a train moves along.
4 A line of writing is the words that are written next to each other on a page. *I don't know the next line of the poem.*
5 A fishing line is a piece of special thin string that you use for catching fish.

link noun plural links
The links in a chain are the rings that are all joined together to make the chain.

link verb links, linking, linked
To link two things means to join them together. *The Channel Tunnel links Britain to France.*

lion noun plural lions
A lion is a big, light brown wild cat that lives in Africa and India. A female lion is called a **lioness**.

lip noun plural lips
Your lips are the parts round the edges of your mouth.

liquid noun plural liquids
any substance that is like water, and is not a solid or a gas

lisp verb lisps, lisping, lisped
If you lisp, you say the sound 's' as if it was 'th'.

list noun plural lists
a number of words or names that are written down one after the other

listen verb listens, listening, listened
When you listen, you pay attention so that you can hear something.

lit verb past tense of light **verb**

literacy noun
Literacy is being able to read and write.

a b c d e f g h i j k l m n o p q r s t u v w x y z

121

literature noun
stories, plays, and poetry

litre noun *plural* litres
We can measure liquids in litres.

litter noun *plural* litters
1 Litter is rubbish that people have dropped or left lying about.
2 A litter is all the young animals that are born to the same mother at the same time.

little adjective
1 Something that is little is not very big. *We set out in our little rowing boat.*
2 If you have little of something, you do not have very much. *I've got very little money left as I spent so much on sweets at lunch time.*

live verb lives, living, lived
1 To live means to be alive. *Dinosaurs lived millions of years ago.*
2 If you live somewhere, that is where your home is.

live adjective (rhymes with *dive*)
1 A live animal is alive. *You can see live animals in the zoo.*
2 A live television programme is not recorded, but is shown as it is happening.

lively adjective livelier, liveliest
Someone who is lively has a lot of energy and enjoys having fun.

liver noun *plural* livers
Your liver is the part inside your body that keeps your blood clean and healthy.

living noun
When you earn a living, you earn enough money to live.

living room noun
plural living rooms
the room in a house with comfortable chairs, where people sit and talk or watch television

lizard noun *plural* lizards
A lizard is an animal with skin like a snake and four legs. Lizards are reptiles and live in warm countries.

load noun *plural* loads
A load of things is an amount that someone is carrying. *The lorry brought another load of sand.*

load verb loads, loading, loaded
1 When you load things into a car or lorry, you put them in. *Load the suitcases into the car.*
2 When you load a gun, you put bullets in it.
3 When you load a program onto a computer, you put it on so that you can use it.

loaf noun *plural* loaves
A loaf of bread is a large piece of bread that you cut into slices to eat.

local adjective
Something that is local is near where you live. *You can borrow books from your local library.*

loch noun *plural* lochs
a lake in Scotland

lock noun *plural* locks
1 The lock on a door, gate, or window is the part that you can open and shut with a key.
2 A lock of hair is a small piece of hair.

lock verb locks, locking, locked
When you lock something, you shut it and fasten it with a key. *Don't forget to lock the door when you go out.*

loft noun *plural* lofts
a room in the roof of a house, where you can store things

log noun *plural* logs
A log is a part of a tree that has been chopped down. You can burn logs on a fire.

log verb logs, logging, logged
When you log in to a computer, you switch it on so that you can use it. When you log out, you shut it down and switch it off.

lolly noun *plural* lollies
a sweet on the end of a stick

lonely adjective lonelier, loneliest
1 If you feel lonely, you feel sad because you are on your own.
2 A lonely place is far away from people and houses.

long adjective longer, longest
1 Something that is long measures a lot from one end to the other. *This piece of string isn't long enough.*
2 Something that is long takes a lot of time. *We looked forward to a lovely long holiday.*

long verb longs, longing, longed
If you long for something, you want it a lot. *I have always longed to own a sweet shop.*
— Roald Dahl, *The Giraffe and the Pelly and Me*

look verb looks, looking, looked
1 When you look at something, you point your eyes at it so that you can see it. *Hey! Look at me!*
2 The way something looks is the way it seems. *That dog doesn't look very friendly.*
3 When you look for something, you try to find it.
4 When you look after someone, you take care of them.
5 When you look forward to something, you feel excited that it is going to happen.

loop noun *plural* loops
a ring made in a piece of string or rope

loose adjective looser, loosest
1 Something that is loose is not fixed firmly in place. *I've got a loose tooth.*
2 Loose clothes do not fit tightly.
3 If a wild animal is loose, it has escaped and is free.
loosely adverb If you do something loosely, you do it so that is not fixed firmly in place. *He loosely tied the horse to the fence.*

lord noun *plural* lords
a title that is given to some important men

lorry noun *plural* lorries
a big truck that is used for carrying heavy things by road

a
b
c
d
e
f
g
h
i
j
k
l
m
n
o
p
q
r
s
t
u
v
w
x
y
z

A
B
C
D
E
F
G
H
I
J
K
L
M
N
O
P
Q
R
S
T
U
V
W
X
Y
Z

lose verb loses, losing, lost
1 When you lose something, you do not have it and do not know where it is. *I've lost my coat.*
2 When you lose a game, someone else wins. *We were really disappointed that our team had lost the match.*

lost adjective
If you are lost, you do not know where you are or where you should go. *Don't get lost in the woods!*

lot noun *plural* lots
A lot means a large number or a large amount. *I've got lots of friends.*

lottery noun *plural* lotteries
a competition in which people buy tickets or choose numbers, and win a prize if their tickets or numbers are picked

loud adjective louder, loudest
Something that is loud makes a lot of noise. *Suddenly there was a loud bang.*
loudly adverb If you do or say something loudly, you do it or say it so that it makes a lot of noise. *I called his name as loudly as I could.*

lounge noun *plural* lounges
a room with comfortable chairs in it, where people can sit and talk or watch television

love noun
the strong feeling you have when you like someone very much

love verb loves, loving, loved
1 If you love someone, you like them very much.
2 If you love something, you like it a lot.

lovely adjective lovelier, loveliest
Something that is lovely is beautiful or very nice *What lovely flowers!*

low adjective lower, lowest
1 Something that is low is not high. *We sat down on the low bench by the swings.*
2 A low price is a small price.
3 A low voice or sound is deep.

lower case adjective
Lower case letters are small letters, not capital letters.

abcdefg
abcdefg

loyal adjective
If you are loyal to someone, you always help them and support them.

luck noun
Luck is when something happens by chance, without anyone planning it.

lucky adjective luckier, luckiest
If you are lucky, you have good luck. *We were lucky we got home before the storm started.*

luggage noun
bags and suitcases that you take with you on a journey

Mm

lump noun *plural* lumps
1 A lump of something is a piece of it. *He took some bread and a lump of cheese.*
2 A lump is a bump on your skin that you get when you have knocked it.

lunar adjective
Lunar means to do with the moon. *Have you ever seen a lunar eclipse?*

lunch noun *plural* lunches
a meal that you eat in the middle of the day

lung noun *plural* lungs
Your lungs are the parts inside your chest that you use for breathing.

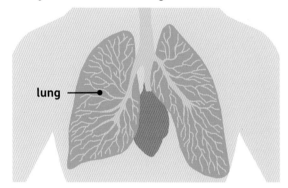

lung

luxury noun *plural* luxuries
something expensive that you like but do not really need

lying verb a tense of lie

machine noun *plural* machines
something that has an engine and moving parts, and can do a job or make things

mad adjective madder, maddest
1 Someone who is mad is ill in their mind.
2 If you are mad about something, you like it a lot. *Jake's mad about football.*
3 If you are mad, you are very angry. *My mum was really mad with me.*

made verb past tense of make

magazine noun *plural* magazines
a thin book that is made and sold every week or month with different stories and pictures in it

magic noun
In stories, magic is the power that some people have to make impossible and wonderful things happen.
magical adjective If something is magical, it has the power to make impossible and wonderful things happen. *She has special magical powers.*

magician noun *plural* magicians
1 a person who does magic tricks to entertain people
2 a person in stories who has the power to use magic

a
b
c
d
e
f
g
h
i
j
k
l
m
n
o
p
q
r
s
t
u
v
w
x
y
z

magnet noun plural magnets
a piece of metal that attracts pieces of iron or steel towards it
magnetic adjective If something is magnetic, it attracts pieces of iron or steel towards it. *A huge magnetic crane lifts the cars up.*

magnificent adjective
Something that is magnificent is very good or beautiful.

magnify verb magnifies, magnifying, magnified
To magnify something means to make it look bigger. *We magnified the insect under the microscope.*

mail noun
letters, cards, and parcels that are sent through the post and delivered to people's houses

main adjective
the main thing is the biggest or most important one *You shouldn't cycle on the main road.*

major adjective
A major thing is very important or serious. *There has been a major accident on the motorway.*

make verb makes, making, made
1 When you make something, you create it. *Please don't make too much mess.*
2 To make something happen means to cause it to happen. *The horrible smell made me feel sick.*
3 If you make someone do something, you force them to do it.
4 If you make something up, you invent it and it is not true.

male adjective
A male person or animal can become a father.

mammal noun plural mammals
A mammal is an animal that gives birth to live babies and feeds its young with its own milk. Cats, dogs, whales, lions, and people are all mammals.

man noun plural men
a grown-up male person

manage verb manages, managing, managed
1 If you manage to do something difficult, you do it after trying very hard. *At last I managed to get the door open.*
2 To manage a shop or business means to be in charge of it.

mane noun plural manes
An animal's mane is the long hair on its neck.

mango noun plural mangoes
a fruit with sweet, yellow flesh, which grows in hot countries

manner noun
The manner in which you do something is the way you do it.

A B C D E F G H I J K L **M** N O P Q R S T U V W X Y Z

manners noun
Your manners are the ways in which you behave when you are talking to people or eating your food.

many determiner, pronoun
Many means a large number. *Were there many people on the bus?*

map noun *plural* maps
a drawing of a town, a country, or the world

marathon noun *plural* marathons
a running race which is about forty kilometres long

marble noun *plural* marbles
1 Marbles are small glass balls that you use to play games with.

2 Marble is a type of smooth stone that is used for building or making statues.

March noun
the third month of the year

march verb marches, marching, marched
When you march, you walk with regular steps like a soldier.

mare noun *plural* mares
a female horse

margarine noun
a food that looks and tastes like butter, but is made from vegetable oils

margin noun *plural* margins
an empty space on the side of a page, where there is no writing

mark noun *plural* marks
1 a dirty stain or spot on something
2 The mark that you get for a piece of work is the number or letter that shows how well you have done.

mark verb marks, marking, marked
To mark a piece of work means to give it a number or letter to show how good it is.

market noun *plural* markets
a group of stalls where people sell food and other things

marmalade noun
jam made from oranges or lemons

marry verb marries, marrying, married
When you marry someone, you become their husband or wife.

marsh noun *plural* marshes
a piece of very wet, soft ground

marsupial noun *plural* marsupials
(say mar-**soo**-pee-al)
A marsupial is an animal that carries its young in a special pouch on the front of its body. Kangaroos are marsupials.

marvellous adjective
Something that is marvellous is wonderful.

masculine adjective
Something that is masculine looks as if it is suitable for boys and men, not girls and women.

a b c d e f g h i j k l **m** n o p q r s t u v w x y z

127

mask noun *plural* masks
something that you wear over your face to hide it or protect it

mass noun *plural* masses
A mass is a large amount of something, or a large number of things.

massive adjective
Something that is massive is very big.
I remembered a huge toyshop and a big Ferris wheel and a museum with massive dinosaurs.
— Jacqueline Wilson, *Best Friends*

mast noun *plural* masts
a tall pole that holds up a ship's sails

mat noun *plural* mats
1 a small carpet
2 something that you put under a hot plate on a table

match noun *plural* matches
1 a small, thin stick that makes a flame when you rub it against something rough
2 a game that two people or teams play against each other

match verb matches, matching, matched
Things that match are the same or go well together.

material noun *plural* materials
1 A material is something that you use to make things with.
2 Material is cloth.

mathematics, maths noun
the subject in which you learn about numbers, measurement, and shapes

matter noun *plural* matters
1 something that you need to talk about or deal with
2 When you ask someone what the matter is, you are asking what is wrong.

matter verb matters, mattering, mattered
If something matters, it is important.
It doesn't matter if you are a bit late.

mattress noun *plural* mattresses
the soft part of a bed that you lie on

May noun
the fifth month of the year

may verb
1 If you may do something, you are allowed to do it. *May I have a drink, please?*
2 If something may happen, it is possible that it will happen. *It may rain later.*

maybe adverb
perhaps

mayor noun *plural* mayors
A mayor is the person in charge of the council of a town or city. A woman who is a mayor can also be called a **mayoress**.

maze noun *plural* mazes
a set of lines or paths that twist and turn so much that it is very easy to lose your way

me pronoun

You use **me** to talk about yourself. *Can you pass me the pencil? The ball hit me on the nose.*

meadow noun *plural* meadows

a field of grass and flowers

meal noun *plural* meals

the food that you eat at breakfast, lunch, dinner, tea, or supper

mean verb means, meaning, meant

When you say what a word means, you say what it describes or shows. *What does the word 'delicious' mean?*

mean adjective meaner, meanest

1 Someone who is mean does not like sharing things.
2 Someone who is mean is unkind. *That was a really mean thing to do!*

meaning noun *plural* meanings

The meaning of a word is what it means.

meanwhile adverb

during the time something else is happening *Ben went to phone the fire brigade. Meanwhile I made sure there was no one left in the building.*

measles noun

an illness that gives you red spots all over your body

measure verb measures, measuring, measured

When you measure something, you find out how big it is or how much there is.

measurement noun

plural measurements

a number that you get when you measure something

meat noun

the flesh from animals that we can eat

mechanical adjective

Something that is mechanical has parts that move like a machine. *They used a mechanical digger to dig a deep ditch.*

medal noun *plural* medals

a special piece of metal that is given to someone who has won a competition or done something very brave

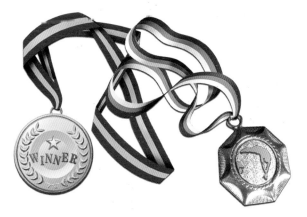

medicine noun *plural* medicines

a special liquid or tablet that you take when you are ill to make you better

medium adjective

Medium means not very big and not very small, but in the middle.

meet verb meets, meeting, met

1 When people meet, they see each other and talk to each other. *Let's meet at two o'clock.*
2 When two roads or rivers meet, they join together.

meeting noun *plural* meetings

When people have a meeting, they meet to talk about something.

megabyte noun (in ICT)

A megabyte is a piece of information on a computer. *The picture I'd attached to the email was about 10 megabytes, which was too big.*

a
b
c
d
e
f
g
h
i
j
k
l
m
n
o
p
q
r
s
t
u
v
w
x
y
z

A
B
C
D
E
F
G
H
I
J
K
L
M
N
O
P
Q
R
S
T
U
V
W
X
Y
Z

melt verb melts, melting, melted
When something melts, it becomes a liquid because it has become warm. *Ice melts as it warms up.*

member noun *plural* members
someone who belongs to a club or group

memory noun *plural* memories
1 Your memory is your ability to remember things. *Have you got a good memory?*
2 A memory is something that you can remember.
3 The memory in a computer is the part that stores information.

men noun *plural of* man

mend verb mends, mending, mended
When you mend something that is broken, you fix it or put it right so that you can use it again.

mental adjective
Something that is mental happens in your mind.

mention verb mentions, mentioning, mentioned
If you mention something, you talk about it.

menu noun *plural* menus
1 a list of the different kinds of food you can choose for your meal
2 (in ICT) a list that appears on a computer screen showing the different things you can ask the computer to do.

mercy noun
If you show mercy to someone, you are kind and do not punish them.

mermaid noun *plural* mermaids
In stories, a mermaid is a sea creature that looks like a woman but has a fish's tail instead of legs.

merry adjective merrier, merriest
Someone who is merry is cheerful and laughing.

mess noun
If something is a mess, it is very untidy.
messy **adjective** Something messy is very untidy. *The room was dirty and messy.*

message noun *plural* messages
words that you write down or record for someone when you cannot see them or speak to them yourself

met verb past tense of meet

metal noun *plural* metals
Metal is a strong material. Gold, silver, iron, and tin are all types of metal.

meteor noun *plural* meteors
(say **mee**-tee-or)
A meteor is a piece of rock or metal that flies through space and burns up when it gets near the earth. A piece of rock or metal that falls to earth without burning up is called a **meteorite**.

meter noun *plural* meters
a machine that measures how much of something has been used

method noun *plural* methods
the way in which you do something

metre noun *plural* metres
We can measure length in metres. There are 100 centimetres in a metre.

metric adjective
The metric system of measurement uses units of 10 and 100. Millimetres, centimetres, and metres are all part of the metric system.

miaow verb miaows, miaowing, miaowed
When a cat miaows, it makes a long, high sound.

mice noun *plural of* mouse

microchip noun *plural* microchips
one of the tiny pieces in a computer that makes it work

microphone noun
plural microphones
something that you speak into when you want to record your voice or make it sound louder

microscope noun *plural* microscopes
an instrument that makes tiny things look bigger

microwave noun *plural* microwaves
an oven that cooks food very quickly by passing special radio waves through it

midday noun
twelve o'clock in the middle of the day

middle noun *plural* middles
1 the part near the centre of something, not at the edges *There was a huge puddle in the middle of the playground.*
2 the part that is not near the beginning or end of something *The phone rang in the middle of the night.*

midnight noun
twelve o'clock at night

might verb a tense of may

migrate verb migrates, migrating, migrated
When birds or animals migrate, they travel to another place at the same time each year.

mild adjective milder, mildest
1 Something that is mild is not very strong.
2 Mild weather is quite warm.

mile noun *plural* miles
We can measure distance in miles. One mile is the same as about $1\frac{1}{2}$ kilometres.

military adjective
Military things are used by soldiers.

milk noun
Milk is a white liquid that you can drink. All female mammals make milk to feed their babies.
milky adjective If something is milky, it looks like milk *His eyes were milky.*

mill noun *plural* mills
a place where grain is crushed to make flour

a b c d e f g h i j k l **m** n o p q r s t u v w x y z

131

millennium noun *plural* millenniums, millennia
a period of 1000 years

millilitre noun *plural* millilitres
We can measure liquid in millilitres. There are 1000 millilitres in one litre.

millimetre noun *plural* millimetres
We can measure length in millimetres. There are 1000 millimetres in one metre.

million noun *plural* millions
the number 1,000,000

millionaire noun *plural* millionaires
a very rich person who has more than a million pounds or dollars

mince noun
meat that has been cut into very small pieces

mind noun *plural* minds
Your mind is your ability to think, and all the thoughts and memories that you have.

mind verb minds, minding, minded
If you do not mind about something, it does not upset or worry you.

mine pronoun
You use **mine** when you want to say something belongs to you. *The blue coat is mine.*

mine noun *plural* mines
1 a place where people work to dig coal, metal, or stones out of the ground
2 A mine is a bomb that is hidden in the ground or the sea. It explodes when something touches it.

mineral noun *plural* minerals
Minerals are things such as salt that form naturally in the ground.

minor adjective
A minor thing is not very important or serious. *He only suffered a minor injury.*

mint noun *plural* mints
1 a green plant that is added to food to give it flavour
2 a sweet that tastes of mint

minus adjective, preposition
(in mathematics)
1 take away *Six minus two is four, 6−2 = 4.*
2 A minus number is less than 0. *The temperature outside was minus three.*

minute noun *plural* minutes (say **min**-it)
We measure time in minutes. There are sixty seconds in one minute, and sixty minutes in one hour.

minute adjective (say my-**newt**)
Something that is minute is very small.

miracle noun *plural* miracles
something wonderful that has happened, although it did not seem possible *It's a miracle no one was hurt in the train crash.*

mirror noun *plural* mirrors
a piece of glass, in which you can see yourself

misbehave verb misbehaves, misbehaving, misbehaved
If you misbehave, you behave in a naughty way.

mischief noun
If you get into mischief, you do silly or naughty things.

miserable adjective
If you are miserable, you are very unhappy.

misfortune noun *plural* misfortunes
bad luck

misprint noun *plural* misprints
a small mistake in something that has been printed or typed

miss verb misses, missing, missed
1 If you miss something, you do not catch it or hit it. *I tried to hit the ball but I missed it.*
2 If you miss someone, you feel sad because they are not with you.

missile noun *plural* missiles
a weapon which is thrown or fired through the air

missing adjective
Something that is missing is lost. *My cat's gone missing.*

mist noun
When there is mist, there is a lot of cloud just above the ground, which makes it difficult to see.

mistake noun *plural* mistakes
If you make a mistake, you do something wrong.

mistake verb mistakes, mistaking, mistook, mistaken
If you mistake someone for another person, you think they are the other person.

mix verb mixes, mixing, mixed
When you mix things together, you put them together and stir them.

mixture noun *plural* mixtures
something that is made of different things mixed together

moan verb moans, moaning, moaned
When you moan, you make a low sound because you are in pain. When you moan about something, you complain about it.

moat noun *plural* moats
a deep ditch filled with water round a castle

mobile adjective
Something that is mobile can be moved or carried around easily.

mobile phone noun
plural mobile phones
A mobile phone is a telephone that you can carry around with you. It is also called a **mobile**.

model noun *plural* models
1 a small copy of something. *We built a model of a spaceship.*

2 someone who shows new clothes to people by wearing them and walking around in them

modern adjective
Something that is modern uses new ideas, not old-fashioned ones.

modest adjective
1 Someone who is modest does not boast.
2 Someone who is modest is shy.

moist adjective moister, moistest
Something that is moist is slightly wet.

moisture noun
tiny drops of water in the air or on the surface of something

mole noun *plural* moles
1 a small, furry animal that digs holes and tunnels under the ground
2 a small, brown mark on your skin

a
b
c
d
e
f
g
h
i
j
k
l
m
n
o
p
q
r
s
t
u
v
w
x
y
z

133

moment noun *plural* moments
a very small amount of time

Monday noun *plural* Mondays
the day after Sunday

money noun
the coins and pieces of paper that we use to buy things

mongrel noun *plural* mongrels
a dog that is not one breed, but is a mixture of more than one breed

monitor noun *plural* monitors (in ICT)
a computer screen

monkey noun *plural* monkeys
A monkey is an animal with fur and a long tail. *Monkeys are good at climbing trees.*

monster noun *plural* monsters
a large, fierce animal in stories

month noun *plural* months
A month is a period of 28, 30, or 31 days. There are twelve months in a year.

mood noun *plural* moods
Your mood is the the way you feel, for example whether you are happy or sad.

moon noun
The moon is the large, round thing that you see shining in the sky at night. The moon travels round the earth in space.

moonlight noun
light from the moon

moor noun *plural* moors
an area of high land that has bushes but no trees

mop noun *plural* mops
You use a mop for cleaning floors. It has a bundle of loose strings on the end of a long handle.

more determiner, adverb
a bigger number or amount *My brother's always got more money than I have. You have more than me.*

morning noun *plural* mornings
the time from the beginning of the day until the middle of the day

mosque noun *plural* mosques
a building where Muslims pray and worship

mosquito noun *plural* mosquitoes
a small insect that bites people and animals

moss noun *plural* mosses
a plant that forms soft lumps when it grows on the ground or on old walls

most determiner, adverb
more than any other or the greatest amount *Which story did you like the most? Joseph has the most.*

moth noun *plural* moths
an insect like a butterfly, that flies at night

mother noun *plural* mothers
Your mother is your female parent.

motive noun *plural* motives
Your motive for doing something is your reason for doing it.

motor noun *plural* motors
an engine that makes something move

motorbike, motorcycle noun
plural motorbikes, motorcycles
a large, heavy bicycle with an engine

motorway noun *plural* motorways
a wide, straight road on which people can drive fast and travel a long way

mould noun *plural* moulds
(rhymes with *old*)
1 the grey or green substance that grows on food that has gone bad

2 a container that you use for making liquids set into a particular shape

mount verb mounts, mounting, mounted
When you mount a horse or a bicycle, you get onto it so that you can ride it.

mountain noun plural mountains
a very high hill

mouse noun plural mice
1 a small furry animal with a long tail
2 (in ICT) A computer mouse is the part that you move about on your desk to choose things on the screen.

moustache noun plural moustaches
hair that grows on a man's top lip

mouth noun plural mouths
1 Your mouth is the part of your face that you can open and use for eating and speaking.
2 The mouth of a river is the place where it flows into the sea.

move verb moves, moving, moved
1 When you move something, you take it from one place and put it in another place. *Mum has moved all my books and I can't find the one I'm looking for.*
2 When something moves, it goes from one place to another. *The dog just sat still and didn't move.*
movement noun A movement is when something goes from one place to another. *I got a terrible fright when I saw a sudden movement in the bushes.*

movie noun plural movies
a film that you watch on a screen at the cinema or on television

mow verb mows, mowing, mowed, mown
When you mow grass, you cut it.

MP3 player noun plural MP3 players
a small music player that plays music you have downloaded onto it from the Internet

much determiner
a lot *Hurry up! We haven't got much time!*

mud noun
wet, sticky soil *My boots were covered in mud.*

muddle noun plural muddles
If something is in a muddle, it is messy or untidy.

muffled adjective
A muffled sound is not clear, and is hard to hear.

mug noun plural mugs
a big cup

multiple noun plural multiples
(in mathematics)
The multiples of a number are the numbers that it will divide into exactly. For example, 10, 15, and 20 are multiples of 5.

a
b
c
d
e
f
g
h
i
j
k
l
m
n
o
p
q
r
s
t
u
v
w
x
y
z

A
B
C
D
E
F
G
H
I
J
K
L
M
N
O
P
Q
R
S
T
U
V
W
X
Y
Z

multiply verb multiplies, multiplying, multiplied (in mathematics)
When you multiply a number, you make it a number of times bigger. *Five multiplied by three is fifteen, 5 × 3 = 15.*

mum, mummy noun plural mums, mummies
Your mum is your mother.

mumble verb mumbles, mumbling, mumbled
When you mumble, you speak without saying the words clearly.

mumps noun
an illness that makes the sides of your face swell up

munch verb munches, munching, munched
When you munch something, you chew it noisily. *We munched our way through a whole packet of biscuits.*

murder verb murders, murdering, murdered
To murder someone means to kill them on purpose.

murmur verb murmurs, murmuring, murmured
When you murmur, you speak in a very soft, low voice.

muscle noun *plural* muscles
Your muscles are the strong parts of your body that you use to make your body move.

museum noun *plural* museums
a place where things from the past are kept for people to go and see

mushroom noun *plural* mushrooms
a small plant with a stem and a grey, round top that you can eat

music noun
the nice sound that you make when you sing or play instruments

musical adjective
A musical instrument is an instrument that you use to play music.

musician noun *plural* musician
a person who plays or composes music

Muslim noun *plural* Muslims
someone who follows the religion of **Islam**

must verb
If you must do something, you have to do it. *You must go to school.*

mustard noun
a cold, yellow sauce with a hot, strong taste

mystery noun *plural* mysteries
(say **miss**-ter-ee)
If something is a mystery, it is strange and puzzling and you do not understand it.
mysterious **adjective** If something is mysterious, it is strange and difficult to understand.

my determiner
You use my when you are talking about something that belongs to you. *Have you seen my shoes?*

myth noun *plural* myths
a very old story, often one about gods and goddesses

Nn

nail noun *plural* nails
1 Your nails are the hard parts at the ends of your fingers and toes.
2 A nail is a small thin piece of metal with a sharp point at the end. You bang nails with a hammer to hold pieces of wood together.
nail verb nails, nailing, nailed
When you nail pieces of wood together, you join them together with nails.

name noun *plural* names
Your name is what people call you.
name verb names, naming, named
To name someone means to give them a name.

narrative noun *plural* narratives
a story or an account of something that has happened

narrow adjective narrower, narrowest
Something that is narrow is not very wide. *We drove along a very narrow road.*

nasty adjective nastier, nastiest
1 Something that is nasty is horrible. *There was a nasty smell in the classroom.*
2 Someone who is nasty is mean or unkind.

nation noun *plural* nations
a country

natural adjective
1 Something that is natural has been made by nature, not by people or machines.
2 Something that is natural is normal.
naturally adverb If someone does something naturally, they do it as if they have been born with the ability to do it. *She's a naturally gifted musician. Naturally I hurried to investigate the noise.*

nature noun
1 everything in the world that was not made by people, for example mountains, animals, and plants
2 Your nature is the type of person that you are. *It's not in Salim's nature to be mean and selfish.*

naughty adjective naughtier, naughtiest (say **nor**-tee)
If you are naughty, you behave badly.

navigate verb navigates, navigating, navigated
When you navigate, you make sure that a ship, aeroplane, or car is going in the right direction.

navy noun *plural* navies
an army that fights at sea, in ships

near adjective adverb nearer, nearest
not far away *We live near the school.*

nearly adverb
almost *It's nearly 3 o'clock.*

neat adjective neater, neatest
Something that is neat is clean and tidy.
neatly adverb Something that is done neatly is done tidily. *Mum's dictionaries and reference books sat neatly on the shelves.*

necessary adjective
If something is necessary, it has to be done. *It is necessary to water plants in dry weather.*

neck noun *plural* necks
Your neck is the part of your body that joins your head to your shoulders.

need verb needs, needing, needed
1 If you need something, you have to have it.
2 If you need to do something, you have to do it. *We need to watch him carefully to see where he puts the money.*

a
b
c
d
e
f
g
h
i
j
k
l
m
n
o
p
q
r
s
t
u
v
w
x
y
z

need noun *plural* needs
1 Your needs are the things that you need.
2 If someone is in need, they do not have enough money, food, or clothes.

needle noun *plural* needles
1 a thin, pointed piece of metal with a hole at one end that you use for sewing

2 A knitting needle is a long, thin stick that you use for knitting.
3 The needles on a pine tree are its thin, pointed leaves.

negative adjective
1 (in grammar) A negative sentence is one that has the word *not* or *no* in it. *Rebecca is not very happy* is a negative sentence .
2 (in mathematics) A negative number is less than 0.

neighbour noun *plural* neighbours
(say **nay**-ber)
Your neighbours are the people who live near you.

nephew noun *plural* nephews
Your nephew is the son of your brother or sister.

nerve noun *plural* nerves
The nerves in your body are the parts that carry messages to and from your brain, so that your body can feel and move.

nervous adjective
If you feel nervous, you feel slightly afraid. *To tell the truth, Jack felt a little nervous, because it isn't every day you find a Scarecrow talking to you.* — Philip Pullman, *The Scarecrow and his Servant*

nest noun *plural* nests
a home that a bird or small animal makes for its babies

net noun *plural* nets
1 A net is a piece of material with small holes in it. You use a net for catching fish.
2 (in ICT) The net is the Internet.

netball noun
a game in which two teams of players try to score goals by throwing a ball through a round net on a pole

nettle noun *plural* nettles
a plant with leaves that can sting you if you touch them

network noun *plural* networks (in ICT)
a group of computers that are connected to each other

never adverb
not ever *I will never tell a lie again!*

new adjective newer, newest
1 Something that is new has just been made or bought and is not old. *I got some new trainers for my birthday.*
2 Something that is new is different. *We're moving to a new house.*

news noun
The news is all the things that are happening in the world, which you can see on television or read about in newspapers.

newspaper noun *plural* **newspapers**
A newspaper is a set of large printed sheets of paper that contain articles about things that are happening in the world.

next adjective
1 The next thing is the one that is nearest to you. *My friend lives in the next street.*
2 The next thing is the one that comes after this one. *We're going on holiday next week.*

nibble verb **nibbles, nibbling, nibbled**
When you nibble something, you eat it by biting off a little bit at a time.

nice adjective **nicer, nicest**
1 Something that is nice is pleasant or enjoyable.
2 Someone who is nice is kind.

nickname noun *plural* **nicknames**
a friendly name that your family or friends call you

niece noun *plural* **nieces**
Your niece is the daughter of your brother or sister.

night noun *plural* **nights**
the time when it is dark

nightmare noun *plural* **nightmares**
a very frightening dream

nil noun
nothing, the number 0

nine noun *plural* **nines**
the number 9

nineteen noun
the number 19

ninety noun
the number 90

no
1 interjection You use **no** when you want to give a negative answer to a question. *'Would you like more cake?' 'No, thank you.'*
2 determiner You use **no** to mean not any. *I have no balloons left.*
3 determiner You use **no** to mean not. *I've asked that they come to the meeting no earlier than six o'clock.*

nobody pronoun
no person *There's nobody here.*

nocturnal adjective
Nocturnal animals move around and feed at night.

nod verb **nods, nodding, nodded**
When you nod, you move your head up and down to show that you agree with someone.

noise noun *plural* **noises**
a sound that you can hear, especially a loud or strange one
noisy adjective If something is noisy, it makes a loud sound. If someone is noisy they make a lot of loud sound. *My brother's music is so noisy that I have to shut my bedroom door when I do my homework.*

noisily adverb
If something is done noisily, it is done with a lot of sound. *He eats noisily.*

a
b
c
d
e
f
g
h
i
j
k
l
m
n
o
p
q
r
s
t
u
v
w
x
y
z

A
B
C
D
E
F
G
H
I
J
K
L
M
N
O
P
Q
R
S
T
U
V
W
X
Y
Z

none pronoun
not any *I went into the kitchen to find some food, but there was none there.*

non-fiction noun
books that contain true information

nonsense noun
something silly that does not mean anything

noon noun
twelve o'clock in the middle of the day

no one pronoun
nobody

normal adjective
Something that is normal is ordinary and not different or surprising.

north noun
North is one of the directions in which you can face or travel. On a map, north is the direction towards the top of the page.

nose noun *plural* noses
Your nose is the part of your face that you use for breathing and smelling.

nostril noun *plural* nostrils
Your nostrils are the two holes at the end of your nose, which you breathe through.

not adverb
You use not to talk about the opposite or absence of something. *She is not hungry. Granny is not at home.*

note noun *plural* notes
1 a short letter
2 A musical note is one sound in a piece of music.
3 A note is a piece of paper money.

nothing noun
not anything *There was nothing in the box.*

notice noun *plural* notices
1 a written message that is put up on a wall for people to see

2 If you take no notice of something, you ignore it.

notice verb notices, noticing, noticed
If you notice something, you see it.

nought noun *plural* noughts
nothing, the number 0

noun noun *plural* nouns (in grammar)
A noun is a word that is the name of a person, place, thing, or idea. Words like *chair, cat, London,* and *sport* are all nouns.

novel noun *plural* novels
a book that tells a long story

November noun
the eleventh month of the year

now adverb
at this time *Do you want to go now?*

nowhere adverb
not anywhere

nudge verb nudges, nudging, nudged
When you nudge someone, you push them with your elbow to make them notice something.

nuisance noun plural nuisances
(say **new**-sans)
If something is a nuisance, it is annoying.

numb adjective
If a part of your body is numb, you cannot feel anything with it. *My toes were numb with cold.*

number noun plural numbers
A number is a word or sign that tells you how many things there are. 1, 2, and 3 are numbers.

1 *one* **2** *two* **3** *three*
4 *four* **5** *five* **6** *six*
7 *seven* **8** *eight*

numeracy noun (say **new**-mer-ass-ee)
Numeracy is being able to count and work with numbers.

numerous adjective (say **new**-mer-uss)
If there are numerous things, there are a lot of them.

nurse noun plural nurses
someone who works in a hospital and looks after people who are ill or hurt

nursery noun plural nurseries
1 a place where very young children go to play and be looked after
2 a place where people grow plants to sell

nut noun plural nuts
1 A nut is a hard fruit that grows on some trees and plants. You can eat some types of nuts.
2 a piece of metal with a hole in it which you screw on the end of a long piece of metal called a bolt

Oo

oak noun plural oaks
a large tree that produces nuts called acorns

oar noun plural oars (say **or**)
a pole with a flat part at one end, which you use for rowing a boat

oasis noun plural oases (say oh-**ay**-sis)
a place in a desert where there is water, and where trees and plants grow

obedient adjective
(say oh-**bee**-dee-ent)
If you are obedient, you do what other people tell you to do. *It was a splendid dog, and like all Swiss dogs it was extremely obedient and well-mannered.* — Alexander McCall Smith, *The Chocolate Money Mystery*
obediently adverb If you do something obediently, you do it as others have told you to do it, and without asking questions.

obey verb obeys, obeying, obeyed
When you obey someone, you do what they tell you to do.

object noun plural objects (say **ob**-jikt)
1 anything that you can see, touch, or hold
2 (in grammar) The object in a sentence is the noun that shows which person or thing receives the action of the verb. For example, in the sentence *The cat chased the dog*, *dog* is the object of the verb.

object verb objects, objecting, objected
(say ob-**jekt**)
If you object to something, you say that you do not like it.

oblong noun plural oblongs
An oblong is a shape that looks like a long square. It is also called a rectangle.

A B C D E F G H I J K L M N **O** P Q R S T U V W X Y Z

observe verb observes, observing, observed
When you observe something, you watch it carefully.

obvious adjective
If something is obvious, it is very easy to see or understand.

occasion noun plural occasions
an important event

occupy verb occupies, occupying, occupied
1 If a place is occupied, someone is using it or living in it. *Is this seat occupied?*
2 To occupy someone means to keep them busy. *My mum gave us some jobs to do to keep us occupied.*

occur verb occurs, occurring, occurred
1 When something occurs, it happens. *The accident occurred at six o'clock last night.*
2 When something occurs to you, you think of it.

ocean noun plural oceans
a big sea *They sailed across the Atlantic Ocean.*

o'clock adverb
a word you use to say what time it is *I'll meet you at one o'clock.*

octagon noun plural octagons
a shape with eight straight sides

October noun
the tenth month of the year

octopus noun plural octopuses
a sea creature with eight tentacles

odd adjective odder, oddest
1 Something that is odd is strange.
2 (in mathematics) An odd number cannot be divided by two. *Five is an odd number.*

of preposition
1 made from *He wore a crown of solid gold.*
2 belonging to *The handle of my bag is broken.*

off adverb, preposition
1 down from something or away from something *He fell off the wall.*
2 not switched on *The alarm is off.*

offend verb offends, offending, offended
To offend someone means to hurt their feelings.

offer verb offers, offering, offered
1 If you offer something to someone, you ask if they would like it. *She offered me a piece of cake.*
2 If you offer to do something, you say that you will do it. *I offered to lay the table.*

office noun plural offices
a room with desks, where people work

officer noun plural officers
1 a person in the army, navy, or air force who is in charge of other people and gives them orders
2 a policeman or policewoman

official adjective
Something that is official is decided or done by a person in charge. *I got an official letter about my prize.*

often adverb
many times *We often go swimming on Saturdays.*

oil noun
Oil is a thick, slippery liquid. You can use some types of oil as fuel, or to make machines work more smoothly. You use other types of oil in cooking.

OK, okay adjective
Something that is OK is all right.

old adjective older, oldest
1 Someone who is old has lived for a long time.
2 Something that is old was made a long time ago. *Our car is quite old.*

old-fashioned adjective
Something that is old-fashioned looks old and not modern.

on preposition, adverb
1 on top of *Put your books on your desk.*
2 on the subject of *I've got a new book on dinosaurs.*
3 working *Is the alarm on?*

once adverb
1 one time *I only missed school once last term.*
2 at one time *Once dinosaurs roamed the earth.*

one noun plural ones
the number 1

onion noun plural onions
a round, white vegetable that has a very strong smell and taste

online adjective
When you work online on a computer, the computer is connected to the Internet.

only adjective
An only child is a child who has no brothers or sisters.

only adverb
not more than *It's only four o'clock.*

onomatopoeia noun
(say on-om-at-o-**pee**-a)
the use of words which sound like the thing they describe, for example *hiss* and *plop*

onto preposition
on *I stuck a label onto the parcel.*

opaque adjective (say oh-**pake**)
If something is opaque, you cannot see through it.

open adjective
1 When a door or window is open, it is not shut.
2 When a shop is open, you can go into it and buy things.

a
b
c
d
e
f
g
h
i
j
k
l
m
n
o
p
q
r
s
t
u
v
w
x
y
z

A
B
C
D
E
F
G
H
I
J
K
L
M
N
O
P
Q
R
S
T
U
V
W
X
Y
Z

open verb opens, opening, opened
1 When you open a door or window, you move it so that it is open.
2 When a shop opens, you can go into it and buy things.

opening noun plural openings
a space or hole in something

operation noun plural operations
When you have an operation, doctors mend or take out a part of your body to make you healthy again.

opinion noun plural opinions
Your opinion is what you think about something.

opponent noun plural opponents
Your opponent is the person that you are fighting or playing a game against.

opposite adjective, preposition
1 facing something *Salim is opposite Sarah.*

2 Things that are opposite are completely different. *North is the opposite direction to south.*

opposite noun plural opposites
The opposite of something is the thing that is completely different to it. *Big is the opposite of small.*

optician noun plural opticians
(say op-**tish**-an)
someone who tests people's eyes and sells glasses to help them see better

orange noun plural oranges
a round, juicy fruit with a thick, orange skin and sweet, juicy flesh
orange adjective
Something that is orange is the colour that you make when you mix red and yellow together.

orbit noun plural orbits
When something is in orbit, it is moving round the sun or a planet.

moon   **earth**   orbit

orchard noun plural orchards
a field where a lot of fruit trees grow

orchestra noun plural orchestras
(-**ch**- in this word sounds like -**k**)
a large group of people who play musical instruments together

order noun plural orders
1 When you give someone an order, you tell them what they must do.
2 The order that things are in is the way that they are arranged, one after the other.

order verb orders, ordering, ordered
1 If you order someone to do something, you tell them that they must do it. *'Come with me,' he ordered.*
2 If you order something in a shop or restaurant, you ask for it. *We ordered pizza.*
3 When you order things in a computer file, you ask the computer to arrange them in a particular order.

ordinary adjective
Something that is ordinary is normal and not different or special.

organ noun plural organs
1 a musical instrument like a piano with large air pipes where the sound comes out
2 Your organs are the parts inside your body like your heart and brain, that each do a particular job.

organic adjective
Food that is organic has been grown naturally.

organization noun
plural organizations
a large number of people who work together to do a job

organize verb organizes, organizing, organized
When you organize something, you plan it and arrange it. *I helped to organize the concert.*

origin noun plural origins
The origin of something is the way in which it started.

original adjective
1 An original part of something was there when it was first made. *My dad's old bike still has its original tyres.*
2 Something that is original is new and has not been copied from something else. *Try to think of some original ideas.*

ornament noun plural ornaments
something that you put in a place to make it look pretty

orphan noun plural orphans
a child whose mother and father are dead

other adjective, pronoun
1 The other thing is a different thing, not this one. *I can't find my other shoe.*
2 The other person is a different person. *I wonder where the others are.*

otherwise adverb
or else *Hurry up otherwise we'll be late.*

ought verb (say **ort**)
If you ought to do something, you should do it. *You ought to do your homework now.*

our determiner
Our means belonging to us. *Would you like to come to our house?*

ours pronoun
You use **ours** when you want to say something belongs to you and at least one other person. *That table is ours.*

ourselves pronoun
Ourselves means we or us and nobody else. *We have often asked ourselves that question.*

out adverb
1 away from *I took the letter out of the envelope.*
2 not at home *Minal's out at the moment.*

outing noun plural outings
a trip to a place

outline noun plural outlines
The outline of something is its shape.

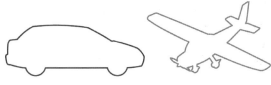

A
B
C
D
E
F
G
H
I
J
K
L
M
N
O
P
Q
R
S
T
U
V
W
X
Y
Z

outside preposition, adverb
not inside *You'll need your coat on if you're going outside.*

oval noun
a shape that looks like an egg

oven noun *plural* ovens
the part of a cooker where you can bake or roast food

over adverb, preposition
1 above or on top of *He put a plaster over the cut.*
2 more than *There were over 200 people there.*
3 about *They were fighting over some sweets.*

overcoat noun *plural* overcoats
a thick, warm coat

overdue adjective
If something is overdue, it is late.

overgrown adjective
A place that is overgrown is covered with messy plants.

overhead adverb
above your head *We saw a plane flying overhead.*

overhear verb overhears, overhearing, overheard
If you overhear something, you hear what other people are saying.

overtake verb overtakes, overtaking, overtook, overtaken
To overtake someone means to catch them up and go past them. *Max overtook me just before I reached the finishing line.*

owe verb owes, owing, owed
If you owe money to someone, you have to pay it to them.

owl noun *plural* owls
a bird with large eyes that hunts at night for small animals

own adjective, pronoun
1 Something that is your own belongs to you.
2 If you are on your own, no one is with you.

own verb owns, owning, owned
If you own something, it is yours and it belongs to you.

oxygen noun (say **ox**-i-jen)
the gas in the air that everyone needs to breathe in order to stay alive

ozone noun (say **oh**-zone)
Ozone is a type of oxygen. The **ozone layer** is a layer of ozone high above the earth which protects us from the dangerous rays of the sun.

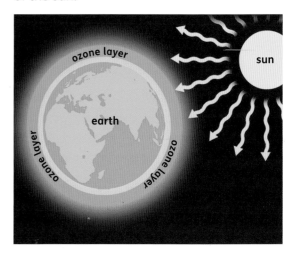

Pp

pace noun *plural* **paces**
a step forwards or backwards

pack noun *plural* **packs**
1 A pack of things is a number of things that you buy together.
2 A pack of cards is a set of cards that you use for playing games.
3 A pack of dogs or wolves is a large group of them.

pack verb **packs, packing, packed**
When you pack things into a box, bag, or suitcase, you put them in.

package noun *plural* **packages**
a parcel

packaging noun
the box or paper that something is wrapped in when you buy it

packet noun *plural* **packets**
a small box or bag that you buy things in

pad noun *plural* **pads**
1 A pad is a piece of thick, soft material that you use as a cushion or to protect something.
2 A helicopter pad is a place on the ground where a helicopter can land.
3 A pad of paper is a set of sheets that are joined together.

pad verb **pads, padding, padded**
If something is padded, it is thick and soft because it is filled with thick, soft material. *Goalkeepers wear special padded trousers.*

paddle verb **paddles, paddling, paddled**
1 When you paddle, you walk about in shallow water. *We went paddling in the sea.*
2 When you paddle a canoe, you make it move through water.

padlock noun *plural* **padlocks**
a lock that you can put on a gate or bicycle

page noun *plural* **pages**
a piece of paper that is part of a book

paid verb past tense of **pay**

pail noun *plural* **pails**
a bucket

pain noun *plural* **pains**
the feeling that you have in your body when something hurts
painful adjective If something is painful it hurts.

paint noun *plural* **paints**
a coloured liquid that you use for making pictures or putting on walls

paint verb **paints, painting, painted**
When you paint, you use paints to make a picture or decorate a wall.

painting noun *plural* **paintings**
A painting is a picture that has been made using paint.

pair noun *plural* **pairs**
two things that belong together *I need a new pair of trainers.*

palace noun *plural* **palaces**
a very large house where a king or queen lives

pale adjective **paler, palest**
1 If you look pale, your face looks white because you are ill.
2 A pale colour is light and not dark. *She was wearing a pale green jumper.*

palm noun *plural* **palms**
1 Your palm is the inside part of your hand.
2 A palm tree is a tree that grows in tropical countries.

a
b
c
d
e
f
g
h
i
j
k
l
m
n
o
p
q
r
s
t
u
v
w
x
y
z

A
B
C
D
E
F
G
H
I
J
K
L
M
N
O
P
Q
R
S
T
U
V
W
X
Y
Z

pan noun *plural* pans
a metal pot that you use for cooking

pancake noun *plural* pancakes
a flat cake that you make by mixing together flour, milk, and eggs and then frying the mixture in a pan

panda noun *plural* pandas
A panda is an animal that looks like a large black and white bear.

pane noun *plural* panes
A pane of glass is a piece of glass in a window.

panic verb panics, panicking, panicked
If you panic, you suddenly feel very frightened and cannot think what to do. *He panicked when he saw the fire.*

pant verb pants, panting, panted
When you pant, you take short, quick breaths because you have been running.

pantomime noun *plural* pantomimes
a special play with jokes and songs, which people perform at Christmas

pants noun
a piece of clothing that you wear over your bottom, underneath your other clothes

paper noun *plural* papers
1 Paper is the thin material that you use to write and draw on.
2 A paper is a newspaper.

parable noun *plural* parables
a short story that tries to teach you something about how to behave

parachute noun *plural* parachutes
(say **pa**-ra-shoot)
a large piece of cloth that opens over your head and stops you from falling too quickly when you jump out of an aeroplane

parade noun *plural* parades
a long line of people marching along, while other people watch them

paragraph noun *plural* paragraphs
A paragraph is one section in a long piece of writing. You begin each new paragraph on a new line.

parallel adjective
Parallel lines are straight lines that go in the same direction and are always the same distance away from each other.

parcel noun *plural* parcels
something that is wrapped up in paper

parent noun *plural* parents
Your parents are your mother and father.

park noun *plural* parks
a large space with grass and trees where people can walk or play

park verb parks, parking, parked
When you park a car, you leave it in a place until you need it again.

parliament noun *plural* **parliaments**
the people who make the laws of a country

parrot noun *plural* **parrots**
a bird with brightly coloured feathers that lives in tropical forests

part noun *plural* **parts**
One part of something is one bit of it. *I've only read the first part of the story.*

participle noun *plural* **participles**
(in grammar)
A participle is part of a verb. You use the present participle to describe something that is happening as you are talking, for example, the word *frightening* in *The noise of the wind is frightening.* You use the past participle to describe something that has happened in the past, for example, *frightened* in *Last night I was frightened by the noise of the wind.*

particular adjective
1 only this one and no other *I like this particular song.*
2 Someone who is particular is fussy and will only choose certain things.

partly adverb
not completely *The school is only partly built.*

partner noun *plural* **partners**
Your partner is the person you are doing something with, for example when you are working or dancing.

part of speech noun
plural **parts of speech** (in grammar)
A part of speech is a name that we give to different types of words. Adjectives, nouns, and verbs are different parts of speech.

party noun *plural* **parties**
a time when people get together to have fun and celebrate something

pass verb **passes, passing, passed**
1 When you pass something, you go past it. *I pass the swimming pool every day.*
2 If you pass something to someone, you pick it up and give it to them. *Please could you pass me the salt?*
3 If you pass a test, you are successful.

passage noun *plural* **passages**
a corridor

passenger noun *plural* **passengers**
a person who is travelling in a bus, train, ship, or aeroplane

Passover noun
a Jewish religious festival

passport noun *plural* **passports**
A passport is a special book or piece of paper with your name and photograph on it. It shows who you are, and you take it with you when you go to another country.

password noun *plural* **passwords**
a secret word that you use to go into a place or to use a computer

past noun
the time that has already gone *In the past people used candles instead of electric lights.*

past preposition
1 If you go past something, you go from one side of it to the other side.
2 If it is past a certain time, it is after that time. *We didn't get home until past midnight.*

a b c d e f g h i j k l m n o **p** q r s t u v w x y z

149

A
B
C
D
E
F
G
H
I
J
K
L
M
N
O
P
Q
R
S
T
U
V
W
X
Y
Z

pasta noun
Pasta is a type of food made from flour and water. Spaghetti is a type of pasta.

paste noun
something that is like a very thick, sticky liquid

paste verb pastes, pasting, pasted
1 When you paste something, you stick it with glue.
2 (in ICT) To paste something into a computer document means to add it into that document after you have copied it from another document.

pastime noun plural pastimes
something that you do to enjoy yourself in your free time

pastry noun
a mixture of flour, fat, and water that you roll flat and use for making pies

pat verb pats, patting, patted
When you pat something, you touch it gently with your hand. *Tom patted the dog gently on the head.*

patch noun plural patches
a small piece of material that you put over a hole in your clothes

path noun plural paths
a narrow road that you can walk along but not drive along

patient noun plural patients
(say pay-shunt)
someone who is ill and being looked after by a doctor

patient adjective (say pay-**shunt**)
If you are patient, you can wait without getting cross or bored. *You will all have to be patient and wait your turn.*

pattern noun plural patterns
a design with lines, shapes, and colours

pause noun plural pauses
a short time when you stop what you are doing

pause verb pauses, pausing, paused
When you pause, you stop what you are doing for a short time.

pavement noun plural pavements
the path that people walk on along the side of a street

paw noun plural paws
An animal's paws are its feet.

pay verb pays, paying, paid
When you pay for something, you give someone money so that you can have it.

PC noun plural PCs
A PC is a small computer for one person to use. PC is short for **personal computer**.

PE noun
PE is a lesson at school in which you do sports and games. PE is short for **physical education**.

pea noun plural peas
a small, round, green vegetable

peace noun
1 When there is peace, there is no war.
2 When there is peace, there is no noise.

peaceful adjective
When a place is peaceful, there is no noise.

peach noun plural peaches
a round, soft, juicy fruit with yellow flesh and a large stone in the middle

peacock noun plural peacocks
a large bird with long, brightly coloured tail feathers

peak noun plural peaks
1 A mountain peak is the top of a mountain.
2 The peak on a cap is the part that sticks out in front.

peanut noun plural peanuts
a small, round nut that grows in a pod in the ground

pear noun plural pears
a sweet, juicy fruit that is narrow at the top and round at the bottom

pearl noun plural pearls
(rhymes with *girl*)
A pearl is a small, shiny, white ball that grows inside the shells of some oysters. People use pearls for making jewellery.

pebble noun plural pebbles
a small, round stone *We collected some pebbles on the beach.*

peck verb pecks, pecking, pecked
When a bird pecks something, it touches it or picks it up with its beak.

peculiar adjective
Something that is peculiar is strange. *The ice cream had a peculiar taste.*

pedal noun plural pedals
a part of a machine that you push with your foot to make it go

peel noun
The peel on a fruit or vegetable is its skin.

peel verb peels, peeling, peeled
When you peel fruit or vegetables, you take their skin off.

peep verb peeps, peeping, peeped
If you peep at something, you look at it quickly.

peg noun plural pegs
1 a small clip that you use for fixing washing onto a line
2 a piece of metal or wood that you can hang things on

pen noun plural pens
something that you hold in your hand and use for writing with ink

pence noun
pennies

a b c d e f g h i j k l m n o p q r s t u v w x y z

151

A B C D E F G H I J K L M N O P Q R S T U V W X Y Z

pencil noun *plural* pencils
something that you hold in your hand and use for writing or drawing

pendown adjective (in ICT)
In some computer programs, when you move the pen on the screen in the pendown position, the pen draws as it moves.

pendulum noun *plural* pendulums
A pendulum is a weight that swings backwards and forwards. Some large old-fashioned clocks have pendulums to make them work.

penguin noun *plural* penguins
A penguin is a large black and white bird that swims in the sea but cannot fly.

penknife noun *plural* penknives
a small knife that folds up so that you can carry it safely

penny noun *plural* pence
a coin

pentagon noun *plural* pentagons
a shape with five straight sides

people noun
men, women, and children

pepper noun
1 Pepper is a powder with a hot taste that you add to food.
2 A pepper is a green, yellow, orange, or red vegetable.

perch noun *plural* perches
a place where a bird rests when it is not flying

percussion noun
Percussion instruments are musical instruments that you play by banging, hitting, or shaking them. Drums, cymbals, and tambourines are percussion instruments.

perfect adjective
Something that is perfect is so good that it cannot be any better.
perfectly adverb Something that is done perfectly is done so well that it cannot be any better. *He could see perfectly without his glasses.*

perform verb performs, performing, performed
When you perform, you do something in front of people to entertain them. *We performed the school play in front of our parents.*

perfume noun *plural* perfumes
a liquid with a nice smell that you put on your skin

perhaps adverb
possibly *Perhaps it will rain tomorrow.*

period noun *plural* periods
a length of time *We all had to leave the building for a period of two hours.*

permanent adjective
Something that is permanent will last for ever.

person noun *plural* people, persons
a man, woman, or child

personal adjective
Your personal things are the things that are to do with just you and no one else.

personality noun *plural* personalities
Your personality is the type of person you are.

personally adverb
If you do something personally, you do it yourself. *I will talk to him personally.*

persuade verb persuades, persuading, persuaded
If you persuade someone to do something, you make them agree to do it. *I managed to persuade my mum to take us swimming.*

persuasive adjective
Persuasive writing is writing that tries to persuade people to do something.

pest noun *plural* pests
a person, animal, or plant that causes damage to things or annoys people

pester verb pesters, pestering, pestered
When you pester someone, you keep annoying them until they do what you want them to do. *Stop pestering me!*

pet noun *plural* pets
an animal which you keep and look after

petal noun *plural* petals
The petals on a flower are the coloured parts.

petrol noun
a liquid that you put in cars to make them go

phone noun *plural* phones
a telephone

phone verb phones, phoning, phoned
When you phone someone, you use a telephone to speak to them.

phonics noun
Phonics are the different sounds that letters represent when they are written down. You can use phonics to help you learn to read by saying the sound of each letter in a word and then putting them all together to make the whole word.

photo noun *plural* photos
a photograph

photocopier noun
plural photocopiers
a machine which can make a copy of a piece of writing or a picture

photograph noun *plural* photographs
a picture that you take with a camera

photograph verb photographs, photographing, photographed
When you photograph something, you take a photograph of it.

phrase noun *plural* phrases
A phrase is a group of words that you use together. *How do you do?* is a phrase.

physical adjective (say **fizz**-ic-al)
Physical activities are activities that you do with your body, for example running and jumping.

piano noun *plural* pianos
a large musical instrument which has white and black keys that you press with your fingers to make different musical notes

a
b
c
d
e
f
g
h
i
j
k
l
m
n
o
p
q
r
s
t
u
v
w
x
y
z

153

A
B
C
D
E
F
G
H
I
J
K
L
M
N
O
P
Q
R
S
T
U
V
W
X
Y
Z

pick verb picks, picking, picked
1 When you pick something, you choose it.
Which one are you going to pick?
2 When you pick something up, you lift it up with your hand.
3 When you pick a flower or fruit, you take it off a plant.

picnic noun *plural* picnics
a meal of cold food that you eat outside

picture noun *plural* pictures
1 a painting, drawing, or photograph
2 When you go to the pictures, you go to a cinema to watch a film.

pie noun *plural* pies
a type of food that has meat, vegetables, or fruit in the middle and pastry on the outside

piece noun *plural* pieces
A piece of something is a bit of it.

pierce verb pierces, piercing, pierced
When you pierce something, you make a hole through it.

pig noun *plural* pigs
an animal with a large snout and a curly tail that is kept on farms for its meat

pigeon noun *plural* pigeons
a grey bird that often lives in towns

pile noun *plural* piles
A pile of things is a lot of things all on top of each other.

pill noun *plural* pills
a small tablet with medicine in, which you swallow when you are ill

pillar noun *plural* pillars
a wooden or stone post that helps to hold up a building

pillow noun *plural* pillows
a cushion that you rest your head on in bed

pilot noun *plural* pilots
someone who flies an aeroplane

pin noun *plural* pins
A pin is a thin piece of metal with a sharp point. You use pins to hold pieces of material together when you are sewing.

pinch verb pinches, pinching, pinched
1 If you pinch someone, you squeeze their skin between your thumb and finger so that it hurts.
2 To pinch something means to steal it.
Who's pinched my pencil?

pine noun *plural* pines
a tree with leaves like needles that do not fall in winter

pineapple noun *plural* pineapples
a large fruit with yellow flesh that grows in hot countries

pink adjective
Something that is pink is very pale red.

PINK

pint noun *plural* pints
We can measure liquids in pints. One pint is about half a litre.

pip noun *plural* pips
a seed of a fruit such as an apple or orange

pipe noun *plural* pipes
a hollow tube that gas or liquid can go along

pirate noun *plural* pirates
someone who sails in a ship and attacks and robs other ships at sea

pit noun *plural* pits
a deep hole in the ground

pitch noun *plural* pitches
A sports pitch is a piece of ground that is marked out so that you can play a game on it.

pity noun
1 If you feel pity for someone, you feel sorry for them. *I felt pity for the children who weren't allowed to go swimming.*
2 If something is a pity, it is a shame. *What a pity you won't be able to come with us!*

pizza noun *plural* pizzas
a food made from a flat, bread-like mixture with tomatoes, cheese, and other things on top

place noun *plural* places
a building or area of land *We found an ideal place to camp.*

place verb places, placing, placed
When you place something somewhere, you put it there. *Place your rubbish in the bin.*

plain adjective plainer, plainest
Something that is plain is ordinary, and not different or special.

plain noun *plural* plains
a large area of flat ground *You can see for miles over the plain.*

plait verb plaits, plaiting, plaited
(say *platt*)
When you plait hair, you twist three pieces together by crossing them over and under each other.

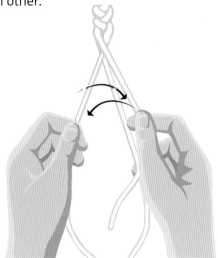

plan noun *plural* plans
1 If you have a plan, you have an idea about how to do something. *A plan was gradually forming in my mind.*
2 a map of a building or a town

plan verb plans, planning, planned
When you plan something, you decide what you are going to do and how you are going to do it.

plane noun *plural* planes
an aeroplane

planet noun *plural* planets
A planet is a very large object in space that moves around a star or around our sun. The earth is a planet.

a
b
c
d
e
f
g
h
i
j
k
l
m
n
o
p
q
r
s
t
u
v
w
x
y
z

plank noun *plural* planks
a long, flat piece of wood

plant noun *plural* plants
A plant is a living thing that grows in the soil. Trees, flowers, and vegetables are all plants.

plant verb plants, planting, planted
When you plant something, you put it in the ground to grow.

plaster noun *plural* plasters
1 a piece of sticky material that you put over a cut to keep it clean
2 Plaster is a soft mixture that goes hard when it dries. Plaster is put onto the walls of buildings. A different sort of plaster is put onto someone's arm or leg when they have broken a bone.

plastic noun
a light, strong material that is made in factories and is used for making all kinds of things

plate noun *plural* plates
a flat dish that you eat food from

platform noun *plural* platforms
1 the place in a station where people wait beside the railway lines for a train to come
2 a small stage in a hall

play verb plays, playing, played
1 When you play, you have fun.
2 When you play an instrument, you use it to make music. *Can you play the piano?*

play noun *plural* plays
a story which people act so that other people can watch

player noun *plural* players
A player is someone who takes part in a sport. *There are seven players on the football pitch today.*

playground noun *plural* playgrounds
a place outside where children can play

pleasant adjective
Something that is pleasant is nice.

please verb pleases, pleasing, pleased
1 To please someone means to make them happy.
2 used when you want to ask for something politely *Please may I have another biscuit?*

pleasure noun
the feeling that you have when you are happy and enjoying yourself

plenty noun
If there is plenty of something, there is as much as you need.

plot noun *plural* plots
1 a secret plan
2 the story of a novel, film, or play

plough noun *plural* ploughs
(rhymes with *how*)
a large machine that is used on farms for digging and turning over the soil

pluck verb plucks, plucking, plucked
1 When you pluck something, you take it from the place where it is growing. *He plucked an apple from the tree.*
2 When you pluck a musical instrument, you play it by pulling on the strings with your fingers.

plug noun *plural* plugs
1 a round piece of plastic that you put into the hole in a bath or sink to stop the water from running out
2 the part of an electric machine or tool that you put into an electric socket to make it work

plum noun *plural* plums
a juicy fruit with a stone in the middle

plumber noun *plural* plumbers
a person whose job is to fit and mend water pipes and taps

plump adjective plumper, plumpest
Someone who is plump is quite fat.

plunge verb plunges, plunging, plunged
If you plunge into water, you jump in.

plural noun *plural* plurals (in grammar)
A plural is the form of a word that you use when you are talking about more than one person or thing. The plural of *book* is *books*.

plus preposition (in mathematics)
add *Three plus three is six, 3 + 3 = 6.*

pocket noun *plural* pockets
a part of a piece of clothing that is like a small bag that you can keep things in

pod noun *plural* pods
A pod is a long thin part of a plant that has seeds inside. Peas grow in pods.

podcast noun *plural* podcasts
a radio programme that you can download from the Internet onto a music player

poem noun *plural* poems
a piece of writing that is written in lines and uses rhythms and rhymes in a clever way

poet noun *plural* poets
someone who writes poems

poetry noun
poems *Do you like reading poetry?*

point noun *plural* points
1 a thin, sharp part on the end of something
2 a particular place or time
3 a mark that you score in a game *Our team scored the most points.*

point verb points, pointing, pointed
1 When you point at something, you show it to someone by holding your finger out towards it.
2 When you point a weapon at something, you aim the weapon towards it.

pointed adjective
something that is pointed has a sharp point at one end

poison noun *plural* poisons
something that will kill you or make you ill if you swallow it
poisonous adjective If something is poisonous it will kill you or make you ill if you swallow it. *Don't touch that plant because it's poisonous.*

poke verb pokes, poking, poked
If you poke something, you push it with your finger or with a stick. *Umpin began to poke at the snow with one foot.* — Jostein Gaarder, *The Frog Castle*

polar bear noun *plural* polar bears
a very large, white bear that lives near the North Pole

pole noun *plural* poles
a long stick

a
b
c
d
e
f
g
h
i
j
k
l
m
n
o
p
q
r
s
t
u
v
w
x
y
z

A
B
C
D
E
F
G
H
I
J
K
L
M
N
O
P
Q
R
S
T
U
V
W
X
Y
Z

police noun
The police are the people whose job is to catch criminals and make sure that people do not break the law.

polish verb polishes, polishing, polished
When you polish something, you rub it to make it shine.

polite adjective politer, politest
Someone who is polite has good manners and is not rude to people.
politely adverb If you do or say something politely you are not rude to people. *'That looks like hard work,' said Pearl politely.*

politician noun *plural* politicians
(say pol-i-**tish**-un)
a person who works in the government of a country

politics noun
the work that the government of a country does

pollen noun
Pollen is a yellow powder that you find inside flowers. Pollen is carried from one flower to another by the wind or by insects so that the flowers can produce seeds.

pollute verb pollutes, polluting, polluted
To pollute air or water means to make it dirty. *Some factories pollute rivers by tipping substances into them.*
pollution noun Pollution is when air or water is made dirty.

polygon noun *plural* polygons
(say **pol**-ee-gon)
A polygon is a flat shape with three or more sides. Triangles, squares, and octagons are all polygons.

polythene noun (say **pol**-i-theen)
a type of plastic material that is used for making bags

pond noun *plural* ponds
a small lake

pony noun *plural* ponies
a small horse

ponytail noun *plural* ponytails
If you wear your hair in a ponytail, you wear it tied in a long bunch at the back of your head.

pool noun *plural* pools
a small area of water

poor adjective poorer, poorest
1 Someone who is poor does not have very much money.
2 Something that is poor is bad. *This is very poor work. You can do better than this!*
3 A poor person is unlucky or unhappy. *You poor child!*

pop verb pops, popping, popped
If something pops, it bursts with a loud bang.

pop noun
Pop is modern music that people dance to.

popcorn noun
a food that is made by heating grains of corn until they burst and become big and fluffy

popular adjective
If something is popular, a lot of people like it. *Football is the most popular sport in the world.*

population noun
The population of a place is the number of people who live there.

porch noun *plural* porches
a place in front of the door of a building where people can wait before they go in

pork noun
meat from a pig

port noun *plural* ports
a place on the coast where ships can come to the land to load or unload goods

portable adjective
If something is portable, you can carry it or move it easily. *I've got a new portable TV for my room.*

portion noun *plural* portions
A portion of food is an amount that you give to one person.

portrait noun *plural* portraits
a painting or drawing of a person

position noun *plural* positions
1 The position of something is the place where it is. *We don't know the exact position of the ship at the moment.*
2 Your position is the way that you are standing, sitting, or lying. *I had to sit in a very uncomfortable position.*

possess verb possesses, possessing, possessed
If you possess something, you own it.

possible adjective
If something is possible, it might happen, or it might be true. *It's possible that someone has stolen the money.*
possibly **adverb** You use possibly to mean perhaps. *Could we possibly leave for the park after lunch?*

possibility noun
A possibility is something that might happen or might be true. *There's still a possibility that we can win.*

post noun *plural* posts
1 A post is a pole that is fixed in the ground.
2 The post is all the letters and parcels that are delivered to people's houses.

post verb posts, posting, posted
When you post a letter or parcel, you send it to someone.

postcard noun *plural* postcards
A postcard is a piece of card with a picture on one side. You write on the other side and send it to someone.

postcode noun *plural* postcodes
letters and numbers that you put at the end of someone's address when you are sending them a letter

poster noun *plural* posters
a large picture or notice that you put up on a wall

a
b
c
d
e
f
g
h
i
j
k
l
m
n
o
p
q
r
s
t
u
v
w
x
y
z

159

A
B
C
D
E
F
G
H
I
J
K
L
M
N
O
P
Q
R
S
T
U
V
W
X
Y
Z

postman noun *plural* postmen

A postman is a man who delivers letters and parcels to people's houses. A woman who does this is a **postwoman**.

post office noun *plural* post offices

a place where you can go to buy stamps, and post letters and parcels

postpone verb postpones, postponing, postponed

If you postpone something, you decide to do it later.

pot noun *plural* pots

a round container that you can put or keep things in

potato noun *plural* potatoes

a round white vegetable that you dig out of the ground

pottery noun

cups, plates, and other things that are made from clay

pouch noun *plural* pouches

1 a small bag that you can keep things in
2 a pocket of skin that some animals have on their bodies for carrying their young

pounce verb pounces, pouncing, pounced

To pounce on something means to attack it by jumping on it suddenly.

pound noun *plural* pounds

1 We can measure weight in pounds. One pound is about half a kilogram.
2 A pound is a unit of money. Pounds are used in Britain and some other countries.

pour verb pours, pouring, poured

1 When you pour a liquid, you tip it into a container. *Dad poured some milk into a glass.*
2 When a liquid is pouring out of something, it is coming out very quickly. *Water was pouring out of the burst pipe.*

powder noun

a substance like flour that is dry and made of lots of tiny bits

power noun *plural* powers

1 If you have power, you can do what you want, or make other people do what you want.
2 If you have special powers, you are able to do magic things.
3 Power is energy that makes machines work.

powerful adjective

1 Someone who is powerful has a lot of power over other people. *He was a rich and powerful king.*
2 Something that is powerful is very strong. *They had to use a very powerful crane to lift the lorry out of the ditch.*

practical adjective

A practical person is good at working with their hands and doing useful things.

practice noun

Practice is when you do something again and again so that you will get better at it.

practise verb practises, practising, practised

When you practise, you keep doing something over and over again so that you will get better at it. *If you keep practising the piano you'll soon get better at it.*

praise verb praises, praising, praised
To praise someone means to tell them that they have done well.

pram noun plural prams
a bed on wheels in which you can push a baby along

prawn noun plural prawns
A prawn is a small sea creature with a shell. You can cook and eat prawns.

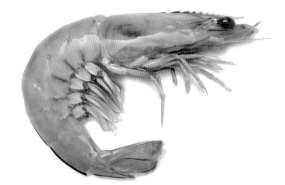

pray verb prays, praying, prayed
When people pray, they talk to a god.

precious adjective (say **presh**-uss)
Something that is precious is worth a lot of money, or is very special to someone.
She hid the precious jewels under her bed.

precise adjective
Something that is precise is exact and correct.

predator noun plural predators
an animal that hunts and kills other animals for food

predict verb predicts, predicting, predicted
If you predict something, you say that it will happen in the future.

prefer verb prefers, preferring, preferred
If you prefer one thing to another, you like it more. *I don't like wearing skirts. I prefer to wear jeans.*

prefix noun plural prefixes (in grammar)
A prefix is a group of letters that are added to the front of a word to change its meaning *Un-* and *dis-* are prefixes.

prehistoric adjective
Prehistoric times were times long ago.

prepare verb prepares, preparing, prepared
When you prepare something, you get it ready.

preposition noun plural prepositions (in grammar)
a word such as *in* or *on* that goes in front of a noun

present adjective (say **prez**-ent)
1 If you are present in a place, you are there.
2 The present time is the time that is happening now.

present noun
plural presents (say prez-**ent**)
1 something that you give to someone

2 The present is the time that is happening now.

present verb presents, presenting, presented (say pri-**zent**)
1 If you present something to someone, you give it to them. *The head presented the prizes to the winners.*
2 When someone presents a show, they introduce it.

a
b
c
d
e
f
g
h
i
j
k
l
m
n
o
p
q
r
s
t
u
v
w
x
y
z

161

A B C D E F G H I J K L M N O P Q R S T U V W X Y Z

president noun *plural* presidents
someone who rules a country

press verb presses, pressing, pressed
When you press something, you push it with your finger. *What will happen if I press this button?*

press noun
The press is a general name for newspapers.

pressure noun (say **presh**-er)
1 Pressure is a force which pushes against something. *Apply pressure to the cut to stop it bleeding.*
2 If you put pressure on someone, you try to make them do something.

pretend verb pretends, pretending, pretended
When you pretend, you say things or do things that are not really true. *Jacob was only pretending to be hurt.*

pretty adjective prettier, prettiest
1 Something that is pretty is nice to look at. *That's a very pretty dress.*
2 A pretty girl or woman has a beautiful face.

prevent verb prevents, preventing, prevented
If you prevent something from happening, you stop it from happening. *He shut the door to prevent anyone from leaving.*

prey noun
An animal's prey is the animal that it hunts and kills.

price noun *plural* prices
The price of something is the amount of money you have to pay for it.

prick verb pricks, pricking, pricked
When you prick something, you make a tiny hole in it with something sharp.

prickle noun *plural* prickles
Prickles are sharp points on a plant.
prickly adjective Something that is prickly has lots of sharp points. *He fell down the steep bank and landed in a prickly bush.*

pride noun
the feeling you have when you are proud

prime minister noun
plural prime ministers
the leader of a country's government

prince noun *plural* princes
the son of a king or queen

princess noun *plural* princesses
1 the daughter of a king or queen
2 the wife of a prince

print verb prints, printing, printed
1 When you print words, you write them with letters that are not joined together. *Please print your name at the top of the page.*
2 When a machine prints words or pictures, it puts them onto paper.

print-out noun *plural* print-outs
a printed copy of a computer document

prison noun *plural* prisons
a place where people are kept as a punishment

prisoner noun *plural* prisoners
someone who is locked up in a place and not allowed to leave

private adjective
Something that is private is only for some people, not for everyone. *The hotel has its own private beach.*

prize noun plural prizes
something that you get if you win a game or competition

probable adjective
If it is probable that something will happen, it is very likely that it will happen.
probably adverb You say that something will probably happen or is probably true when you think it is likely to happen or be true. *We'll probably go to Spain on holiday again this year.*

problem noun plural problems
something that is difficult *I would love to come to the cinema with you, but the problem is I can't get there.*

process noun plural processes
a series of actions that you do one after the other, and that take a long time *Making computers is quite a complicated process.*

produce verb produces, producing, produced
1 To produce something means to make it. *Cows produce milk.*
2 If you produce something, you bring it out of a box or bag. *The woman produced a camera from her bag.*

product noun plural products
1 something that has been made so that it can be sold to people in shops
2 (in mathematics) the number you get when you multiply two numbers together *The product of 2 and 3 is 6.*

profit noun plural profits
If you make a profit, you make money by selling something for more than you paid to buy it or make it.

program noun plural programs
A computer program is a list of instructions that the computer follows.

programme noun plural programmes
1 a show on the radio or television
2 a small book that tells you what will happen at an event

progress noun
When you make progress, you get better at doing something. *You have made a lot of progress with your maths this term.*

project noun plural projects
a piece of work where you find out as much as you can about something interesting and write about it

promise verb promises, promising, promised
If you promise to do something, you say that you will definitely do it. *Don't forget—you promised to help me wash the car.*

pronoun noun plural pronouns
(in grammar)
A pronoun is a word that you use instead of a noun. *He, she,* and *it* are all pronouns.

pronounce verb pronounces, pronouncing, pronounced
The way you pronounce a word is the way you say it. *How do you pronounce your name?*

A
B
C
D
E
F
G
H
I
J
K
L
M
N
O
P
Q
R
S
T
U
V
W
X
Y
Z

proof noun
If there is proof that something happened, there is something that shows that it definitely happened. *We think we know who stole the books, but we have no proof.*

prop verb props, propping, propped
If you prop something somewhere, you lean it there so that it does not fall over. *He propped his bicycle against the wall.*

propeller noun *plural* propellers
a set of blades that spin round to make something move

proper adjective
The proper thing is the correct or right one. *Put the books back in their proper places.*
properly adverb Something that is done properly is done in the correct or right way. *Make sure you brush your teeth properly.*

proper noun noun
plural proper nouns (in grammar)
A proper noun is a noun that is the name of a person or place. For example, *London* and *Tom* are proper nouns.

property noun *plural* properties
If something is your property, it belongs to you.

prophet noun *plural* prophets
(**-ph-** in this word sounds like **-f-**)
1 someone who says what will happen in the future
2 a great religious teacher

prose noun
writing which is not poetry or a play

protect verb protects, protecting, protected
To protect someone means to keep them safe and stop them being hurt.

protein noun
Protein is a substance that is found in some types of food, for example meat, eggs, and cheese. Your body needs protein to help you grow.

protest verb protests, protesting, protested
If you protest about something, you say that you do not like it or do not agree with it. *'No, no! Don't do that!' protested the Scarecrow. — Philip Pullman, The Scarecrow and his Servant*

proud adjective prouder, proudest
If you are proud of something, you are pleased with it and think that it is very good. *I'm very proud of this painting.*

prove verb proves, proving proved
(say **proov**)
To prove that something is true means to show that it is definitely true. *These footprints prove that someone has been in the garden.*

proverb noun *plural* proverbs
a short, well-known saying which gives you advice about something

provide verb provides, providing, provided
If you provide something for people, you give it to them. *The school provides us with books and pencils.*

pub noun *plural* pubs
a place where people can go to have a drink and meet friends

public adjective
Something that is public can be used by everyone. *Is there a public swimming pool in your town?*

publish verb publishes, publishing, published
To publish a book means to print it and sell it.

pudding noun *plural* puddings
any sweet food which you eat after the main part of a meal

puddle noun *plural* puddles
a small pool of water

pull verb pulls, pulling, pulled
When you pull something, you get hold of it and move it towards you.

pullover noun *plural* pullovers
a jumper

pump noun *plural* pumps
a machine that pushes air or water into something or out of something *You use a bicycle pump to put air into tyres.*

pump verb pumps, pumping pumped
When you pump water or air, you force it into something or out of something. *The firemen pumped all the water out of the flooded house.*

pumpkin noun *plural* pumpkins
a very large, round orange vegetable

pun noun *plural* puns
A pun is a joke that is funny because it uses words that sound the same, or words that have two different meanings. For example, *eggs are very eggs-pensive* is a pun.

punch verb punches, punching, punched
If you punch someone, you hit them with your fist.

punctuation noun
all the marks such as commas and full stops that you put into a piece of writing to make it easier to read

puncture noun *plural* punctures
a small hole in a tyre

punish verb punishes, punishing, punished
To punish someone means to make them suffer because they have done something wrong. *The teacher punished us by keeping us inside at lunch time.*
punishment noun Punishment is when someone makes you suffer because you have done something wrong. *I wondered what punishment he would give us.*

pupil noun *plural* pupils
1 A pupil is a child who goes to school.
2 Your pupils are the black circles in the middle of your eyes.

puppet noun *plural* puppets
a small doll that you can move by pulling on strings, or by putting it over your hand like a glove and then moving your hand

puppy noun *plural* **puppies**
a young dog

pure adjective **purer, purest**
Something that is pure is one thing only, with nothing else mixed in. *She was wearing a necklace made of pure gold.*

purple adjective
Something that is purple is the colour that you make by mixing red and blue together.

PURPLE

purpose noun *plural* **purposes**
The purpose of something is the reason why you are doing it.
on purpose If you do something on purpose, you do it deliberately. *I'm sorry, I didn't do it on purpose.*

purr verb **purrs, purring, purred**
When a cat purrs, it makes a low, rumbling sound because it is happy.

purse noun *plural* **purses**
a small bag that you carry money in

push verb **pushes, pushing, pushed**
When you push something, you use your hands to move it away from you.

put verb **puts, putting, put**
1 When you put something in a place, you move it so that it is there. *Please put the books back on the shelf.*
2 If you put something off, you decide to do it later instead of now.

puzzle noun *plural* **puzzles**
1 a game in which you have to do something difficult or find the answer to a difficult question
2 If something is a puzzle, no one can explain it or understand it.

puzzle verb **puzzles, puzzling, puzzled**
If something puzzles you, it seems strange and you do not understand it.

pyjamas noun
loose trousers and a top that you wear in bed

pyramid noun *plural* **pyramids**
1 a large, stone building that was made by the ancient Egyptians to bury a dead king or queen

2 a solid shape with a square base and four triangular sides that come together in a point at the top

Qq

quack verb quacks, quacking, quacked
When a duck quacks, it makes a loud sound.

quadrilateral noun
plural quadrilaterals
A quadrilateral is any shape that has four straight sides. A square is a type of quadrilateral.

quaint adjective quainter, quaintest
Something that is quaint is pretty and old-fashioned. *What a quaint little cottage!*

qualify verb qualifies, qualifying, qualified
1 When you qualify, you pass a test or exam so that you are allowed to do a job.
2 When you qualify in a competition, you get enough points to go on to the next part of the competition. *England managed to qualify for the World Cup.*

quality noun plural qualities
The quality of something is how good or bad it is. *You need good quality paper for model-making.*

quantity noun plural quantities
A quantity is an amount. *We measured the quantity of water in the jug.*

quarrel verb quarrels, quarrelling, quarrelled
When people quarrel, they argue with each other in an angry way. *Ben and Alice have been quarrelling about where to sit for ages.*

quarry noun plural quarries
a place where people cut stone out of the ground so that it can be used for building

quarter noun plural quarters
One quarter of something is one of four equal parts that the thing is divided into. It can also be written as $\frac{1}{4}$.

quay noun plural quays (say key)
a place where ships can be loaded and unloaded

queen noun plural queens
A queen is a woman who rules a country.

query noun plural queries (say queer-ee)
a question

question noun plural questions
When you ask a question, you ask someone something because you want to know the answer.

question mark noun
plural question marks
A question mark is a mark like this ? that you use in writing.

questionnaire noun
plural questionnaires
a sheet of paper with a lot of questions on it to collect information from people

queue verb queues, queueing, queued
When people queue, they wait in a line.

a b c d e f g h i j k l m n o p q r s t u v w x y z

A
B
C
D
E
F
G
H
I
J
K
L
M
N
O
P
Q
R
S
T
U
V
W
X
Y
Z

quick adjective quicker, quickest
Something that is quick does not take very long. *We had a quick lunch and then set out.*
quickly adverb Something that is done quickly does not take very long. *I quickly got dressed and ran out of the house.*

quiet adjective quieter, quietest
1 If a place is quiet, there is no noise there. *The school was deserted and all the classrooms were quiet.*
2 Something that is quiet is not very loud
quietly adverb Something that is done quietly is done with no or little noise. *'I want to go home,' he said quietly.*

quilt noun *plural* quilts
a thick, warm cover for a bed

quit verb quits, quitting, quitted
1 If you quit doing something, you stop doing it.
2 When you quit a file or program on a computer, you close it.

quite adverb
1 slightly, but not very *The film was quite good.*
2 completely *We haven't quite finished.*

quiz noun *plural* quizzes
a game in which people try to answer a lot of questions

quotation marks noun
Quotation marks are marks like this ' ' or this " " that you use in writing. You put these marks round words to show that someone has spoken them.

quote verb quotes, quoting, quoted
When you quote words from a book or poem, you repeat them. *He quoted some lines from an old poem.*

Rr

rabbi noun *plural* rabbis (say **ra**-bye)
a Jewish religious leader

rabbit noun *plural* rabbits
A rabbit is a small furry animal with long ears. Rabbits live in holes in the ground and use their strong back legs to hop about.

race verb races, racing, raced
When people race, they run or swim against each other to find out who is the fastest.

race noun *plural* races
1 a competition in which people run or swim against each other to find out who is the fastest
2 a group of people who come from the same part of the world and look the same because they have the same colour skin, the same type of hair, and so on

racist noun *plural* racists
someone who treats other people unfairly because they have different colour skin or come from a different country

rack noun *plural* racks
a shelf made of bars that you put things on

racket noun *plural* rackets
1 A racket is a bat that you use for hitting a ball in a game of tennis or badminton.
2 If someone is making a racket, they are making a lot of loud noise.

radar noun
a way of finding where a ship or aeroplane is when you cannot see it, by using radio waves

radiator noun *plural* radiators
a metal heater which hot water flows through to keep a room warm

radio noun *plural* radios
a machine that picks up signals that are sent through the air and changes them into music or talking that you can listen to

radius noun *plural* radii
The radius of a circle is how much it measures from the centre to the edge.

raffle noun *plural* raffles
A raffle is a competition in which people buy tickets with numbers on them. If their tickets are chosen, they win a prize.

raft noun *plural* rafts
a flat boat made of logs joined together

rag noun *plural* rags
A rag is a torn piece of cloth.

rage noun *plural* rages
a feeling of very strong anger

rail noun *plural* rails
1 A rail is a metal or wooden bar that is part of a fence.
2 Rails are the long metal bars that trains travel on.
3 When you travel by rail, you travel in a train.

railings noun
a fence made of a row of metal bars that stand upright next to each other

railway noun *plural* railways
1 A railway line is the long metal bars that trains travel on.
2 When you travel on the railway, you travel by train.

rain noun
drops of water that fall from the sky

rain verb rains, raining, rained
When it rains, drops of water fall from the sky. *We'll go out when it stops raining.*

rainbow noun *plural* rainbows
a curved band of different colours you see in the sky when the sun shines through rain

rainforest noun *plural* rainforests
a large forest in a tropical part of the world, where there is a lot of rain

raise verb raises, raising, raised
1 When you raise something, you lift it up so that it is higher.
2 When you raise money, you collect it so that you can give it to a school or charity.

raisin noun *plural* raisins
a dried grape that you use to make fruit cakes

rake noun *plural* rakes
a tool that you use in the garden for making the soil smooth

rake verb rakes, raking, raked
When you rake the ground, you pull a rake over it to make it smooth. *We raked up the dead leaves.*

RAM noun
RAM is one of the types of memory on a computer. RAM stands for **random-access memory**.

a
b
c
d
e
f
g
h
i
j
k
l
m
n
o
p
q
r
s
t
u
v
w
x
y
z

169

A
B
C
D
E
F
G
H
I
J
K
L
M
N
O
P
Q
R
S
T
U
V
W
X
Y
Z

ram noun *plural* **rams**
a male sheep

Ramadan noun

Ramadan is the ninth month of the Muslim year. During Ramadan, Muslims do not eat or drink anything from the time the sun comes up each morning until it sets in the evening.

ramp noun *plural* **ramps**
a slope that you can walk or drive up to go from one level to another level

ran verb past tense of **run**

ranch noun *plural* **ranches**
a large farm in America where a lot of cows or horses are kept

rang verb past tense of **ring** verb

range noun *plural* **ranges**
1 A range of mountains or hills is a line of them.
2 A range of things is a collection of different things.

rank noun *plural* **ranks**
Someone's rank is the title that they have, which shows how important they are.

rap verb **raps, rapping, rapped**
When you rap on a door, you knock on it.

rap noun *plural* **raps**
1 A rap on a door is a knock on a door.
2 Rap is a type of poetry that you speak aloud with a strong rhythm.

rapid adjective
Something that is rapid happens very quickly.

rare adjective **rarer, rarest**
If something is rare, you do not see it or find it very often. *Pandas are very rare animals.*

rash noun *plural* **rashes**
If you have a rash, you have red spots on your skin.

raspberry noun *plural* **raspberries**
a soft, sweet, red berry

rat noun *plural* **rats**
an animal that looks like a large mouse

rate noun *plural* **rates**
The rate at which something happens is how quickly it happens.

rather adverb
1 quite *I was rather annoyed.*
2 If you would rather do something, you would prefer to do it. *I don't like shopping—I'd rather stay at home.*

rattle verb **rattles, rattling, rattled**
When something rattles, it makes a loud noise because it is being shaken.

rattle noun *plural* **rattles**
a toy for a baby which makes a noise when you shake it

raw adjective
Food that is raw has not been cooked. *Do you like raw carrots?*

ray noun *plural* **rays**
A ray of light or heat is a beam of it that shines onto something.

razor noun *plural* **razors**
a very sharp blade that people use for shaving hair off their body

reach verb **reaches, reaching, reached**
1 When you reach a place, you get there. *We reached home by six o'clock.*

2 When you reach for something, you put out your hand to touch it or pick it up. *He reached across for a cake.*

react verb reacts, reacting, reacted
The way that you react to something is the way that you behave when it happens. *How did Ali react when you told him about the fire?*

read verb reads, reading, read
When you read words that are written down, you look at them and understand them. *Samir loves reading.*

ready adjective
1 If you are ready, you are prepared so that you can do something straight away. *Are you ready to leave?*
2 If something is ready, it is finished and you can have it or use it straight away. *Is dinner ready?*

real adjective
1 Something that is real is true, and not made up or imaginary. *There are no unicorns in real life.*
2 Something that is real is genuine, and not a copy. *Is this a real diamond?*

realize verb realizes, realizing, realized
When you realize something, you suddenly notice it or know that it is true. *I suddenly realized that everyone was looking at me.*

really adverb
1 very *The water's really cold!*
2 If something is really true, it is true in real life. *Are you really moving to Spain?*

rear noun
The rear of something is the part at the back of it.

reason noun plural reasons
The reason for something is why it happens. *She was very upset, but I didn't know the reason why.*

reasonable adjective
Something that is reasonable is fair and right.

receive verb receives, receiving, received
When you receive something, someone gives it to you or sends it to you. *I haven't received your letter yet.*

recent adjective (say ree-sent)
Something that is recent happened only a short time ago. *They are still celebrating their recent victory.*
recently **adverb** Something that happened recently happened only a short time ago. *We moved here quite recently.*

recipe noun plural recipes (say ress-ip-ee)
a list of the things you need to cook something, and instructions that tell you how to cook it

recite verb recites, reciting, recited
When you recite something, you say it out loud from memory. *I've got to recite a poem in the school concert.*

a b c d e f g h i j k l m n o p q **r** s t u v w x y z

171

A
B
C
D
E
F
G
H
I
J
K
L
M
N
O
P
Q
R
S
T
U
V
W
X
Y
Z

recognize verb recognizes, recognizing, recognized

If you recognize someone, you know who they are because you have seen them before.

recommend verb recommends, recommending, recommended

1 When you recommend something, you tell people that it is good. *I would recommend this book to anyone who loves adventure stories.*

2 When you recommend something, you tell someone that they should do it. *I recommend that you see a doctor.*

record noun plural records (say **rek**-ord)

1 The record for something is the best that anyone has ever done. *She has set a new world record for the women's high jump.*

2 If you keep a record of something, you write it down.

3 A record in a computer database is one of the individual pieces of information that is stored in it.

record verb records, recording, recorded (say ree-**kord**)

1 When you record music or pictures, you store them on a tape or CD. *We can record the film and watch it later.*

2 When you record information, you write it down.

recorder noun plural recorders

a musical instrument that you play by blowing into one end and covering holes with your fingers to make different notes

recover verb recovers, recovering, recovered

1 When you recover, you get better after you have been ill.

2 When you recover something that you have lost, you get it back. *The police recovered the stolen car.*

rectangle noun plural rectangles

A rectangle is a shape with four straight sides and four right angles. A rectangle looks like a long square and is also called an oblong.

recycle verb recycles, recycling, recycled (say ree-**sye**-kal)

To recycle things means to use them again instead of throwing them away.

red adjective

Something that is red is the colour of blood.

reduce verb reduces, reducing, reduced

When you reduce something, you make it smaller or less. *Reduce speed when you approach a corner.*

reed noun plural reeds

a plant that looks like tall grass and grows near water

refer verb refers, referring, referred

When you refer to something, you talk about it. *She had never referred to her uncle before.*

referee noun plural referees

someone who is in charge of a game and makes sure that all the players keep to the rules

reference book noun
plural reference books
A reference book is a book that gives you information. Dictionaries are reference books.

reflex noun *plural* reflexes
a way in which your body moves without you thinking about it or controlling it

refresh verb refreshes, refreshing, refreshed
If something refreshes you, it makes you feel fresh and less tired.

refreshments noun
drinks and snacks

refrigerator noun *plural* refrigerators
a fridge

refugee noun *plural* refugees
someone who has had to leave their own country because of a war

refuse verb refuses, refusing, refused
(say ri-**fewz**)
If you refuse to do something, you say that you will not do it. *He refused to go home.*

region noun *plural* regions
one part of a country *These snakes live in the desert regions of Africa.*

register noun *plural* registers
a book in which people write down lists of names or other important information

regret verb regrets, regretting, regretted
If you regret doing something, you are sorry that you did it.

regular adjective
1 Something that is regular happens at the same time every day or every week. *There is a regular bus service into the city centre.*

2 A regular pattern stays the same and does not change.
3 A regular shape has sides and angles that are all equal.
regularly **adverb** *We go swimming regularly.*

rehearse verb rehearses, rehearsing, rehearsed
When you rehearse, you practise something before you do it in front of an audience.

reign verb reigns, reigning, reigned
(say **rain**)
When a king or queen reigns, they rule over a country.

reign noun *plural* reigns (say **rain**)
The reign of a king or queen is the time when they are ruling a country.

reindeer noun reindeer (say **rain**-deer)
a deer with large antlers that lives in very cold countries.

relate verb relates, relating, related
When you relate a story, you tell it.

related adjective
People who are related belong to the same family.

relation noun *plural* relations
Your relations are all the people who belong to your family.

a b c d e f g h i j k l m n o p q **r** s t u v w x y z

A
B
C
D
E
F
G
H
I
J
K
L
M
N
O
P
Q
R
S
T
U
V
W
X
Y
Z

relative noun *plural* **relatives**
Your relatives are all the people who belong to your family.

relax verb **relaxes, relaxing, relaxed**
1 When you relax, you do things that make you calm and happy. *Sometimes I just want to sit down and relax in front of the TV.*

2 When a muscle relaxes, it becomes looser and softer.

release verb **releases, releasing, released**
To release someone means to set them free.

reliable adjective
If someone is reliable, you can trust them.

relief noun
the feeling you have when you are no longer worried about something *It was such a relief when we got home safely!*

relieved adjective
If you feel relieved, you feel happy because you are no longer worried about something.

religion noun *plural* **religions**
A religion is a set of ideas that people have about a god or gods. Different religions worship different gods, and have different festivals and traditions.
religious **adjective** If someone is religious they have a set of ideas about a god or gods. If something is religious it is to do with religion. *He went to church every Sunday as he was religious.*

rely verb **relies, relying, relied**
If you rely on something, you need it. If you rely on someone, you need them to do something for you. *The young birds rely on their mother for food.*

remain verb **remains, remaining, remained**
To remain means to stay. *Please remain in your seats.*

remainder noun (in mathematics) an amount that is left over after you have worked out a sum

remark verb **remarks, remarking, remarked**
To remark means to say something.

remark noun *plural* **remarks**
something that you say *He made some rude remarks about my clothes.*

remember verb **remembers, remembering, remembered**
If you can remember something, you can think of it and have not forgotten it. *Can you remember his name?*

remind verb **reminds, reminding, reminded**
If you remind someone about something, you tell them about it again so that they do not forget it. *My mum reminded me that I needed to take my PE kit to school.*

remote adjective remoter, remotest
A place that is remote is far away from towns and cities.

remove verb removes, removing, removed
When you remove something, you take it off or take it away. *Please remove your muddy boots.*

rent noun *plural* rents
an amount of money that you pay each week to live in a house that belongs to another person

repair verb repairs, repairing, repaired
When you repair something, you mend it. *Can you repair my bike?*

repeat verb repeats, repeating, repeated
When you repeat something, you say it or do it again.

replace verb replaces, replacing, replaced
1 When you replace something, you put it back in the place where it was before. *He replaced the book on the shelf.*
2 When you replace something, you change it for something else. *This computer is getting quite old now, so we will have to replace it soon.*

reply noun *plural* replies
an answer

reply verb replies, replying, replied
When you reply to someone, you answer them. *I asked him his name, but he didn't reply.*

report verb reports, reporting, reported
to tell someone about something that has happened *We reported the accident to the police.*

report noun *plural* reports
1 an account of something that has happened, for example in a newspaper
2 A school report is something that teachers write about each child, to say how well they have been working.

represent verb represents, representing, represented
If a drawing or picture represents something, it is meant to be that thing. *These red lines on the map represent roads.*

reptile noun *plural* reptiles
A reptile is an animal that has a dry, smooth skin, and lays eggs. Snakes and crocodiles are reptiles.

request verb requests, requesting, requested
When you request something, you ask for it politely.

require verb requires, requiring, required
If you require something, you need it.

a
b
c
d
e
f
g
h
i
j
k
l
m
n
o
p
q
r
s
t
u
v
w
x
y
z

175

A
B
C
D
E
F
G
H
I
J
K
L
M
N
O
P
Q
R
S
T
U
V
W
X
Y
Z

rescue verb rescues, rescuing, rescued
If you rescue someone, you save them from danger. *We managed to rescue all the animals from the fire.*

research noun
When you do research, you find out about something so that you can learn about it.

resent verb resents, resenting, resented
If you resent something, you feel angry about it. *I resent having to tidy up other people's mess!*

reserve verb reserves, reserving, reserved
If you reserve something, you ask someone to keep it for you.

reservoir noun *plural* reservoirs
a big lake that has been built to store water in

resign verb resigns, resigning, resigned
When someone resigns, they give up their job.

resist verb resists, resisting, resisted
When you resist something, you fight against it.

resource noun *plural* resources
something that is useful to people *Oil is an important natural resource.*

respect noun
If you have respect for someone, you admire them and think that their ideas and opinions are important.

respect verb respects, respecting, respected
If you respect someone, you admire them and think that their ideas and opinions are important.

respond verb responds, responding, responded
When you respond, you answer someone. *I called his name, but he didn't respond.*

responsibility noun
plural responsibilities
something that you have to do because it is your job or duty to do it

responsible adjective
1 If you are responsible for doing something, it is your job to do it. *You are responsible for feeding the fish.*
2 If you are responsible for something, you did it or made it happen. *Who is responsible for all this mess?*
3 Someone who is responsible behaves in a sensible way.

rest noun *plural* rests
1 When you have a rest, you sleep or sit still for a while.
2 The rest means all the others. *Only half the children are here, so where are the rest?*

rest verb rests, resting, rested
When you rest, you sit or lie still for a while. *We sat down to rest.*

restaurant noun *plural* restaurants
a place where you can buy a meal and eat it

result noun *plural* results
1 If something happens as a result of something else, it happens because of it.
2 The result at the end of a game is the score.

retire verb retires, retiring, retired
When someone retires, they stop working because they are too old or ill.

retreat verb retreats, retreating, retreated
If you retreat, you go back because it is too dangerous to go forwards.

return verb returns, returning, returned
1 If you return to a place, you go back there. *We returned home at tea time.*
2 If you return something to someone, you give it back to them. *You must return all your books to the library by next week.*

reveal verb reveals, revealing, revealed
To reveal something means to uncover it so that people can see it.

revenge noun
If you take revenge on someone, you do something nasty to them because they have hurt you or one of your friends.

reverse verb reverses, reversing, reversed
When you reverse, you go backwards in a car.

revise verb revises, revising, revised
When you revise, you learn something again so that you are ready for a test.

revolting adjective
Something that is revolting is horrible and disgusting.

reward noun *plural* rewards
something that is given to someone because they have done something good, or done something to help someone

rhinoceros noun *plural* rhinoceroses
(say rye-**noss**-er-us)
A rhinoceros is a very big, wild animal that lives in Africa and Asia and has one or two large horns on its nose. It is also called a **rhino**.

rhyme noun *plural* rhymes (say **rime**)
A rhyme is a word that has the same sound as another word. *Can you think of a rhyme for 'hat'?*

rhyme verb rhymes, rhyming, rhymed
If two words rhyme, they sound the same. *Fish rhymes with dish.*

rhythm noun *plural* rhythms
(say **rith**-um)
The rhythm in a piece of music is its regular beat. The rhythm in a poem is the regular pattern that the words make as you read them.

rib noun *plural* ribs
Your ribs are the curved bones in your chest that protect your heart and lungs.

ribbon noun *plural* ribbons
a strip of coloured material that you tie round a parcel or in your hair

rice noun
white or brown grains that you cook and eat

rich adjective richer, richest
Someone who is rich has a lot of money.

a b c d e f g h i j k l m n o p q r s t u v w x y z

177

A
B
C
D
E
F
G
H
I
J
K
L
M
N
O
P
Q
R
S
T
U
V
W
X
Y
Z

rid verb
When you get rid of something, you throw it away or give it to someone else so that you no longer have it.

riddle noun *plural* **riddles**
a clever question or puzzle that is difficult to answer because it is a trick or joke

ride verb **rides, riding, rode, ridden**
1 When you ride on a horse or bicycle, you sit on it while it moves along.
2 When you ride in a car, bus, or train, you sit in it while it moves along.

ride noun *plural* **rides**
When you go for a ride, you ride on a horse or bicycle, or in a bus, train, or car.

ridiculous adjective
Something that is ridiculous is very silly and makes people laugh.

right adjective
1 The right side of something is the side that is opposite the left side. Most people write with their right hand, not their left hand.
She was holding a torch in her right hand.
2 Something that is right is correct.
Yes, that's the right answer.
3 Something that is right is fair and honest.
It is not right to cheat.

right angle noun *plural* **right angles**
A right angle is an angle that measures 90 degrees. A square has four right angles.

rim noun *plural* **rims**
1 The rim of a cup or jug is the edge around the top of it.

2 The rim of a wheel is the edge around the outside of it.

ring noun *plural* **rings**
1 a circle *The dogs formed a ring around us.*
2 a circle of gold or silver that you wear on your finger

ring verb **rings, ringing, rang, rung**
1 When something rings, it makes a sound like a bell. *The doorbell rang.*
2 When you ring someone, you phone them.

rinse verb **rinses, rinsing, rinsed**
When you rinse something, you wash it in clean water after you have washed it using soap.

rip verb **rips, ripping, ripped**
If you rip something, you tear it.

ripe adjective **riper, ripest**
Fruit that is ripe is soft and ready to eat.

ripple noun *plural* **ripples**
a tiny wave on the surface of water
The rain was making ripples on the surface of the pond.

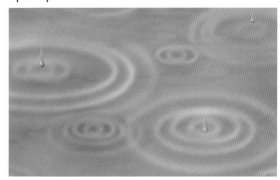

rise verb **rises, rising, rose, risen**
1 When something rises, it moves upwards.
2 When you rise, you stand up.
3 When the sun or moon rises, it moves up into the sky.

risk noun *plural* **risks**
If there is a risk, there is a danger that something bad or dangerous might happen.

rival noun *plural* rivals
someone who is trying to beat you in a competition or game

river noun *plural* rivers
a large stream of water that flows into the sea

road noun *plural* roads
a wide path that cars, buses, and lorries go along

roam verb roams, roaming, roamed
When you roam, you travel around without going in any particular direction. *The animals are free to roam wherever they want.*

roar verb roars, roaring, roared
When an animal like a lion roars, it makes a loud, fierce sound.

roast verb roasts, roasting, roasted
When you roast meat or vegetables, you cook them in the oven. *We'll roast the chicken in the oven.*

rob verb robs, robbing, robbed
To rob someone means to steal something from them. *A band of thieves attacked him and robbed him.*

robin noun *plural* robins
a small, brown bird with a red patch on its chest

robot noun *plural* robots
a machine that can do some of the jobs that a person can do

rock noun *plural* rocks
1 A rock is a very big stone. *They hurled huge rocks into the sea.*
2 Rock is the hard, stony substance that mountains, hills, and the ground are made of.

rock verb rocks, rocking, rocked
When something rocks, it moves gently backwards and forwards or from side to side.

rocket noun *plural* rockets
1 a firework that shoots high into the air and then explodes with bright lights and a loud bang
2 A rocket is something that can travel very fast through the air or into space. Some rockets are used as weapons, and some are used to take people up into space.

rod noun *plural* rods
A fishing rod is a long, thin piece of wood or metal. You attach a piece of thin fishing line to it and use it for catching fish.

rode verb past tense of ride verb

rodent noun *plural* rodents
A rodent is an animal that has big front teeth, which it uses for biting and chewing things. Rats and mice are rodents.

a b c d e f g h i j k l m n o p q **r** s t u v w x y z

A
B
C
D
E
F
G
H
I
J
K
L
M
N
O
P
Q
R
S
T
U
V
W
X
Y
Z

roll verb rolls, rolling, rolled
When something rolls, it moves along on wheels or by turning over and over like a ball. *The barrel rolled down the hill.*

roll noun plural rolls
1 A roll of cloth or paper is a piece that has been rolled up into the shape of a tube.
2 A roll is a very small loaf of bread for one person. *We had warm rolls for breakfast.*

Rollerblade noun plural Rollerblades
(trademark) Rollerblades are boots with wheels on the bottom.

roller skate noun plural roller skates
Roller skates are special shoes with wheels on the bottom.

ROM noun
ROM is one of the types of memory on a computer. ROM stands for **read-only memory**.

roof noun plural roofs
the sloping part on the top of a building

room noun plural rooms
1 The rooms in a building are the different parts inside it.
2 If there is room for something, there is enough space for it.

root noun plural roots
the part of a plant that grows under the ground

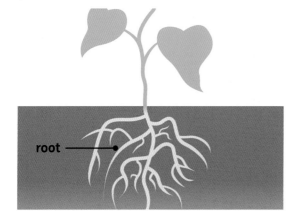

root ———

rope noun plural ropes
a long piece of thick, strong material which you use for tying things together

rose noun plural roses
a flower which has a sweet smell and sharp thorns on its stem

rose verb a tense of rise

rot verb rots, rotting, rotted
When something rots, it goes bad and soft and sometimes smells nasty.

rotate verb rotates, rotating, rotated
When something rotates, it turns round in a circle, like a wheel.

rotten adjective
1 Something that is rotten is not fresh, but has gone bad and soft.
2 Something that is rotten is bad or nasty. *That was a rotten thing to do!*

rough adjective rougher, roughest
(say **ruff**)
1 Something that is rough is not smooth or flat. *With this bike, you can ride over rough ground.*
2 Someone who is rough is not gentle.
3 Something that is rough is more or less right, but not exactly right. *He looks about fifteen, but that's only a rough guess.*

roughly adverb
1 If you touch or hold something roughly, you do it in a way that is not gentle.
2 about, but not exactly *There will be roughly twenty people at my party.*

round adjective
Something that is round is shaped like a circle or ball.

round adverb, preposition
1 turning in a circle *The wheels spun round and round.*
2 on all sides of something *There was a high wall round the garden.*

round verb rounds, rounding, rounded
(in mathematics)
When you round a number up or down, you raise it or lower it to the nearest 10, 100, or 1000. *If you round 18 to the nearest ten, the answer is 20.*

rounders noun
a game in which two teams try to hit a ball with a special bat and score points by running round a square

route noun *plural* routes (say **root**)
The route that you follow is the way you go to get to a place

routine noun *plural* routines
(say roo-**teen**)
Your routine is the way in which you usually do things at the same time and in the same way.

row noun *plural* rows (rhymes with *toe*)
A row of people or things is a long, straight line of them.

row verb rows, rowing, rowed
(rhymes with *toe*)
When you row a boat, you push oars through the water to make it move along.

row noun *plural* rows (rhymes with *how*)
1 When you make a row, you make a lot of loud noise.
2 When people have a row, they have an angry, noisy argument.

royal adjective
Royal things belong to a king or queen.

rub verb rubs, rubbing, rubbed
1 When you rub something, you move your hands backwards and forwards over it. *She woke up and rubbed her eyes.*
2 When you rub out something that you have written, you make it disappear by rubbing it.

rubber noun *plural* rubbers
1 Rubber is a type of soft material that stretches, bends, and bounces. Rubber is used for making car tyres.
2 A rubber is a small piece of rubber that you use for rubbing out marks.

rubbish noun
1 things that you have thrown away because you do not want them any more
2 If something that you say is rubbish, it is silly and not true.

rucksack noun *plural* rucksacks
a bag that you carry on your back

rude adjective ruder, rudest
Someone who is rude says or does things that are not polite.

rug noun *plural* rugs
1 a small carpet
2 a thick blanket

rugby noun
a game in which two teams throw, kick, and carry a ball, and try to score points by taking it over a line at one end of the pitch

a
b
c
d
e
f
g
h
i
j
k
l
m
n
o
p
q
r
s
t
u
v
w
x
y
z

181

A
B
C
D
E
F
G
H
I
J
K
L
M
N
O
P
Q
R
S
T
U
V
W
X
Y
Z

ruin noun *plural* ruins
a building that has fallen down

ruin verb ruins, ruining, ruined
To ruin something means to spoil it completely. *You've ruined my picture!*

rule noun *plural* rules
something that tells you what you must and must not do

rule verb rules, ruling, ruled
The person who rules a country is in charge of it.

ruler noun *plural* rulers
1 someone who rules a country
2 a flat, straight piece of wood, metal, or plastic that you use for measuring things and drawing lines

rumour noun *plural* rumours
(say **room**-er)
something that a lot of people are saying, although it might not be true *There's a rumour that our teacher might be leaving at the end of this term.*

run verb runs, running, ran, run
1 When you run, you move along quickly by taking very quick steps.
2 When you run something, you control it and are in charge of it. *Who runs the school shop?*

rung noun *plural* rungs
The rungs on a ladder are the bars that you step on.

rung verb past tense of **ring** verb

runway noun *plural* runways
a strip of land where an aeroplane can take off and land

rush verb rushes, rushing, rushed
When you rush, you run or do something very quickly. *'I'm come, your Majesty,' said Edmund, rushing eagerly forward.* — C. S. Lewis, *The Lion, the Witch and the Wardrobe*

rust noun
a rough, red stuff that you see on metal that is old and has got wet

rustle verb rustles, rustling, rustled
When something rustles, it makes a soft sound like the sound of dry leaves or paper being squashed.

Ss

sack noun *plural* **sacks**
a large, strong bag

sad adjective **sadder, saddest**
If you feel sad, you feel unhappy.

saddle noun *plural* **saddles**
the seul that you sit on when you are riding a bicycle or a horse

safari noun *plural* **safaris**
a trip to see lions and other large animals in the wild

safe adjective **safer, safest**
1 If you are safe, you are not in any danger.
2 If something is safe, you will not get hurt if you go on it or use it. *The bridge wasn't safe.*

safe noun *plural* **safes**
a strong metal box with a lock where you can keep money and jewellery

safely adverb
Something done safely is done without the chance of harm or danger. *It's important to use tools safely.*

safety noun
Safety is being safe and not in danger. *After crossing the river we finally reached safety.*

said verb past tense of **say**

sail noun *plural* **sails**
A sail is a large piece of strong cloth which is attached to a boat. The wind blows into the sail and makes the boat move along.

sail verb **sails, sailing, sailed**
When you sail, you go somewhere in a boat. *We sailed across the lake to the island.*

sailor noun *plural* **sailors**
someone who works on a ship

salad noun *plural* **salads**
a mixture of vegetables that you eat raw or cold

sale noun *plural* **sales**
1 If something is for sale, people can buy it.
2 When a shop has a sale, it sells things at lower prices than usual.

saliva noun
the liquid in your mouth

salmon noun *plural* **salmon**
a large fish that you can eat

salt noun
a white powder that people often add to food for its flavour

a
b
c
d
e
f
g
h
i
j
k
l
m
n
o
p
q
r
s
t
u
v
w
x
y
z

A
B
C
D
E
F
G
H
I
J
K
L
M
N
O
P
Q
R
S
T
U
V
W
X
Y
Z

salute verb salutes, saluting, saluted
When you salute, you touch your forehead with your fingers to show that you respect someone.

same adjective
1 Things that are the same are like each other. *Your jeans are the same as mine.*
2 If two people share the same thing, they share one thing and do not have two different ones. *We both go to the same school.*

sample noun *plural* samples
a small amount of something that you can try to see what it is like

sand noun *plural* sands
Sand is a powder made from tiny bits of crushed rock. You find sand in a desert or on a beach.

sandal noun *plural* sandals
Sandals are shoes with straps that you wear in warm weather.

sandwich noun *plural* sandwiches
two slices of bread and butter with a layer of a different food in between them

sang verb past tense of sing

sank verb past tense of sink verb

sap noun
Sap is the sticky liquid inside a plant.

sardine noun *plural* sardines
a small sea fish you can eat

sari noun *plural* saris
A sari is a type of dress that women and girls from India and other countries in Asia wear. It is a long piece of cloth that you wrap round your body.

sat verb past tense of sit

satellite noun *plural* satellites
A satellite is a machine that is sent into space to collect information and send signals back to earth. Satellites travel in orbit round the earth.

satellite dish noun
plural satellite dishes
an aerial shaped like a large dish which can receive television signals sent by satellite

satisfactory adjective
Something that is satisfactory is not very good, but is good enough.

satisfy verb satisfies, satisfying, satisfied
If something satisfies you, it is good enough to make you feel pleased or happy.

Saturday noun *plural* Saturdays
the day after Friday

sauce noun *plural* sauces
a thick liquid that you put over food

saucepan noun *plural* saucepans
a metal pan that you use for cooking

saucer noun *plural* saucers
a small plate that you put a cup on

sausage noun *plural* sausages
minced meat that has been made into a long, thin shape and cooked

savage adjective
A savage animal is wild and fierce.

save verb saves, saving, saved
1 If you save someone, you take them away from danger and make them safe.
2 When you save money, you keep it so that you can use it later.
3 (in ICT) When you save a computer file, you instruct the computer to keep a copy of it on its hard disk.

savings noun
Your savings are money that you have saved to use later.

saw noun *plural* saws
A saw is a tool that you use to cut wood. It has a row of sharp teeth which you push backwards and forwards over the wood to cut it.

saw verb saws, sawing, sawed, sawn
When you saw wood, you cut it with a saw.

saw verb past tense of see

say verb says, saying, said
When you say something, you speak. *'Hello,' he said.*

scald verb scalds, scalding, scalded
If you scald yourself, you burn yourself with very hot liquid.

scale noun *plural* scales
1 A scale is a line of numbers that you use for measuring something.
2 The scale of a map is how big things on the map are compared to how big they are in real life.
3 The scales on a fish are the small, round pieces of hard skin all over its body.

scales noun
something that you use for weighing things

scamper verb scampers, scampering, scampered
To scamper around means to run around quickly. *A harvest mouse goes scamper by, / with silver claws and silver eye.* — Walter de la Mare, *'Silver'*

scan verb scans, scanning, scanned
1 When a machine scans something, it moves a beam of light over it to make a picture of it.
2 When you scan a piece of writing, you read it quickly.

scar noun *plural* scars
a mark that is left on your skin after a cut or burn has healed

scarce adjective scarcer, scarcest
If something is scarce, there is not very much of it. *Water is scarce in the desert.*

scare verb scares, scaring, scared
If something scares you, it makes you feel frightened.

scarecrow noun *plural* scarecrows
something that looks like a person and is put in a field to frighten away birds

scarf noun *plural* scarves
a piece of material that you wear round your neck to keep you warm

scatter verb scatters, scattering, scattered
1 When you scatter things, you throw them all around you. *She scattered some crumbs for the birds.*
2 When people scatter, they all run away in different directions.

scene noun *plural* scenes (say **seen**)
1 The scene of something is the place where it happens. *Police are still examining the scene of the crime.*
2 A scene in a play is one part of the play.

a
b
c
d
e
f
g
h
i
j
k
l
m
n
o
p
q
r
s
t
u
v
w
x
y
z

scenery noun (say **seen**-er-ee)
1 things that you can see around you when you are out in the country
2 things that you put on the stage of a theatre to make it look like a real place

scent noun plural scents (say **sent**)
1 perfume that you put on your skin so that you will smell nice
2 a pleasant smell
3 An animal's scent is its smell.

scheme noun plural schemes (say **skeme**)
a clever plan

school noun plural schools
1 a place where children go to learn things
2 A school of fish is a large group of them swimming together.

science noun plural sciences
the subject in which you study the things in the world around you, for example plants and animals, wood and metal, light, and electricity

scissors noun
a tool that you use for cutting paper or cloth

scoop noun plural scoops
a deep spoon that you use for serving ice cream

scoop verb scoops, scooping, scooped
If you scoop something up, you pick it up with both hands.

score noun plural scores
The score in a game is the number of points that each player or team has.

score verb scores, scoring, scored
When you score in a game, you get a point or a goal.

scowl verb scowls, scowling, scowled (rhymes with owl)
When you scowl, you look cross.

scramble verb scrambles, scrambling, scrambled
If you scramble over things, you climb over them using your hands and feet.

scrap noun plural scraps
1 A scrap of paper or cloth is a small piece.
2 Scrap is anything that you do not want any more.

scrape verb scrapes, scraping, scraped
1 If you scrape something off, you get it off by pushing it with something sharp. *Scrape the mud off your shoes.*
2 If you scrape a part of your body, you cut it by rubbing it against something. *I fell over and scraped my knee.*

scratch verb scratches, scratching, scratched
1 To scratch something means to cut it or make a mark on it with something sharp. *Don't scratch the paint on the new car!*

2 When you scratch, you rub your skin because it is itching.

scream verb screams, screaming, screamed
When you scream, you shout or cry loudly because you are frightened or hurt.

screech verb screeches, screeching, screeched
When you screech, you shout or cry in a loud, high voice.

screen noun plural screens
1 the part of a television or computer where the words and pictures appear
2 the large, flat surface at a cinema, on which films are shown

screw noun plural screws
A screw is a pointed piece of metal that you use for fixing pieces of wood together.

screw verb screws, screwing, screwed
1 When you screw things together, you fix them together using screws.
2 When you screw a lid on or off, you put it on or take it off by turning it round and round.

screwdriver noun plural screwdrivers
a tool that you use for fixing screws into wood

scribble verb scribbles, scribbling, scribbled
When you scribble, you write or draw something quickly, in an untidy way.

script noun plural scripts
The script of a play is all the words that the characters say.

scroll verb scrolls, scrolling, scrolled
(in ICT)
When you scroll up or down on a computer screen, you move up or down on the screen to see what comes before or after.

scrub verb scrubs, scrubbing, scrubbed
When you scrub something, you rub it hard to clean it.

sculpture noun plural sculptures
a statue made out of stone or wood

sea noun plural seas
The sea is the salty water that covers large parts of the earth.

seal noun plural seals
A seal is an animal that has flippers and lives in the sea. Seals have thick fur to keep them warm in cold water.

seam noun plural seams
a line of sewing that joins two pieces of material together

search verb searches, searching, searched
When you search for something, you look for it very carefully.

search engine noun plural search engines
a computer program that helps you find information on the Internet

a
b
c
d
e
f
g
h
i
j
k
l
m
n
o
p
q
r
s
t
u
v
w
x
y
z

A
B
C
D
E
F
G
H
I
J
K
L
M
N
O
P
Q
R
S
T
U
V
W
X
Y
Z

seaside noun
a place by the sea where people go on holiday to enjoy themselves

season noun *plural* seasons
1 The four seasons are the four parts of the year, which are spring, summer, autumn, and winter.
2 The season for a sport is the time of year when it is played. *When does the cricket season start?*

spring

summer

autumn

winter

seat noun *plural* seats
anything that you can sit on

seat belt noun *plural* seat belts
a strap that you wear round your body to keep you safe in a car

seaweed noun
a plant that grows in the sea

second adjective
The second thing is the one that comes after the first.

second noun *plural* seconds
We measure time in seconds. There are sixty seconds in one minute.

secret adjective
A secret thing is one that not very many people know about. *There is a secret passage leading into the castle.*

secret noun *plural* secrets
If something is a secret, not many people know about it and you must not tell anyone.
secretly adverb Something done secretly is done so that not many people know about it. *He had secretly hoped she would think he was funny.*

secretary noun *plural* secretaries
someone whose job is to type letters and answer the telephone in an office

section noun *plural* sections
one part of something *The front section of the aeroplane broke off.*

secure adjective securer, securest
1 Something that is secure is safe and firm. *Make sure the ladder is secure before you climb it.*
2 If you feel secure, you feel safe.

see verb sees, seeing, saw, seen
1 When you see something, you notice it with your eyes.
2 When you can see something, you can understand it. *Do you see what I mean?*

seed noun *plural* seeds
a small thing that a new plant grows from

seem verb seems, seeming, seemed
To seem means to look, sound, or appear. *Everyone seemed very happy and relaxed.*

see-saw noun *plural* see-saws
A see-saw is a toy that children can play on. It is made of a long piece of wood that is balanced on something in the middle so that someone can sit on each end and make it go up and down.

segment noun *plural* **segments**
one small part of something *Would you like a segment of orange?*

seize verb **seizes, seizing, seized**
(rhymes with *sneeze*)
When you seize something, you grab it roughly. *The thief seized the bag and ran away.*

select verb **selects, selecting, selected**
When you select something, you choose it.

selfish adjective
If you are selfish you only think about yourself and do not care what other people want.

sell verb **sells, selling, sold**
When you sell something, you give it to someone and they give you money for it.

Sellotape noun (trademark)
a type of sticky tape that you use for sticking pieces of paper together

semicircle noun *plural* **semicircles**
half of a circle

semi-colon noun *plural* **semi-colons**
a mark like this ; that you use in writing

send verb **sends, sending, sent**
1 When you send something somewhere, you arrange for someone to take it there. *My grandma sent me a birthday card.*
2 When you send someone somewhere, you tell them to go there. *He was sent to the headteacher for behaving badly.*

senior adjective
Someone who is senior is older or more important than other people.

sensation noun *plural* **sensations**
If you have a sensation in your body, you have a feeling.

sense noun *plural* **senses**
1 Your senses are your ability to see, hear, smell, feel, and taste. *Dogs have a good sense of smell.*
2 If you have good sense, you know what is the right thing to do. *She had the sense to call an ambulance.*

sensible adjective
If you are sensible, you think carefully and you do the right thing.

sensitive adjective
1 Someone who is sensitive is easily upset by other people.
2 Something that is sensitive reacts to things around it. *Some people have very sensitive skin.*

sent verb past tense of **send**

sentence noun *plural* **sentences**
1 (in grammar) A sentence is a group of words that mean something together. A sentence begins with a capital letter and ends with a full stop.
2 a punishment that is given to someone by a judge

a
b
c
d
e
f
g
h
i
j
k
l
m
n
o
p
q
r
s
t
u
v
w
x
y
z

A
B
C
D
E
F
G
H
I
J
K
L
M
N
O
P
Q
R
S
T
U
V
W
X
Y
Z

separate adjective
Things that are separate are not joined together or not next to each other.

separate verb separates, separating, separated
When you separate people or things, you take them away from each other so that they are no longer together.

September noun
the ninth month of the year

sequence noun plural sequences
A sequence is a series of numbers that come after each other in a regular order.
For example, 2, 4, 6, 8 is a sequence.

series noun plural series
1 a number of things that come one after another We have had a series of accidents in the playground.
2 a television show that is on regularly and is about the same thing each week

serious adjective
1 Something that is serious is very important. *This is a very serious matter.*
2 Someone who is serious does not smile or joke, but thinks carefully about things.
3 Something that is serious is very bad. *There has been a serious accident on the motorway.*
seriously adverb If someone is seriously ill, injured, or hurt it means that they are very badly ill, injured, or hurt.

servant noun plural servants
someone who works at another person's home, doing jobs such as cleaning and cooking

serve verb serves, serving, served
1 To serve someone in a shop means to help them find and buy the things that they want.
2 To serve food means to put it on people's plates.
3 When you serve in a game of tennis, you start the game by hitting the ball to the other player.

service noun plural services
something that is done to help people or give them something that they need *Letters are delivered by the post service.*

set verb sets, setting, set
1 When you set a machine, you change the controls to a particular position. *We set the alarm clock for six o'clock.*
2 When something sets, it goes hard. *Has the glue set yet?*
3 When the sun sets, it goes down at the end of the day.
4 To set off means to leave.

set noun plural sets
a group of people or things that belong together *I'm trying to collect the whole set of these cards.*

settle verb settles, settling, settled
1 When you settle an argument, you agree and decide what to do about it.
2 When you settle down somewhere, you sit or lie down comfortably.

seven noun plural sevens
the number 7

seventeen noun
the number 17

seventy noun
the number 70

several determiner
Several things means quite a lot of them. *The teacher told him several times to be quiet.*

severe adjective severer, severest
Something that is severe is very bad. *The Mathematical Master frowned and looked very severe, for he did not approve of children dreaming.* — Oscar Wilde, *The Happy Prince*

sew verb sews, sewing, sewed, sewn
(say *so*)
When you sew, you use a needle and thread to join pieces of cloth together.

sex noun *plural* sexes
The sex of a person or an animal is whether they are male or female.

shade noun *plural* shades
1 If a place is in the shade, it is quite dark because the light of the sun cannot get to it.
2 The shade of a colour is how light or dark it is.

shade verb shades, shading, shaded
When you shade something, you stop the sun from shining onto it.

shadow noun *plural* shadows
the dark shape that forms on the ground when something is blocking out the light

shake verb shakes, shaking, shook, shaken
1 When you shake something, you move it about quickly.
2 When something shakes, it moves about. *The ground shook as the giant came nearer.*
3 When you shake, you cannot keep your body still because you are very cold or frightened.

shall verb
I shall do something means that I will do it.

shallow adjective
Something that is shallow is not very deep. *The water is quite shallow here.*

shame noun
the feeling you have when you are unhappy because you have done wrong

shampoo noun *plural* shampoos
liquid soap that you use to wash your hair

shape noun *plural* shapes
The shape of something is what its outline looks like, for example whether it is square, round, or oval. *What shape is this room?*

share verb shares, sharing, shared
1 When you share something, you give some of it to other people. *I hope you're going to share your food with us!*
2 When people share something, they both use it. *I share a bedroom with my sister.*

shark noun *plural* sharks
a big, fierce sea fish that has sharp teeth and hunts and kills other fish to eat

a
b
c
d
e
f
g
h
i
j
k
l
m
n
o
p
q
r
s
t
u
v
w
x
y
z

A B C D E F G H I J K L M N O P Q R S T U V W X Y Z

sharp *adjective* sharper, sharpest
1 Something that is sharp can cut things because it is thin or pointed.
2 If you have sharp eyes or ears, you see or hear things easily.
3 If someone speaks in a sharp voice, they say something angrily.
4 A sharp turn is very sudden. *There was a sharp bend in the road.*
sharply *adverb* If you say something sharply, you say it angrily.

shatter *verb* shatters, shattering, shattered
When something shatters, it breaks into tiny pieces *A tiny stone shattered the glass.*

shave *verb* shaves, shaving, shaved
If you shave a part of your body, you cut all the hair off it to make it smooth.

she *pronoun*
You use **she** to talk about a girl, woman, or female animal. *She likes her new hat.*

shed *noun* plural sheds
a small wooden building
shed *verb* sheds, shedding, shed
To shed something means to let it fall off. *Trees shed their leaves in winter.*

sheep *noun* sheep
an animal that is kept on farms for its wool and meat

sheet *noun* plural sheets
1 a large piece of cloth that you put on a bed
2 A sheet of something is a thin, flat piece of it. *I need another sheet of paper.*

shelf *noun* plural shelves
a piece of wood that is fastened to a wall so that you can put things on it

shell *noun* plural shells
A shell is a hard part on the outside of something. Eggs and nuts have shells, and some animals such as snails and tortoises have a shell on their back.

shelter *noun* plural shelters
a place that protects people from bad weather or from danger
shelter *verb* shelters, sheltering, sheltered
1 To shelter someone means to keep them safe from bad weather or danger.
2 When you shelter, you stay in a place that is safe from bad weather or danger. *We sheltered from the storm in an old barn.*

shepherd *noun* plural shepherds
someone whose job is to look after sheep

sheriff *noun* plural sheriffs
In America, a sheriff is a person who makes sure that people do not break the law.

shield *noun* plural shields
something that soldiers or the police hold in front of their bodies to protect themselves during a battle

shift *verb* shifts, shifting, shifted
When you shift something, you move it. *I can't shift this rock.*

shin *noun* plural shins
Your shins are the front parts of your legs below your knees.

shine *verb* shines, shining, shone
When something shines, it gives out light or looks very bright. *The sun shone all day.*
shiny *adjective* Something that is shiny looks very bright and gives out light. *He bought a shiny red sports car.*

ship *noun* plural ships
a very large boat

shirt *noun* plural shirts
A shirt is a piece of clothing that you wear on the top half of your body. It has buttons down the front, sleeves, and a collar.

shiver verb shivers, shivering, shivered
When you shiver, you shake because you are cold or frightened.

shoal noun plural shoals
A shoal of fish is a big group of fish all swimming together.

shock noun plural shocks
1 If something is a shock, you were not expecting it and it upsets you when it happens. *It was a terrible shock when my grandmother died.*
2 If you get an electric shock, electricity gets into your body and hurts you.

shock verb shocks, shocking, shocked
If something shocks you, it gives you a nasty surprise and upsets you. *The terrible news shocked us all.*

shoe noun plural shoes
something that you wear on your feet to keep them warm and dry when you go outside

shone verb past tense of shine

shook verb past tense of shake

shoot noun plural shoots
a new part of a plant that has just grown

shoot verb shoots, shooting, shot
1 When you shoot with a gun or other weapon, you fire it.
2 When you shoot in a game such as football, you try to score a goal.

shop noun plural shops
a place where you can go to buy things

shop verb shops, shopping, shopped
When you shop, you go into a shop to buy something.

shore noun plural shores
the land by the edge of the sea

short adjective shorter, shortest
1 Someone who is short is not very tall.
2 Something that is short is not very long. *The rope is too short.*
3 Something that is short does not last very long.

shorts noun
short trousers that only cover the top part of your legs

shot noun plural shots
1 the sound of someone firing a gun *Suddenly, we heard a shot.*
2 a photograph *There are some lovely shots of you.*
3 one kick or hit of the ball in a game such as football or tennis *That was a brilliant shot!*

shot verb past tense of shoot verb

should verb
If you should do something, you ought to do it. *I should go home now.*

shoulder noun plural shoulders
Your shoulders are the parts of the body between your neck and your arms.

a
b
c
d
e
f
g
h
i
j
k
l
m
n
o
p
q
r
s
t
u
v
w
x
y
z

193

A
B
C
D
E
F
G
H
I
J
K
L
M
N
O
P
Q
R
S
T
U
V
W
X
Y
Z

shout verb shouts, shouting, shouted
When you shout, you speak in a very loud voice.

show noun plural shows
something that people perform for other people to watch at the theatre or on television

show verb shows, showing, showed, shown
1 When you show something to someone, you let them see it.
2 If you show someone how to do something, you do it so that they can watch you and learn how to do it. *Can you show me how to print this out from the computer?*
3 If something shows, people can see it.

shower noun plural showers
1 When there is a shower, it rains or snows for a short time.
2 When you have a shower, you stand under a stream of water to wash yourself.

shrank verb past tense of shrink

shriek verb shrieks, shrieking, shrieked
If you shriek, you shout or scream in a high voice. *The girls were shrieking with laughter.*

shrill adjective shriller, shrillest
A shrill sound is high and loud.

shrimp noun plural shrimps
a small sea animal that you can eat

shrink verb shrinks, shrinking, shrank, shrunk
When something shrinks, it gets smaller.

shrug verb shrugs, shrugging, shrugged
When you shrug your shoulders, you lift them up to show that you do not know something or do not care about it.

shrunk verb past tense of shrink

shuffle verb shuffles, shuffling, shuffled
1 When you shuffle, you walk slowly, without lifting your feet off the ground.
2 When you shuffle cards, you mix them up so that they are ready for a game.

shut verb shuts, shutting, shut
1 When you shut something, you close it. *Don't forget to shut the door when you go out.*
2 When a shop shuts, it closes and people cannot use it.
3 When you shut down a computer, you close all the programs and switch it off.

shy adjective shyer, shyest
If you are shy, you feel frightened and nervous when you meet people you do not know.

sick adjective sicker, sickest
1 If you are sick, you are ill.
2 If you are sick, food comes back up out of your mouth after you have eaten it.

side noun *plural* sides
1 The sides of something are the parts on the left and right of it, not at the back or the front. *There were some people standing at one side of the field.*
2 Your sides are the parts of your body on your left and right. *He had a big bruise on his right side.*
3 The sides of something are its edges. *A triangle has three sides.*
4 The two sides of a piece of paper or cloth are its front and back. *You can write on both sides of the paper.*
5 One side in a game or fight is one group that is playing or fighting against another group. *Whose side are you on?*

sideways adverb
If you move sideways, you move towards the side rather than forwards or backwards.

sigh verb sighs, sighing, sighed
(rhymes with *by*)
When you sigh, you breathe out heavily because you are sad or tired.

sight noun
1 Your sight is how well you can see things. *You are lucky to have good sight.*
2 A sight is something that you see. *I've never seen such a funny sight in all my life!*

sign noun *plural* signs (rhymes with *mine*)
1 a picture or mark that means something *The sign for a dollar is $.*
2 a notice that tells you something *The sign said 'Keep off the grass'.*
3 If you give someone a sign, you move your body to tell them something. *He raised his arm as a sign that the race was about to start.*

sign verb signs, signing, signed
When you sign something, you write your name on it.

signal noun *plural* signals
a light, sound, or movement that tells people what they should do, or tells them that something is going to happen *A red light is a signal for cars to stop.*

signature noun *plural* signatures
Your signature is your own special way of writing your name.

sign language noun
a way of communicating by using your hands to make words

Sikh noun *plural* Sikhs
a person who follows the Indian religion of **Sikhism**

silent adjective
1 Something that is silent does not make any noise. Someone who is silent does not speak or make a noise. *For a few moments everyone was silent.*
2 If a place is silent, there is no noise in it.

silk noun
a type of smooth cloth that is made from threads spun by insects called silkworms
silky adjective Something that is silky feels smooth and soft. *She stroked the rabbit's silky brown ears.*

silly adjective sillier, silliest
Something that is silly is stupid, not clever or sensible.

silver noun
a shiny, white metal that is very valuable

A
B
C
D
E
F
G
H
I
J
K
L
M
N
O
P
Q
R
S
T
U
V
W
X
Y
Z

similar adjective
Things that are similar are the same in some ways, but not exactly the same. *Your dress is quite similar to mine.*

simile noun *plural* similes (say **sim**-i-li)
A simile is an expression in which you describe something by comparing it to something else. For example, the expression *as brave as a lion* is a simile.

simple adjective simpler, simplest
1 Something that is simple is very easy. *That's a really simple question.*
2 Something that is simple is plain and clear. *I did quite a simple design for my poster.*

since adverb, conjunction, preposition
1 from that time *We have been friends since last summer.*
2 because *We couldn't play outside since it was raining.*

sincere adjective
If you are sincere, you really mean what you say.

sing verb sings, singing, sang, sung
When you sing, you use your voice to make music.

single adjective
1 only one *The tree had a single apple on it.*
2 Someone who is single is not married.

singular noun (in grammar)
The singular is the form of a word you use when you are talking about only one person or thing. *Children is a plural, and the singular is child.*

sink noun *plural* sinks
a large bowl with taps where you can wash things

sink verb sinks, sinking, sank, sunk
1 When something sinks, it goes under water.
2 When something sinks, it goes downwards. *The sun sank behind the mountains.*

sip verb sips, sipping, sipped
When you sip a drink, you drink it slowly, a little bit at a time.

sir noun
a word you use when you are speaking politely to a man

siren noun *plural* sirens
a machine that makes a loud sound to warn people about something

sister noun *plural* sisters
Your sister is a girl who has the same parents as you.

sit verb sits, sitting, sat
1 When you sit you rest on your bottom.
2 If something is sitting somewhere, it is there. *My school bag was sitting by the back door.*

site noun *plural* sites
A site is a piece of ground that is used for something. For example, a campsite is a place where people can camp.

situation noun *plural* situations
all the things that are happening to you and to the people around you *We are now in a very difficult situation.*

six noun *plural* sixes
the number 6

sixteen noun
the number 16

sixty noun
the number 60

size noun *plural* sizes
The size of something is how big or small it is. *These trousers are the wrong size for me.*

skate noun *plural* skates
1 a boot with a special blade on the bottom, which you use for skating on ice
2 a special shoe or boot with wheels on the bottom

skate verb skates, skating, skated
When you skate, you move smoothly over ice or over the ground wearing ice skates or roller skates.

skateboard noun *plural* skateboards
a small board on wheels that you can stand on and ride

skeleton noun *plural* skeletons
Your skeleton is all the bones that are in your body.

sketch verb sketches, sketching, sketched
When you sketch something, you draw it quickly and roughly.

ski noun *plural* skis (say **skee**)
Skis are long, flat sticks that you strap to your feet and use for moving over snow.

ski verb skis, skiing, skied
When you ski, you move over snow on skis.

skid verb skids, skidding, skidded
If a car skids, it slides out of control because the road is wet or slippery.

skill noun *plural* skills
If you have skill, you can do something well.

skin noun *plural* skins
1 Your skin is the part of you that covers all of your body.
2 The skin on a fruit or vegetable is the tough part on the outside of it.

skip verb skips, skipping, skipped
1 When you skip, you run along lightly taking a little jump with each step.
2 When you skip, you turn a rope over your head and under your feet and jump over it each time it goes under your feet.

a
b
c
d
e
f
g
h
i
j
k
l
m
n
o
p
q
r
s
t
u
v
w
x
y
z

197

A
B
C
D
E
F
G
H
I
J
K
L
M
N
O
P
Q
R
S
T
U
V
W
X
Y
Z

skirt noun *plural* skirts
A skirt is a piece of clothing that a woman or girl wears. It fastens around her waist and hangs down over her legs.

sky noun *plural* skies
The sky is the space above the earth where you can see the sun, moon, and stars.

skyscraper noun *plural* skyscrapers
a very tall building

slab noun *plural* slabs
A slab of something is a flat, thick piece of it.

slack adjective slacker, slackest
If something is slack, it is not pulled tight. *Some of the ropes round the tent were too slack.*

slam verb slams, slamming, slammed
If you slam a door, you push it shut so that it makes a loud bang.

slang noun
words that you use when you are talking to your friends, but not when you are writing or talking politely to people

slant verb slants, slanting, slanted
If something slants, it slopes and is not straight.

slap verb slaps, slapping, slapped
To slap someone means to hit them with the front of your hand.

slate noun *plural* slates
Slate is a type of smooth, grey rock. Pieces of slate are sometimes used to cover the roofs of houses.

sledge noun *plural* sledges
a piece of wood or plastic, which you sit on to slide along on snow or ice

sleek adjective sleeker, sleekest
Sleek hair or fur is smooth and shiny.

sleep verb sleeps, sleeping, slept
When you sleep, you close your eyes and rest your body and your mind.

sleet noun
a mixture of rain and snow

sleeve noun *plural* sleeves
The sleeves on a shirt, jumper, or coat are the parts that cover your arms.

sleigh noun *plural* sleighs (say **slay**)
a large sledge that is pulled along by animals

slept verb past tense of sleep

slice noun *plural* slices
A slice of something is a thin piece that has been cut off.

slide verb slides, sliding, slid
When something slides, it moves along smoothly. *My skis slid across the snow.*

slide noun *plural* slides
1 A slide is a toy that children can play on. It is made of steps that you climb up, and a long sloping part that you can slide down.

2 a clip that girls sometimes wear in their hair to keep it tidy

slight adjective slighter, slightest
Something that is slight is small and not very important or not very bad.
slightly adjective If you do something slightly, you do it by a small amount.

slim adjective slimmer, slimmest
Someone who is slim is thin.

slime noun
nasty wet, slippery stuff

sling noun plural slings
A sling is a piece of cloth that goes round your arm and is tied round your neck. You wear a sling to support your arm if you have hurt it.

slip verb slips, slipping, slipped
1 If you slip, your foot accidentally slides on the ground. *I slipped and fell over.*
2 When you slip somewhere, you go there quickly and quietly.

slipper noun plural slippers
Slippers are soft shoes that you wear indoors.

slippery adjective
If something is slippery, it is smooth or wet and difficult to get hold of or walk on. *We had to drive slowly because the road was slippery.*

slit noun plural slits
a long, narrow cut in something

slope verb slopes, sloping, sloped
Something that slopes is not flat but goes up or down at one end. *The field slopes slightly down towards the river.*

slope noun plural slopes
a piece of ground that goes up or down like the side of a hill

slot noun plural slots
a narrow opening that you can put a coin into

slow adjective slower, slowest
1 Something that is slow does not move very quickly. Someone who is slow does not do things quickly.

2 If a clock or watch is slow, it shows a time that is earlier than the right time. *I'm sorry I'm late, but my watch is slow.*
slowly adverb Something that moves slowly does not move quickly.

slug noun plural slugs
a small, soft animal that looks like a snail but has no shell

sly adjective slyer, slyest
Someone who is sly is clever at tricking people secretly to get what they want.

smack verb smacks, smacking, smacked
To smack someone means to hit them with the front of your hand.

small adjective smaller, smallest
Something that is small is not very big. *We live in quite a small house.*

smart adjective smarter, smartest
1 If you look smart, you look clean and neat and have nice clothes on.
2 Someone who is smart is clever.

smash verb smashes, smashing, smashed
When something smashes, it breaks into a lot of pieces with a loud noise. *I dropped a glass and it smashed.*

smell verb smells, smelling, smelled, smelt
1 When you smell something, you notice it through your nose. *I can smell something burning.*
2 If something smells, you can notice it through your nose. *Your feet smell!*

smell noun plural smells
1 A smell is something that you can notice with your nose. *There was a strange smell in the kitchen.*
2 Your sense of smell is how well you can smell things. *Dogs have a very good sense of smell.*

a
b
c
d
e
f
g
h
i
j
k
l
m
n
o
p
q
r
s
t
u
v
w
x
y
z

199

A
B
C
D
E
F
G
H
I
J
K
L
M
N
O
P
Q
R
S
T
U
V
W
X
Y
Z

smile verb smiles, smiling, smiled
When you smile, you move your mouth to show that you are happy.

smoke noun
grey or black gas from a fire

smoke verb smokes, smoking, smoked
1 When something smokes, smoke comes off it. *The bonfire was still smoking the next morning.*
2 If someone smokes they breathe in the smoke from rolled up leaves of a plant.

smooth adjective smoother, smoothest
Something that is smooth is flat and level, with no bumps or rough parts. *Babies have lovely, smooth skin.*
smoothly adverb Something that moves smoothly moves without bumps. *The car moved smoothly away from the scene.*

smoothie noun
A smoothie is a thick, smooth drink with fresh and milk, yogurt, or ice cream. *I had a banana smoothie for breakfast.*

SMS noun
SMS is a system for sending text messages to mobile phones. SMS stands for **short message service**.

smudge noun plural smudges
a dirty mark on something

smudge verb smudges, smudging, smudged
If you smudge paint or ink, you touch it while it is still wet and make it messy.

smuggle verb smuggles, smuggling, smuggled
To smuggle something into a place or out of a place means to take it there secretly.

snack noun plural snacks
something you can eat quickly instead of a meal

snail noun plural snails
a small animal with a soft body, no legs, and a hard shell on its back

snake noun plural snakes
an animal with a long, thin body and no legs

snap verb snaps, snapping, snapped
1 If something snaps, it breaks suddenly. *The rope snapped.*

2 If an animal snaps at you, it tries to bite you.

3 To snap at someone means to shout at them angrily.

snarl **verb** snarls, snarling, snarled
When an animal snarls, it makes a fierce sound and shows its teeth.

snatch **verb** snatches, snatching, snatched
If you snatch something, you grab it quickly.

sneak **verb** sneaks, sneaking, sneaked
When you sneak somewhere, you go there quietly so that people do not see you or hear you. *I sneaked round to the back of the school, while the dinner ladies weren't looking.* — Narinder Dhami, *Bindi Babes*

sneeze **verb** sneezes, sneezing, sneezed
When you sneeze, air suddenly comes out of your nose with a loud noise. *The dust made me sneeze.*

sniff **verb** sniffs, sniffing, sniffed
When you sniff, you breathe in noisily through your nose.

snooze **verb** snoozes, snoozing, snoozed
When you snooze, you have a short sleep.

snore **verb** snores, snoring, snored
If you snore, you breathe very noisily while you are asleep.

snow **noun**
small, light flakes of frozen water that fall from the sky when it is very cold

snowball **noun** *plural* snowballs
a ball of snow that you throw at someone

snowboard **noun** *plural* snowboards
a narrow board that you stand on to slide down a slope over snow

snowflake **noun** *plural* snowflakes
Snowflakes are small light pieces of snow that fall from the sky.

snug **adjective** snugger, snuggest
If you feel snug, you feel warm, cosy, and comfortable.

snuggle **verb** snuggles, snuggling, snuggled
When you snuggle somewhere, you curl up there so that you are warm and comfortable.

so **conjunction**
You use so to mean for that reason. *I have no money left so can't buy any more sweets.*

soak **verb** soaks, soaking, soaked
1 To soak something means to make it very wet. *The rain got in and soaked the carpet.*
2 If something soaks up water, the water goes into it.

soap **noun** *plural* soaps
1 Soap is something that you use with water for washing yourself.
2 A soap or a soap opera is a regular television series about the lives of ordinary people.

soar **verb** soars, soaring, soared
When something soars, it goes high up into the air.

sob **verb** sobs, sobbing, sobbed
If you sob, you cry in a noisy way.

a
b
c
d
e
f
g
h
i
j
k
l
m
n
o
p
q
r
s
t
u
v
w
x
y
z

201

A B C D E F G H I J K L M N O P Q R **S** T U V W X Y Z

soccer noun
the game of football

society noun *plural* **societies**
(say so-**sye**-et-ee)
1 A society is all the people who live together in the same country.
2 A society is a club.

sock noun *plural* **socks**
a piece of clothing that you wear over your feet

socket noun *plural* **sockets**
a place on a wall that an electric plug fits into

sofa noun *plural* **sofas**
a long, comfortable seat for more than one person

soft adjective **softer, softest**
1 Something that is soft is not hard or stiff. *I slept on a lovely soft bed.*
2 A soft sound is not very loud.
softly adverb If you say something softly, you say it quietly. *'Don't worry,' Alice whispered softly.*

software noun (in ICT)
the programs that you put into a computer to make it work

soggy adjective **soggier, soggiest**
Something that is soggy is wet and soft. *The cardboard box had gone all soggy in the rain.*

soil noun
the brown earth that plants grow in

solar adjective
Solar means to do with the sun. *Some houses now use solar energy.*

sold verb past tense of **sell**

soldier noun *plural* **soldiers**
someone who is a member of an army

sole noun *plural* **soles**
The sole of your foot or shoe is the part underneath it.

solid adjective
1 Something that is solid is not hollow in the middle. *Tennis balls are hollow but cricket balls are solid.*
2 Something that is solid is hard and firm. *Water becomes solid when it freezes.*

solid noun *plural* **solids**
A solid is any substance that is hard and is not a liquid or a gas. Wood, rock, and plastic are all solids.

solo noun *plural* **solos**
a piece of music or a dance that one person performs on their own

solution noun *plural* **solutions**
1 The solution to a puzzle or problem is the answer.

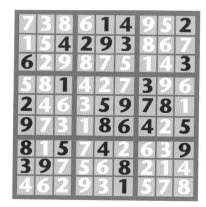

2 (in science) A solution is a liquid in which something has been dissolved. *In the beaker we had a solution of sugar and water.*

solve verb solves, solving, solved
When you solve a puzzle or problem, you find the answer to it.

some determiner, pronoun
1 a few *Some of us can swim, but the others can't.*
2 an amount of something *Would you like some cake?*

somebody, someone pronoun
a person *Somebody's taken my pencil!*

somehow adverb
in some way *We must get away somehow.*

somersault noun plural somersaults
When you do a somersault, you roll over forwards or backwards.

something pronoun
a thing *I'm sure I've forgotten something.*

sometimes adverb
at some times *Sometimes I cycle to school, sometimes I walk.*

somewhere adverb
in some place *I put the book somewhere but I've forgotten where.*

son noun plural sons
Someone's son is their male child.

song noun plural songs
a piece of music with words that you sing

soon adverb
in a very short time *We must go home soon.*

soot noun
black powder that is left behind after coal or wood has been burnt

sore adjective sorer, sorest
If a part of your body is sore, it hurts. *I've got a sore throat.*

sorry adjective sorrier, sorriest
1 If you are sorry that you did something, you are sad about it and wish that you had not done it. *I'm very sorry that I broke your window.*
2 If you feel sorry for someone, you feel sad because something nasty has happened to them.

sort noun plural sorts
a kind *Which sort of ice cream do you like?*

sort verb sorts, sorting, sorted
When you sort things, you put them into different groups. *We sorted the books into different piles.*

sound noun plural sounds
anything that you can hear

sound verb sounds, sounding, sounded
If a bell or alarm sounds, it makes a noise.

soup noun plural soups
a hot liquid made from meat or vegetables

sour adjective sourer, sourest
Something that is sour has a nasty bitter taste, like a lemon.

source noun plural sources
The source of something is the place where it comes from, or the place where it starts. *The source of the river is up in the hills.*

south noun
South is one of the directions in which you can face or travel. On a map, south is the direction towards the bottom of the page.

a
b
c
d
e
f
g
h
i
j
k
l
m
n
o
p
q
r
s
t
u
v
w
x
y
z

A
B
C
D
E
F
G
H
I
J
K
L
M
N
O
P
Q
R
S
T
U
V
W
X
Y
Z

souvenir noun *plural* souvenirs
something that you keep because it reminds you of a person or place *We brought back some shells as a souvenir.*

sow verb sows, sowing, sowed, sown
(rhymes with *low*)
When you sow seeds, you put them into the ground so that they will grow.

space noun *plural* spaces
1 Space is the place around the earth and far beyond the earth, where the stars and planets are. *Would you like to go up into space?*
2 A space is a place with nothing in it. *There is a space here for you to write your name.*

spade noun *plural* spades
a tool with a long handle and a wide blade that you use for digging

spaghetti noun
a type of pasta that is made in long, thin pieces

spanner noun *plural* spanners
a tool that you use for tightening and undoing nuts

spare verb spares, sparing, spared
If you can spare something, you have some extra that you can give to someone else. *Can you spare a bit of money for our collection?*

spare adjective
If something is spare, you are not using it at the moment but you can use it if you need it. *I always have a spare pencil in my pencil case.*

spark noun *plural* sparks
1 a tiny flash of electricity *There was a spark as the wires touched.*
2 a tiny piece of something burning that shoots out from a fire

sparkle verb sparkles, sparkling, sparkled
When something sparkles, it shines brightly. *The sea sparkled in the sunlight.*

sparrow noun *plural* sparrows
a small, brown bird that you often see in people's gardens

spawn noun
Frog spawn is eggs that look like jelly and are laid by frogs in water.

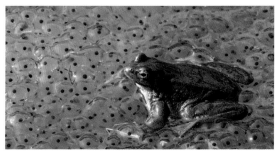

speak verb speaks, speaking, spoke, spoken
When you speak, you say something. *I spoke to my grandmother on the phone.*

speaker noun *plural* speakers
the part of a radio, television, or music player that the sound comes out of

spear noun *plural* spears
a long stick with a sharp point that is used as a weapon

special adjective
1 Something that is special is different and more important than other things.
2 A special thing is for one particular person or job. *You use a special tool to get the strings on a piano in tune.*

spectator noun *plural* spectators
Spectators are people who watch a sporting event or game.

speech noun *plural* speeches
1 Speech is the ability to speak. *People use speech to communicate with each other.*
2 A speech is a talk that someone gives to a group of people.

speech bubble noun
plural speech bubbles
A speech bubble is a circle containing words, which you draw next to a person in a picture to show what that person is saying.

speechless adjective
If you are speechless, you cannot say anything because you are so surprised, angry, or afraid.

speech marks noun
Speech marks are marks like this ' ' or " " this that you use in writing. You put these marks round words to show that someone has spoken them.

speed noun
The speed of something is how fast it moves or how quickly it happens. *We were driving along at a speed of 100 kilometres an hour.*

speed verb speeds, speeding, sped
To speed means to run or go along very fast. *He sped past me on his bike.*

spell verb spells, spelling, spelled, spelt
The way in which you spell a word is the letters that you use when you write it. *I can't spell your name.*

spell noun *plural* spells
A spell is a set of words that people say in stories when they want something magic to happen.

spellcheck noun *plural* spellchecks
When you do a spellcheck on a computer, you tell the computer to check the spellings of all the words you have typed.

spend verb spends, spending, spent
1 When you spend money, you use it to pay for things. *I've already spent all my money.*
2 When you spend time doing something, you use the time to do that thing. *We spent all day trying to mend the boat.*

sphere noun *plural* spheres (say **sfeer**)
the shape of a ball

spice noun *plural* spices
A spice is a powder or seed which is added to food to give it a strong flavour.

spicy adjective spicier, spiciest
Something spicy has a strong flavour and a hot taste. *She cooked a dish of spicy vegetables.*

spider noun *plural* spiders
a small animal with eight legs that spins sticky webs to catch insects for food

a
b
c
d
e
f
g
h
i
j
k
l
m
n
o
p
q
r
s
t
u
v
w
x
y
z

A
B
C
D
E
F
G
H
I
J
K
L
M
N
O
P
Q
R
S
T
U
V
W
X
Y
Z

spike noun plural spikes
a thin piece of metal with a sharp point

spill verb spills, spilling, spilled, spilt
If you spill something, you let some of it fall out onto the floor. *Mind you don't spill your drink.*

spin verb spins, spinning, spun
1 Something that spins turns round and round.
2 To spin thread from wool or cotton means to make it.
3 To spin a web means to make it. *The spider spun a web.*

spine noun plural spines
1 Your spine is the long line of bones down the middle of your back.
2 The spines on a plant or animal are sharp points on it.

spiral noun plural spirals
a line that keeps going round and round in circles, with each circle getting slightly bigger

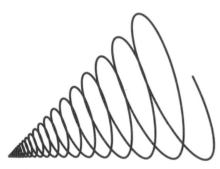

spire noun plural spires
a tall, pointed part on the top of a tower on a building

spite noun
If you do something out of spite, you do it to hurt or upset someone.

spiteful adjective
Someone who is spiteful does nasty things to hurt or upset other people.

splash verb splashes, splashing, splashed
If you splash water, you hit it so that it makes a noise and flies up into the air.

splinter noun plural splinters
a small, sharp bit of wood or glass

split verb splits, splitting, split
1 When something splits, it breaks or tears. *The bag split open and all the shopping fell out.*
2 When you split something, you break it into pieces. *He split the log with an axe.*

spoil verb spoils, spoiling, spoiled, spoilt
1 To spoil something means to damage it so that it is not as good or as nice as it was before *You'll spoil your new trainers if you get them all muddy.*
2 To spoil a child means to give them everything that they want so that they always expect to get their own way and behave badly if they do not.

spoke noun plural spokes
The spokes on a wheel are the pieces of metal that go from the centre of the wheel to the edge.

spoke, spoken verb
past tense of speak

sponge noun plural sponges
1 A sponge is a thick, soft thing with a lot of small holes in. A sponge soaks up water easily, and you use it for washing things.
2 a type of cake

sponsor verb sponsors, sponsoring, sponsored
If you sponsor someone, you promise to give them money if they do something difficult.

spoon noun plural spoons
a thing that you use for eating soft or liquid foods such as soup and ice cream

sport noun *plural* sports
A sport is a game that you play or something difficult that you do to exercise your body.

spot noun *plural* spots
1 a small round mark on something
Leopards have spots all over their bodies.
2 a small, sore, red lump on your skin
Teenagers often get spots on their faces.

spot verb spots, spotting, spotted
If you spot something, you see it.

spotless adjective
Something that is spotless is perfectly clean.

spout noun *plural* spouts
The spout of a jug or teapot is the part that you pour liquid out of.

sprang verb past tense of spring verb

spray verb sprays, spraying, sprayed
When you spray water on something, you cover it with tiny drops of water.

spread verb spreads, spreading, spread
1 To spread something means to open it out to its full size. *The huge bird spread its wings and flew away.*
2 When you spread butter or jam, you put a thin layer of it onto bread.

spring verb springs, springing, sprang, sprung
To spring means to jump. *Just inside the gate, with the moonlight shining on it, stood an enormous lion crouched as if it was ready to spring.* — C. S. Lewis, *The Lion, the Witch and the Wardrobe*

spring noun *plural* springs
1 a piece of metal that is wound into rings so that it jumps back into shape after it has been pressed down
2 the time of the year when plants start to grow and the days get lighter and warmer

sprinkle verb sprinkles, sprinkling, sprinkled
When you sprinkle something, you shake a few drops or small pieces of it over something else.

sprint verb sprints, sprinting, sprinted
When you sprint, you run as fast as you can over a short distance.

sprout verb sprouts, sprouting, sprouted
When a plant sprouts, it starts to grow new parts.

sprung verb past tense of spring verb

spun verb past tense of spin

spy noun *plural* spies
someone who works secretly to find out information about another person or country

spy verb spies, spying, spied
1 When you spy on someone, you watch them secretly.
2 When you spy something, you see it.

square noun *plural* squares
1 A square is a shape with four straight sides and four right angles. The sides of a square are all the same length.

2 (in mathematics) The square of a number is the number you get when you multiply it by itself. *The square of 4 is 16.*
3 an open space in a town with buildings all round it *We ate lunch in the square.*

a
b
c
d
e
f
g
h
i
j
k
l
m
n
o
p
q
r
s
t
u
v
w
x
y
z

207

A
B
C
D
E
F
G
H
I
J
K
L
M
N
O
P
Q
R
S
T
U
V
W
X
Y
Z

squash verb squashes, squashing, squashed
When you squash something, you press it hard so that it becomes flat. *My sandwiches got squashed at the bottom of my bag.*

squash noun
a sweet drink made from fruit juice and sugar *Would you like some orange squash?*

squat verb squats, squatting, squatted
When you squat, you bend your knees under you so that your bottom is almost touching the ground.

squawk verb squawks, squawking, squawked
When a bird squawks, it makes a loud, rough sound in its throat.

squeak verb squeaks, squeaking, squeaked
To squeak means to make a very high sound. *The door squeaked as I opened it.*

squeal verb squeals, squealing, squealed
When you squeal, you shout or cry in a high voice. *The girls were squealing with delight.*

squeeze verb squeezes, squeezing, squeezed
1 When you squeeze something, you press it hard with your hands. *Squeeze the tube to get everything out.*

2 If you squeeze something into a place, you push it in even though there is not very much room. *Can we squeeze six people in the car?*

squirrel noun plural squirrels
A squirrel is a small animal with a thick, tail. Squirrels live in trees and eat nuts and seeds.

squirt verb squirts, squirting, squirted
When water squirts out of something, it shoots out quickly.

stable noun plural stables
a building in which horses are kept

stack noun plural stacks
A stack of things is a neat pile of them.

stadium noun plural stadiums
a large building where people can watch sports and games

staff noun
The staff in a school, shop, or office are all the people who work there.

stag noun plural stags
a male deer

stage noun plural stages
The stage in a theatre or hall is the raised part on which people act, sing, or dance to entertain other people.

stagger verb staggers, staggering, staggered
1 When you stagger, you walk with unsteady legs, almost falling over with each step.
2 If something staggers you, it surprises you a lot.

stain noun *plural* stains
a dirty mark on something that does not come out when you wash it or rub it

stair noun *plural* stairs
Stairs are steps inside a building.

staircase noun *plural* staircases
a set of stairs inside a building

stale adjective staler, stalest
Something that is stale is not fresh. *We had nothing to eat except stale bread.*

stalk noun *plural* stalks
The stalk of a flower, leaf, or fruit, is the part that joins it to the plant.

stall noun *plural* stalls
1 a table that things are arranged on so that they can be sold, for example in a market
2 a place for one animal in a stable

stallion noun *plural* stallions
a male horse

stammer verb stammers, stammering, stammered
If you stammer, you keep repeating the sounds at the beginning of words when you speak.

stamp noun *plural* stamps
A stamp is a small piece of sticky paper with a picture on it. You stick a stamp on a letter or parcel to show that you have paid to post it.

stamp verb stamps, stamping, stamped
When you stamp your feet, you bang them heavily on the ground.

stand verb stands, standing, stood
1 When you stand, you are on your feet, not sitting or lying down. *The teacher asked us all to stand up.*
2 If you cannot stand something, you do not like it at all.

stand noun *plural* stands
something that you can put things on
Put your music on the music stand.

standard noun *plural* standards
The standard of something is how good or bad it is.

standard adjective
Something that is standard is ordinary and not special. *This software will run on any standard computer.*

stank verb past tense of stink

star noun *plural* stars
1 Stars are the tiny, bright lights you see in the sky at night.
2 A star is a shape that has five or more points sticking out all round it.

3 A star is a famous person.
star verb stars, starring, starred
If someone stars in a film or show, they have an important part in it.

starch noun *plural* starches
Starch is a substance in food that gives you energy. There is starch in bread and potatoes.

a
b
c
d
e
f
g
h
i
j
k
l
m
n
o
p
q
r
s
t
u
v
w
x
y
z

A
B
C
D
E
F
G
H
I
J
K
L
M
N
O
P
Q
R
S
T
U
V
W
X
Y
Z

stare verb stares, staring, stared
If you stare at something, you keep looking at it for a long time, without moving your eyes.

start verb starts, starting, started
1 When you start to do something, you begin to do it. *Georgina started to cry.*
2 When something starts, it begins. *What time does the concert start?*

start noun plural starts
The start of something is when it begins.

startle verb startles, startling, startled
If something startles you, it gives you a sudden shock. *The sudden noise startled me.*

starve verb starves, starving, starved
To starve means to be ill or to die because you have not got enough food.

state noun plural states
1 The state that something is in is the condition it is in, for example whether it is clean, tidy, or broken. *The house was in a terrible state.*
2 A state is a country or one part of a country that has its own laws and government.

statement noun plural statements
a sentence that is not a question or an exclamation

station noun plural stations
1 a place where trains and buses stop so that people can get on and off
2 a building where the police or firefighters work

stationary adjective
If a car is stationary, it is not moving.

stationery noun
paper, pens, and other things that you use for writing and drawing

statue noun plural statues
a model of a person made from stone, wood, or metal

stay verb stays, staying, stayed
1 If you stay somewhere, you remain there and do not go away. *Please stay in your seats.*
2 If you stay in a place, you live there for a while. *I'm going to stay with my grandma for the summer holidays.*
3 To stay means to remain. *I hope it stays dry for sports day.*

steady adjective steadier, steadiest
1 Something that is steady is firm and does not shake or move about.
2 If something moves in a steady way, it moves along at the same speed all the time.

steak noun plural steaks
a thick slice of meat or fish

steal verb steals, stealing, stole, stolen
To steal something means to take something that belongs to someone else. *Someone's stolen my phone!*

steam noun
the hot gas that comes off water when it boils

steel noun
a type of strong, shiny metal

steep adjective steeper, steepest
Something that is steep slopes sharply up or down.

steer verb steers, steering, steered
When you steer a car or bicycle, you make it go in the direction you want.

stem noun plural stems
the long, thin part of a plant that grows up out of the ground

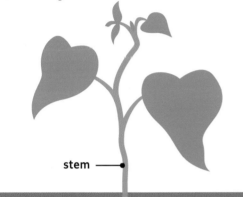

stem

step noun plural steps
1 When you take a step, you move one foot forwards or backwards.
2 Steps are stairs.

stepbrother noun
plural stepbrothers
A stepbrother is a boy whose father or mother has married your father or mother.

stepfather noun plural stepfathers
Your stepfather is a man who has got married to your mother but is not your real father.

stepmother noun plural stepmothers
Your stepmother is a woman who has got married to your father but is not your real mother.

stepsister noun plural stepsisters
A stepsister is a girl whose father or mother has married your father or mother.

stereo noun plural stereos
a machine that plays music from tapes or CDs through two speakers

stern adjective sterner, sternest
Someone who is stern is serious and strict. *Mr Robinson had a very stern expression on his face.*

stew noun plural stews
a mixture of meat or vegetables cooked in a sauce

stick noun plural sticks
a long, thin piece of wood
stick verb sticks, sticking, stuck
1 If you stick a pin or nail into something, you push it in.
2 When you stick things together, you fix them together using glue. *I stuck the pictures into my book.*
3 If something sticks, it gets jammed and you cannot move it. *Sometimes the door sticks a bit.*

sticker noun plural stickers
a small piece of paper with a picture or writing on one side and glue on the other side

sticky adjective stickier, stickiest
Something that is sticky will stick to things when it touches them.

stiff adjective stiffer, stiffest
Something that is stiff is hard and does not bend easily. *Use a piece of stiff cardboard for the base of your model.*

a
b
c
d
e
f
g
h
i
j
k
l
m
n
o
p
q
r
s
t
u
v
w
x
y
z

A B C D E F G H I J K L M N O P Q R **S** T U V W X Y Z

still adjective stiller, stillest
1 Something that is still is not moving. *The water in the lake was still and calm.*
2 A still drink is not fizzy.

still adverb
1 When you stand, sit, or lie still, you do not move.
2 even now *He's still asleep.*

sting verb stings, stinging, stung
If an insect stings you, it jabs you with a sharp part of its body and hurts you.

stink verb stinks, stinking, stank, stunk
If something stinks, it smells nasty.

stir verb stirs, stirring, stirred
When you stir something, you move it about with a spoon.

stitch noun plural stitches
1 Stitches are the loops of thread that you make when you are sewing or knitting.
2 A stitch is a sudden pain in your side that you sometimes get when you have been running.

stole, stolen verb past tense of steal

stomach noun plural stomachs
Your stomach is the part inside your body where your food goes after you have eaten it.

stone noun plural stones
1 Stone is rock. *The castle is built of solid stone.*
2 A stone is a small piece of rock.
3 A stone is the hard seed in the middle of some fruits such as a cherry or peach.

4 We can measure weight in stones. One stone is just under $6\frac{1}{2}$ kilograms.

stood verb past tense of stand verb

stool noun plural stools
a small seat without a back

stoop verb stoops, stooping, stooped
When you stoop, you bend your body forwards. *The giraffe stooped low and went out through the tall door.* — Roald Dahl, *The Giraffe and Pelly and Me*

stop verb stops, stopping, stopped
1 When you stop something, you make it stand still. *The policeman stopped the traffic.*
2 When something stops, it stands still. *The bus stopped outside the school.*
3 When you stop doing something, you no longer do it. *The baby finally stopped crying.*

store verb stores, storing, stored
When you store things, you keep them until you need them.

store noun plural stores
a large shop

storey noun *plural* **storeys**
One storey of a tall building is one floor.

storm noun *plural* **storms**
When there is a storm, there is a strong wind and a lot of rain or snow.
stormy adjective If the weather is stormy, there is a strong wind and a lot of rain or snow. *It was a very stormy night.*

story noun *plural* **stories**
something in a book that tells you about things that have happened

straight adjective **straighter, straightest**
Something that is straight does not bend or curl. *Have you got straight hair or curly hair?*

strain verb **strains, straining, strained**
1 If you strain a muscle, you hurt it by stretching it too much.
2 If you strain to do something, you try very hard to do it by pushing or stretching with your body. *I had to strain to reach the top cupboard.*
3 When you strain a liquid, you take out any lumps.

strange adjective **stranger, strangest**
1 Something that is strange is unusual and surprising. *What a strange animal!*
2 A strange place is one that you have not seen before. *She was very frightened to find herself alone in a strange place.*

stranger noun *plural* **strangers**
A stranger is someone you do not know. *You shouldn't talk to strangers.*

strap noun *plural* **straps**
a strip of leather or cloth that you hold when you are carrying something or use for fastening things

straw noun *plural* **straws**
1 Straw is dry stalks of corn or wheat that you put on the ground for animals to lie on.
2 A straw is a thin tube that you sometimes put into a drink and use to drink through.

strawberry noun *plural* **strawberries**
a small, red, juicy fruit

stray adjective
A stray dog or cat does not have a home but lives outside.

stream noun *plural* **streams**
1 a small river
2 A stream of things is a moving line of them. *There was a stream of cars coming out of the car park.*

street noun *plural* **streets**
a road in a town or city with houses along each side

strength noun
The strength of something is how strong it is. *We need to test the strength of the rope.*

stretch verb **stretches, stretching, stretched**
1 When you stretch something, you pull it so that it becomes longer or bigger. *He had to stretch the trousers a bit to get them on.*
2 When you stretch, you move your arms or legs as far as you can. *I stretched over to reach the telephone.*

a
b
c
d
e
f
g
h
i
j
k
l
m
n
o
p
q
r
s
t
u
v
w
x
y
z

213

strict adjective stricter, strictest
Someone who is strict does not allow people to behave badly.

stride verb strides, striding, strode
When you stride along, you walk with long steps.

stride noun plural strides
a long step

strike verb strikes, striking, struck
1 To strike something means to hit it. To strike someone means to hit or slap them. *His father had never struck him.*
2 When you strike a match, you rub it so that it makes a flame.
3 When a clock strikes, it makes a sound.

string noun plural strings
1 String is thin rope.
2 The strings on a guitar or violin are the parts that you touch to make music.

strip verb strips, stripping, stripped
When you strip, you take off all your clothes.

strip noun plural strips
A strip of something is a long, narrow piece of it.

stripe noun plural stripes
A stripe is a band of colour on something. *He was wearing a blue shirt with white stripes.*

strode verb past tense of stride verb

stroke verb strokes, stroking, stroked
When you stroke something, you move your hand over it gently. *I like stroking the cat.*

stroll verb strolls, strolling, strolled
When you stroll, you walk along slowly.

strong adjective stronger, strongest
1 If you are strong, you can lift and move heavy things.
2 Something that is strong will not break easily.
3 A strong taste or smell is not mild or weak.
strongly adverb If something is built strongly, it will not break easily. If something smells strongly, it doesn't smell mild or weak.

struck verb past tense of strike

structure noun plural structures
A structure is anything that has been built. *Next to the house is a small wooden structure.*

struggle verb struggles, struggling, struggled
1 When you struggle, you fight with your arms and legs to try to get free.
2 If you struggle to do something, you work hard to do it because it is difficult. *I struggled a bit with some of the maths questions.*

stubborn adjective
Someone who is stubborn will not change their mind even though they might be wrong.

stuck verb past tense of stick verb

student noun plural students
someone who is studying at college or university

studio noun plural studios
(say **stew**-dee-oh)
1 a place where people make films or radio or television programmes
2 a room where an artist or photographer works

study verb studies, studying, studied
1 When you study a subject, you learn about it. *We are studying rivers in geography.*
2 When you study something, you look at it very carefully. *He studied the map, looking for the farm and the house.*

study noun *plural* studies
a room in a house where someone works or studies

stuff noun
anything that you can see and touch *There was some nasty, slimy stuff on the floor.*

stuff verb stuffs, stuffing, stuffed
1 When you stuff something, you fill it with things.
2 When you stuff something somewhere, you push it there roughly. *She stuffed the sweets into her pocket.*

stuffy adjective stuffier, stuffiest
A room that is stuffy smells nasty because there is no fresh air in it.

stumble verb stumbles, stumbling, stumbled
If you stumble, you trip and fall over.

stump noun *plural* stumps
1 A stump is the part of something that is left after the main part has been broken off.
2 The stumps in a game of cricket are the three sticks that you put at each end of the pitch.

stun verb stuns, stunning, stunned
If something stuns you, it hits you on the head and makes you feel dizzy or weak.

stung verb past tense of sting

stunk verb past tense of stink

stupid adjective
1 Something that is stupid is very silly. *That was a really stupid thing to do.*
2 Someone who is stupid is not very clever.

stutter verb stutters, stuttering, stuttered
If you stutter, you keep repeating the sounds at the beginning of words when you speak.

sty noun *plural* sties
a building where a pig is kept

style noun *plural* styles
The style of something is its shape and design. *I like the colour of this sweatshirt, but I don't like the style.*

subject noun *plural* subjects
1 A subject is something that you learn about at school. Maths, English, history, and art are all subjects.
2 (in grammar) The subject of a sentence is the person or thing that does the action of the verb. In the sentence *William ate an apple*, *William* is the subject of the sentence.
3 The subjects of a king or queen are the people they rule over.

submarine noun *plural* submarines
a ship that can go under the water

a b c d e f g h i j k l m n o p q r **s** t u v w x y z

215

A
B
C
D
E
F
G
H
I
J
K
L
M
N
O
P
Q
R
S
T
U
V
W
X
Y
Z

substance noun *plural* substances
anything that is a liquid, solid, or gas *Glue is a sticky substance.*

subtract verb subtracts, subtracting, subtracted (in mathematics)
When you subtract one number from another, you take it away to make a smaller number. *If you subtract 6 from 9, you get 3.*

suburb noun *plural* suburbs
a part of a city that is a long way from the city centre *A lot of people live in the suburbs of London.*

subway noun *plural* subways
A subway is a path or tunnel under a busy road or railway.

succeed verb succeeds, succeeding, succeeded (say suk-**seed**)
If you succeed, you manage to do something. *I finally succeeded in getting the door open.*

success noun *plural* successes (say suk-**sess**)
If something is a success, it works well and people like it. *The concert was a great success.*

successful adjective
1 If you are successful, you manage to do something.
2 If something is successful, it works well and people like it. *Our trip to France was very successful.*
successfully adverb Something done successfully works well. If someone does something successfully they manage to do it. *She finished the test successfully.*

such determiner
so much *That was such fun!*

suck verb sucks, sucking, sucked
1 When you suck something into your mouth, you pull it in. *Sarah sucked some squash up through the straw.*

2 When you suck on something, you keep moving it about in your mouth without chewing it or swallowing it. *Ben was sucking on a sweet.*

sudden adjective
Something that is sudden happens quickly without any warning. *There was a sudden change in the weather.*
suddenly adverb If something happens suddenly, it happens quickly and without warning. *He heard a noise and suddenly he was frightened.*

suffer verb suffers, suffering, suffered
When you suffer, something hurts you or upsets you.

suffix noun *plural* suffixes (in grammar)
A suffix is a group of letters that are added to the end of a word to change its meaning or make it into a different word class.

sugar noun
a sweet powder that you add to drinks and other foods to make them taste sweet

suggest verb suggests, suggesting, suggested
If you suggest something, you say that it would be a good idea.

suggestion noun *plural* suggestions
A suggestion is an idea or possibility that you can think about. *His suggestion was that they go to the cinema.*

suit noun *plural* suits
a jacket and a pair of trousers or a skirt that are made of the same material and meant to be worn together

suit verb suits, suiting, suited
If something suits you, it looks nice on you. *Blue really suits you.*

suitable adjective
Something that is suitable is the right type of thing. *Are these shoes suitable for wearing in wet weather?*

suitcase noun *plural* suitcases
a bag with stiff sides that you use for carrying clothes and other things on journeys

sulk verb sulks, sulking, sulked
When you sulk, you are bad-tempered and do not speak to people because you are cross about something.

sum noun *plural* sums
1 The sum of two numbers is the number that you get when you add them together. *The sum of 7 and 3 is 10.*
2 When you do a sum, you find an answer to a question by working with numbers. *Have you done all your sums yet?*
3 A sum of money is an amount of money.

summarize verb summarizes, summarizing, summarized
To summarize something means to give a summary of it.

summary noun *plural* summaries
When you give a summary of something, you describe the important parts of it and leave out the parts that are not so important.

summer noun *plural* summers
the time of the year when the weather is hot and it stays light for longer in the evenings

sun noun
1 The sun is the star that we see shining in the sky during the day. The sun gives the earth heat and light.
2 If you are in the sun, the sun is shining on you. *You shouldn't stay out in the sun for too long or you will burn.*

sunburn noun
If you have sunburn, your skin becomes red and painful because you have spent a long time in the sun.

Sunday noun *plural* Sundays
the day of the week after Saturday

sunflower noun *plural* sunflowers
a big yellow flower that grows very tall and always turns to face the sun

sung verb past tense of sing

sunglasses noun
dark glasses that you wear to protect your eyes from the bright sun

sunk verb past tense of sink verb

sunlight noun
light from the sun

sunny adjective sunnier, sunniest
When the weather is sunny, the sun is shining.

a
b
c
d
e
f
g
h
i
j
k
l
m
n
o
p
q
r
s
t
u
v
w
x
y
z

sunrise noun
the time in the morning when the sun comes up and it becomes light

sunset noun
the time in the evening when the sun goes down and it becomes dark

sunrise   sunset

sunshine noun
the light and heat that come from the sun

super adjective
Something that is super is very good. *That's a super drawing!*

superlative adjective (in grammar)
The superlative form of an adjective is the part that means 'most', for example *biggest* is the superlative form of *big*.

supermarket noun
plural supermarkets
a large shop where you can buy food and other things

superstition noun
good luck or bad luck

supper noun *plural* suppers
a meal or snack that you eat in the evening

supply verb supplies, supplying, supplied
If someone supplies you with something, they give it or sell it to you.

supply noun *plural* supplies
If you have a supply of things, you are keeping them ready to use.

support verb supports, supporting, supported
1 To support something means to hold it up and stop it from falling down. *These pieces of wood support the roof.*
2 If you support someone, you help them and encourage them to do well. *Which football team do you support?*

suppose verb supposes, supposing, supposed
If you suppose that something is true, you think that it is true although you do not know for sure.

sure adjective
1 If you are sure about something, you know that it is definitely true. *Are you sure you locked the door?*
2 If something is sure to happen, it will definitely happen.

surf verb surfs, surfing, surfed
1 When you surf, you stand on a special board called a surfboard and ride in towards the shore on big waves.

2 (in ICT) When you surf the Internet, you look at different websites to find information.

surface noun *plural* surfaces
The surface of something is the top or outside part, not the middle. *We polished the tables to give them a shiny surface.*

surgery noun *plural* surgeries
the room where you go to see a doctor or dentist

surname noun *plural* surnames
Your surname is your last name, which is the name you share with other members of your family.

surprise noun *plural* surprises
1 If something is a surprise, you were not expecting it to happen. *It was a complete surprise when my name was called out.*
2 Surprise is the feeling you have when something happens that you were not expecting. *She looked at me in surprise.*

surprise verb surprises, surprising, surprised
If something surprises you, you were not expecting it to happen. *It surprised everyone when Ben won the race.*

surrender verb surrenders, surrendering, surrendered
When people surrender, they stop fighting or hiding and give themselves up.

surround verb surrounds, surrounding, surrounded
To surround a place means to form a circle all around it.

survey noun *plural* surveys
a set of questions that you ask people to find out information about something

survive verb survives, surviving, survived
1 If you survive, you do not die but carry on living. *A few people survived the plane crash.*
2 If something survives, it is not destroyed.

suspect verb suspects, suspecting, suspected
If you suspect that something is true, you have a feeling that it might be true.

suspense noun
excitement that you feel because you do not know what is going to happen next

suspicious adjective
(say sus-**pish**-uss)
1 If someone behaves in a suspicious way, they behave in a strange, secret way which makes you think they are doing something wrong.
2 If you are suspicious of someone, you have a feeling that they have done something wrong and you do not trust them.

swallow verb swallows, swallowing, swallowed
When you swallow something, you make it go down your throat.

swam verb past tense of swim

swan noun *plural* swans
a big white bird with a long neck that lives near water and often swims on the water

swap verb swaps, swapping, swapped
When you swap something, you give it to someone and get something else in return.

swarm noun *plural* swarms
A swarm of insects is a lot of them all flying together.

a
b
c
d
e
f
g
h
i
j
k
l
m
n
o
p
q
r
s
t
u
v
w
x
y
z

A B C D E F G H I J K L M N O P Q R S T U V W X Y Z

sway verb sways, swaying, swayed
To sway means to move gently from side to side. *The tall trees swayed in the wind.*

sweat verb sweats, sweating, sweated
When you sweat, salty liquid comes out from your skin when you are very hot.

sweater noun *plural* sweaters
a warm jumper

sweatshirt noun *plural* sweatshirts
a jumper made of thick cotton cloth

sweep verb sweeps, sweeping, swept
When you sweep a floor, you clean it by pushing a brush over it.

sweet adjective sweeter, sweetest
1 Something that is sweet tastes of sugar.
2 Something or someone that is sweet is very nice. *What a sweet little girl!*

sweet noun *plural* sweets
1 something small and sweet which you eat as a snack *You shouldn't eat too many sweets.*

2 a pudding

sweetcorn noun
the yellow seeds of a corn plant, which you cook and eat as a vegetable

swell verb swells, swelling, swelled, swollen
When something swells, it gets bigger.

swept verb *see* sweep

swerve verb swerves, swerving, swerved
If a car swerves, it suddenly moves to the side so that it does not hit something. *The bus swerved to avoid a dog in the road.*

swift adjective swifter, swiftest
Something that is swift moves very quickly.

swim verb swims, swimming, swam, swum
When you swim, you move through water by floating and moving your arms and legs.

swimming costume noun
plural swimming costumes
a piece of clothing that a woman or girl wears when she goes swimming

swimming pool noun
plural swimming pools
a large pool that has been built for people to swim in

swimming trunks noun
a piece of clothing that a man or boy wears when he goes swimming

swing verb swings, swinging, swung
When something swings, it moves backwards and forwards in the air. *There were monkeys swinging in the trees above us.*

swing noun *plural* swings
A swing is a seat that hangs down from a frame. You can sit on it and move backwards and forwards.

switch noun *plural* switches
something that you turn or press to make a machine work or a light come on

switch verb switches, switching, switched
When you switch something on, you turn or press a control so that it starts working. When you switch something off, you turn or press a control so that it stops working. *It was getting dark so he switched the light on so that he could read his book.*

swollen verb a tense of swell

swoop verb swoops, swooping, swooped
When a bird swoops down, it flies downwards quickly.

swop verb swops, swopping, swopped
Swop is another spelling of swap.

sword noun *plural* swords
a weapon that has a handle and a long, thin, sharp blade

swum verb past tense of swim

swung verb past tense of swing verb

syllable noun *plural* syllables
(say **sil**-a-bal)
A syllable is one of the sounds or beats in a word. The word chim-pan-zee has three syllables. The word sweet-corn has two syllables.

symbol noun *plural* symbols
A symbol is a sign which stands for something or means something. The + symbol means that you add numbers together.

symmetrical adjective
A shape that is symmetrical has two halves that are exactly alike.

symmetry noun
If a shape or object has symmetry, its two halves are exactly alike. The line of symmetry in a shape is the line through the middle, which divides the two symmetrical halves.

sympathy noun
If you have sympathy for someone, you feel sorry for them.

synagogue noun *plural* synagogues
(say **sin**-a-gog)
a building where Jewish people pray and worship

synonym noun *plural* synonyms
(say **sin**-a-nim)
a word that means the same as another word, *courageous* is a synonym of *brave*

syrup noun *plural* syrups
a very sweet, sticky, liquid

system noun *plural* systems
1 If you have a system for doing something, you do it in a particular order or way every time.
2 A system is a set of machines that work together. *The school has a new heating system.*

a
b
c
d
e
f
g
h
i
j
k
l
m
n
o
p
q
r
s
t
u
v
w
x
y
z

Tt

table noun *plural* **tables**
1 a piece of furniture with a flat top that you can put things on
2 a list of numbers or words arranged in rows or columns

tablet noun *plural* **tablets**
a small pill with medicine in, which you swallow when you are ill

tackle verb **tackles, tackling, tackled**
1 When you tackle a difficult job, you start doing it.
2 If you tackle someone in a game such as football or rugby, you try to get the ball from them.

tactful adjective
If you are tactful, you are careful not to upset someone by saying something unkind. *Mum and Dad and Callum and Jack were very tactful and didn't ask any awkward questions.* — Jacqueline Wilson, *Best Friends*

tadpole noun *plural* **tadpoles**
A tadpole is a tiny animal that lives in water and will turn into a frog or toad.

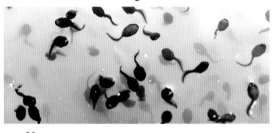

tail noun *plural* **tails**
1 An animal's tail is the long part at the end of its body.
2 The tail of something is the part at the back of it. *There was smoke coming out from the tail of the aeroplane.*

take verb **takes, taking, took, taken**
1 When you take something, you get hold of it. *I offered him a sweet, and he took one.*
2 If you take something to a place, you have it with you when you go there.
3 If someone takes something, they steal it.
4 If someone takes you to a place, you go there with them. *Dad promised to take us to the cinema.*
5 (in mathematics) If you take one number away from another, you subtract it.
6 When a rocket takes off, it goes up into space.

tale noun *plural* **tales**
a story

talent noun *plural* **talents**
If you have a talent for something, you can do it very well.

talk verb **talks, talking, talked**
When you talk, you speak to someone.

tall adjective **taller, tallest**
1 Someone who is tall measures a lot from their head to their feet. *I'm quite tall for my age.*
2 A tall tree or building is very high.

Talmud noun
The Talmud is a book of writings about the Jewish religion.

tame adjective **tamer, tamest**
An animal or bird that is tame is not wild or fierce, and is not afraid of people.

tan noun
When you have a tan, your skin is darker than usual because you have been in the hot sun.

tangle noun *plural* **tangles**
If things are in a tangle, they are all twisted or knotted together and it is difficult to separate them.

tank noun *plural* tanks
1 a very large container that you keep liquid in
2 a very strong, heavy truck that is used in war and moves on metal tracks, not wheels

tanker noun *plural* tankers
1 a large ship that carries oil
2 a large lorry that carries milk or petrol

tap noun *plural* taps
a handle which you turn to start or stop water flowing through a pipe

tap verb taps, tapping, tapped
When you tap something, you hit it gently. *I tapped on the window.*

tape noun *plural* tapes
1 Sticky tape is a strip of sticky paper that you use for sticking things together.
2 Tape is a special magnetic strip that you can record sound and picture on.

tape verb tapes, taping, taped
To tape sound or pictures means to record them. *He taped the conversation so he could remember what everyone had said.*

tape measure noun *plural* tape measures
a long strip of cloth or plastic with measurements marked on it, which you use for measuring things *My mum measured my height with a tape measure.*

target noun *plural* targets
something that you aim at and try to hit when you are shooting or throwing something

tart noun *plural* tarts
a type of food that has pastry on the bottom and fruit, meat, or vegetables on top

task noun *plural* tasks
a job that you have to do *I was given the task of washing up the plates.*

taste verb tastes, tasting, tasted
1 When you taste food, you eat a small amount to see what it is like.
2 The way something tastes is the flavour that it has. *The food tasted horrible.*

taste noun
1 The taste of something is what it is like when you eat it.
2 Your sense of taste is how well you can recognize things when you eat them.

taught verb past tense of teach

tax noun *plural* taxes
money that people have to pay to the government

taxi noun *plural* taxis
a car that you can travel in if you pay the driver

tea noun
1 a hot drink that you make by pouring boiling water over the dried leaves of the tea plant
2 a meal that you eat in the afternoon or early evening

a
b
c
d
e
f
g
h
i
j
k
l
m
n
o
p
q
r
s
t
u
v
w
x
y
z

A
B
C
D
E
F
G
H
I
J
K
L
M
N
O
P
Q
R
S
T
U
V
W
X
Y
Z

teach verb teaches, teaching, taught
When you teach someone something, you tell them about it or show them how to do it. *Miss Cummings teaches us maths.*

teacher noun *plural* teachers
A teacher is someone who teaches someone.

team noun *plural* teams
a group of people who work together or play together on the same side in a game

teapot noun *plural* teapots
a container with a spout that you use for making and pouring tea

tear verb tears, tearing, tore, torn
(rhymes with *fair*)
When you tear something, you pull it apart so that it splits or makes a hole. *Mind you don't tear your dress.*

tear noun *plural* tears (rhymes with *fear*)
Tears are drops of salty water that come from your eyes when you cry.

tease verb teases, teasing, teased
To tease someone means to make fun of them. *People often tease me because I'm short.*

technology noun
Technology is using science and machines to help people in their lives.

teddy bear noun *plural* teddy bears
a stuffed toy bear

teenager noun *plural* teenagers
someone who is between thirteen and nineteen years old

teeth noun plural of tooth

telephone noun *plural* telephones
A telephone is a machine that you use to speak to someone who is far away from you. It is also called a **phone**.

telephone verb telephones, telephoning, telephoned
When you telephone someone, you use a telephone to speak to them.

telescope noun *plural* telescopes
A telescope is a tube with special lenses in. When you look through a telescope, things that are far away look bigger and closer.

television noun *plural* televisions
a machine that picks up signals that are sent through the air and changes them into pictures and sound so that people can watch them

tell verb tells, telling, told
1 When you tell someone something, you speak to them about it. *Uncle Jack told us all about his life at sea.*
2 If you can tell the time, you can look at a clock and say what time it is.
3 To tell someone off means to speak to them angrily because they have done something wrong.

temper noun
1 Your temper is how you are feeling. If you are in a good temper, you are happy and cheerful. If you are in a bad temper, you are cross and grumpy.
2 If you are in a temper, you are very angry. If you lose your temper, you suddenly become very angry.

temperature noun
1 The temperature of something is how hot or cold it is.
2 If you have a temperature, your body is hotter than usual because you are ill.

temple noun *plural* temples
a place where people go to pray and worship a god

temporary adjective
Something that is temporary only lasts for a short time.

tempt verb tempts, tempting, tempted
If something tempts you, it seems nice and you want it, but you think it would be wrong or dangerous.

ten noun *plural* tens
the number 10

tender adjective tenderer, tenderest
1 Someone who is tender is kind and loving.
2 Food that is tender is soft and easy to eat. *The meat was lovely and tender.*

tennis noun
a game in which players use a special racket to hit a ball backwards and forwards over a net

tense noun *plural* tenses
The different tenses of a verb are the different forms that you use to show whether you are talking about the past, present, or future. The past tense of *come* is *came.*

tent noun *plural* tents
A tent is a shelter made of cloth that is stretched over poles. You sleep in a tent when you go camping.

tentacle noun *plural* tentacles
The tentacles of a sea animal such as an octopus are the long parts that it can move about.

term noun *plural* terms
A school term is a time when you go to school and are not on holiday.

terrace noun *plural* terraces
a row of houses that are all joined together

terrible adjective
Something that is terrible is very bad.

terrify verb terrifies, terrifying, terrified
If something terrifies you, it makes you feel very frightened.

territory noun *plural* territories
Someone's territory is the land that they own or use.

terror noun
a feeling of very great fear

test noun *plural* tests
a set of questions that you have to answer to show what you have learned *I got all the words right in my spelling test.*

test verb tests, testing, tested
1 To test someone means to give them questions to answer to show what they have learned.
2 To test something means to use it so that you can find out whether it works. *Now it is time to test our new invention.*

text noun *plural* texts
a piece of writing

text verb texts, texting, texted
When you text someone, you send them a text message.

textbook noun *plural* textbooks
a book which gives you information about a subject

a
b
c
d
e
f
g
h
i
j
k
l
m
n
o
p
q
r
s
t
u
v
w
x
y
z

text message noun
plural **text messages**
a written message that you send to someone on a mobile phone.

texture noun *plural* **textures**
The texture of something is what it feels like when you touch it.

than conjunction, pronoun
compared with another person or thing *My brother is smaller than me.*

thank verb **thanks, thanking, thanked**
When you thank someone, you tell them that you are grateful for something they have given you or done for you. *I thanked my uncle and aunt for their present.*

that determiner, pronoun
plural **those**
the one there *That book is yours.*

thaw verb **thaws, thawing, thawed**
When something thaws, it melts and is no longer frozen.

the determiner
You use **the** in front of a noun when you are talking about that thing in particular *the tree, the bus, the dog.*

theatre noun *plural* **theatres**
a place where plays and shows are performed and people can go to watch them

their determiner
You use **their** when you are talking about something that belongs to one person that isn't, or more people that aren't, you. *Their coats are hanging up in the cloakroom.*

theirs pronoun
You use **theirs** when you want to say something belongs to one person, or more people, that aren't you. *Those coats are theirs.*

them pronoun
You use **them** when you're talking about two or more people. *I asked them to my party.*

theme noun *plural* **themes**
The theme of a book or film is the main idea that it is about.

then adverb
1 after that *I got up and then went to school.*
2 at that time *I was only five years old then.*

there adverb
in that place *You can sit there.*

therefore adverb
so *We haven't got very much money and therefore we can't go on holiday.*

thermometer noun
plural **thermometers**
something that you use for measuring temperature

thesaurus noun *plural* **thesauruses**
a book which gives you lists of words that have similar meanings

these determiner plural of **this**

they pronoun
You use **they** when you are talking about the people or things already mentioned. *Your mum and dad don't have a dog, do they?*

thick adjective **thicker, thickest**
1 Something that is thick is wide and not thin. *He cut himself a thick slice of cake.*
2 Thick clothes are made of heavy material.
3 A thick liquid is not very runny.
thickly adverb If you cut something thickly, you cut it so that it is wide and not thin.

thief noun *plural* **thieves**
someone who steals things

thigh noun *plural* **thighs**
Your thighs are the top parts of your legs.

thin adjective thinner, thinnest
1 Something that is thin is not very thick or wide.
2 Someone who is thin is not very fat.
3 A thin liquid is runny.

thing noun *plural* things
an object, or anything that is not a person, animal, or plant. *A pen is a thing you use to write with.*

think verb thinks, thinking, thought
1 When you think, you have thoughts and ideas in your mind. *Think carefully before you answer the question.*

2 If you think that something is true, you believe that it is true, but you do not know for sure. *I think we break up next Friday.*

third adjective
The third thing is the one that comes after the second.

third noun
One third of something is one of three equal parts that the thing is divided into. It can also be written as $\frac{1}{3}$.

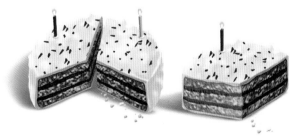

third person noun (in grammar)
When you use the third person, you use the words *he* or *she* to write about someone in a story.

thirsty adjective thirstier, thirstiest
If you are thirsty, you feel that you want to drink something.

thirteen noun
the number 13

thirty noun
the number 30

this determiner, pronoun *plural* these
the one here *This pencil is mine. This is the one that I want. These books are all very interesting.*

thistle noun *plural* thistles
a wild plant that has prickly leaves and purple flowers

thorn noun *plural* thorns
a sharp, prickly point that grows on some plants

those determiner plural of that

though adverb (rhymes with *go*)
although *It was very cold though it didn't snow.*

thought verb past tense of think
thought noun *plural* thoughts
an idea you think of

thoughtful adjective
1 If you look thoughtful, you look quiet, as if you are thinking about something.
2 If you are thoughtful, you are kind and think about what other people want.

a
b
c
d
e
f
g
h
i
j
k
l
m
n
o
p
q
r
s
t
u
v
w
x
y
z

A
B
C
D
E
F
G
H
I
J
K
L
M
N
O
P
Q
R
S
T
U
V
W
X
Y
Z

thousand noun *plural* thousands
the number 1000

thread noun *plural* threads
a long, thin piece of cotton that you use for sewing

thread verb threads, threading, threaded
When you thread a needle, you put a thread through it so that you can use it for sewing.

threaten verb threatens, threatening, threatened
To threaten someone means to say that you will do something nasty to them.

three noun *plural* threes
the number 3

three-dimensional adjective
A three-dimensional object is solid rather than flat. A cube is a three-dimensional shape.

threw verb past tense of throw

thrill noun *plural* thrills
If something gives you a thrill, it is very exciting and enjoyable.

throat noun *plural* throats
Your throat is the part at the back of your mouth where you swallow food and drink.

throb verb throbs, throbbing, throbbed
If a part of your body throbs, it hurts a lot. *My knee was throbbing and I could hardly walk.*

throne noun *plural* thrones
a special chair that a king or queen sits on

through preposition
(rhymes with *threw*)
from one side of something to the other
He climbed through the window.

throw verb throws, throwing, threw, thrown
1 When you throw something, you hold it in your hand and then push it away so that it flies through the air. *Throw the ball to me.*
2 When you throw something away, you get rid of it because you do not want it any more.

thud noun *plural* thuds
a dull banging sound

thumb noun *plural* thumbs
Your thumb is the short, thick finger at the side of your hand.

thump verb thumps, thumping, thumped
To thump someone means to hit them hard.

thunder noun
the loud, rumbling noise that you hear after a flash of lightning in a storm

Thursday noun *plural* Thursdays
the day after Wednesday

tick noun *plural* ticks
a small mark like this ✓ that shows that something is right

tick verb ticks, ticking, ticked
1 When you tick something, you put a tick next to it.
2 When a clock ticks, it makes a regular clicking sound.

ticket noun *plural* tickets
a piece of paper that you buy so that you can travel on a bus or train or get into a place such as a cinema or theatre

tickle verb tickles, tickling, tickled
When you tickle someone, you touch them lightly with your fingers to make them laugh.

tide noun *plural* tides
The tide is the regular movement of the sea towards the land and then away from the land.

tidy adjective tidier, tidiest
If a place is tidy, everything is in the right place and there is no mess.

tie verb ties, tying, tied
To tie something means to fasten it with a knot or a bow. *I tied my laces.*

tie noun *plural* ties
1 a strip of material that you wear round your neck, under the collar of a shirt
2 If there is a tie in a game, two people or teams have the same number of points. *The match ended in a tie.*

tiger noun *plural* tigers
A tiger is a large wild cat that lives in Asia. It has orange fur with black stripes. A female tiger is called a **tigress**.

tight adjective tighter, tightest
1 Tight clothes fit your body closely and are not loose.
2 A tight knot is tied very firmly and is difficult to undo.

tights noun
a piece of clothing that women and girls wear over their feet, legs, and bottom

tile noun *plural* tiles
Tiles are thin pieces of baked clay that people use to cover walls or floors.

till conjunction, preposition
until *Wait till I'm ready!*
till noun *plural* tills
a machine that people use in a shop to keep money in and add up how much customers have to pay

tilt verb tilts, tilting, tilted
To tilt something means to tip it up so that it slopes.

timber noun
wood that people use for making things

time noun *plural* times
1 Time is the thing that we measure in seconds, minutes, hours, days, weeks, months, and years. *What time is it?*
2 If it is time to do something, it should be done now. *It's time to leave.*
3 If you do something one or two times, you do it once or twice. *I've already called you three times!*

times preposition (in mathematics)
One number times another number is one number multiplied by another number. *2 times 4 equals 8.*

timetable noun *plural* timetables
a list of times when things will happen or buses or trains will leave

timid adjective
Someone who is timid is shy and not very brave. *'Who's there?' he said in a timid voice.* — James Riordan, *Retelling of Pinocchio*

a b c d e f g h i j k l m n o p q r s **t** u v w x y z

229

tin noun *plural* tins
1 a round metal container that food is sold in *I'll open a tin of beans for tea.*
2 a metal container for putting things in

tiny adjective tinier, tiniest
Something that is tiny is very small.

tip noun *plural* tips
1 The tip of something long and thin is the part right at the end of it.
2 If you give someone a tip, you give them a small amount of money to thank them for helping you.
3 A tip is a rubbish dump.

tip verb tips, tipping, tipped
When you tip something, you move it so that it is no longer straight. *Don't tip your chair back.*

tiptoe verb tiptoes, tiptoeing, tiptoed
When you tiptoe, you walk quietly on your toes.

tired adjective
1 If you are tired, you feel as if you need to sleep.
2 If you are tired of something, you are bored or fed up with it.

tissue noun *plural* tissues
1 Tissue paper is very thin, soft paper that you use for wrapping up fragile things to stop them breaking.
2 A tissue is a paper handkerchief.

title noun *plural* titles
1 The title of a book, film, picture, or piece of music is its name.
2 Someone's title is the word like *Dr, Mr,* and *Mrs* that is put in front of their name.

to preposition
When you go to a place, you go there. *We're going to Spain next week.*

toad noun *plural* toads
A toad is an animal that looks like a big frog. It has rough, dry skin and lives on land.

toadstool noun *plural* toadstools
a plant that looks like a mushroom but is poisonous to eat

toast noun
a slice of bread that has been cooked until it is crisp and brown

toboggan noun *plural* toboggans
a sledge that you use for sliding down slopes covered in snow

today noun, adverb
this day *I'm not very well today.*

toddler noun *plural* toddlers
a young child who is just beginning to walk

toe noun *plural* toes
Your toes are the parts of your body on the ends of your feet.

together adverb
1 When you join or put things together, you put them with each other. *I stuck two pieces of paper together.*
2 When people do something together, they do it at the same time as each other. *They all sang together.*

toilet noun *plural* toilets
a large bowl with a seat that you use when you need to empty waste from your body

told verb past tense of tell

tomato noun *plural* tomatoes
a soft, round, red fruit that you can eat raw in a salad or cook as a vegetable

tomorrow noun, adverb
the day after today *I'll see you tomorrow.*

ton noun *plural* tons
We can measure weight in tons. One ton is about 1,016 kilograms.

tongue noun *plural* tongues
(rhymes with *sung*)
Your tongue is the part inside your mouth that you can move about and use for speaking.

tonight noun, adverb
this evening or night *I'll phone you tonight.*

tonne noun *plural* tonnes
We can measure weight in tons. One tonne is 1000 kilograms.

too adverb
1 also *Can I come too?*
2 more than you need *Don't use too much salt.*

took verb past tense of take

tool noun *plural* tools
A tool is something that you use to help you to do a job. Hammers and saws are tools.

tooth noun *plural* teeth
1 Your teeth are the hard, white parts inside your mouth which you use for biting and chewing.
2 The teeth on a comb or saw are the sharp, pointed parts.

toothbrush noun
A long-handled brush that you use to clean your teeth. *I need a new toothbrush.*

top noun *plural* tops
1 The top of something is the highest part of it. *We climbed right to the top of the hill.*
2 The top on a bottle or jar is the lid.
3 A top is a piece of clothing that you wear on the top part of your body, over your chest and arms.

topic noun *plural* topics
a subject that you are writing or talking about

torch noun *plural* torches
an electric light that you can carry about with you

A
B
C
D
E
F
G
H
I
J
K
L
M
N
O
P
Q
R
S
T
U
V
W
X
Y
Z

tore, torn verb past tense of **tear** verb

tornado noun *plural* **tornadoes**
(say tor-**nay**-doh)
a very strong wind

tortoise noun *plural* **tortoises**
A tortoise is an animal that has four legs and a hard shell over its body. Tortoises move slowly and hide their head and legs inside their shell when they are in danger.

toss verb **tosses, tossing, tossed**
1 When you toss something, you throw it through the air. *She tossed her apple core into the bin.*
2 When you toss a coin, you throw it into the air to see which way it lands.

total noun
The total is the amount that you get when you have added everything up.
total adjective
complete *There was total silence in the hall.*

touch verb **touches, touching, touched**
1 When you touch something, you feel it with your hand.
2 When two things are touching, they are right next to each other, with no space between them.

tough adjective **tougher, toughest**
(say **tuff**)
1 Something that is tough is very strong. *The ropes are made of tough nylon.*
2 Someone who is tough is brave and strong.

tour noun *plural* **tours**
When you go on a tour, you visit a lot of different places.

tourist noun *plural* **tourists**
someone who is visiting a place on holiday

tournament noun
plural **tournaments**
a competition in which a lot of different people or teams play matches against each other until a winner is found

tow verb **tows, towing, towed**
(rhymes with *low*)
To tow something means to pull it along. *The car was towing a caravan.*

towards preposition
in the direction of *He walked towards the school.*

towel noun *plural* **towels**
a piece of cloth that you use for drying things that are wet

tower noun *plural* **towers**
a tall, narrow part of a building

town noun *plural* **towns**
A town is a place where a lot of people live close to each other. A town is smaller than a city.

toy noun *plural* **toys**
something that children can play with

trace verb traces, tracing, traced
1 When you trace a picture, you copy it using thin paper that you can see through.
2 To trace something means to find it by getting information and following clues.

track noun plural tracks
1 The tracks that a person or animal leaves are the marks that they leave on the ground as they walk.

2 a path
3 A railway track is a railway line.
4 A racing track is a piece of ground with lines marked on it so that people can use it for racing.

tractor noun plural tractors
a strong, heavy truck with large wheels that people drive on a farm and use for pulling farm machines

trade noun
When people do trade, they buy and sell things. *The shops do a lot of trade at Christmas.*

trademark noun plural trademarks
a picture or name that a company always puts on the things that it makes

tradition noun plural traditions
If something is a tradition, people have done it in the same way for a very long time. *Dressing up at Hallowe'en is a tradition.*

traffic noun
cars, buses, bicycles, lorries, and other things that travel on roads *It's dangerous to play on the road because of the traffic.*

tragedy noun plural tragedies
something very sad that happens, especially something in which people are hurt or killed

trail noun plural trails
1 a rough path across fields or through woods
2 the smells or marks that an animal leaves behind as it goes along *We were able to follow the animal's trail.*

trailer noun plural trailers
1 a truck that is pulled along behind a car or lorry and used for carrying things
2 a short part of a film that is shown to people to encourage them to watch it

train noun plural trains
something that carries passengers or goods on a railway

train verb trains, training, trained
1 To train a person or animal means to teach them how to do something. *The dog had been trained to sit up and beg for bits of food.*
2 When you train, you practise the skills you need to do a sport.

trainer noun plural trainers
1 A trainer is someone who trains people or animals.
2 Trainers are shoes that you wear for running or doing sport.

a
b
c
d
e
f
g
h
i
j
k
l
m
n
o
p
q
r
s
t
u
v
w
x
y
z

tram noun *plural* trams
a type of bus which runs along rails in the road

trampoline noun *plural* trampolines
a large piece of thick cloth that is joined to a metal frame and is used for jumping up and down on

transfer verb transfers, transferring, transferred
1 If you transfer something from one place to another, you move it. *I transferred some pencils from the tin into my pencil case.*
2 When you transfer to a new school, you start going there.

translate verb translates, translating, translated
If you translate something, you change it from one language into another.

transparent adjective
If something is transparent, you can see through it. *Glass is a transparent material.*

transport noun
anything that is used to take people, animals, or things from one place to another, for example, buses, trains, and lorries

trap noun *plural* traps
something that is used to catch a person or an animal *The police laid a trap to catch the robbers.*

trapdoor noun *plural* trapdoors
a door in the floor or ceiling which you can open to make people fall through

travel verb travels, travelling, travelled
When you travel, you go from one place to another. *They travelled right across America.*

tray noun *plural* trays
a flat piece of wood, metal, or plastic that you use for carrying cups, plates, and other things

tread verb treads, treading, trod, trodden
If you tread on something, you walk on it. *Mind you don't tread on that spider.*

treasure noun
gold, silver, jewels, and other valuable things

treat verb treats, treating, treated
1 The way in which you treat someone is the way you behave towards them. *Some people don't treat their animals very well.*
2 When doctors treat someone, they give them medicine or do things to them to make them better when they are ill.

treat noun *plural* treats
something special that you enjoy *We went to the cinema as a birthday treat.*

tree noun *plural* trees
a tall plant that has a thick trunk, branches, and leaves

tremble verb trembles, trembling, trembled
When you tremble, your body shakes because you are cold or frightened.

trespass verb trespasses, trespassing, trespassed
To trespass means to go onto someone else's land, without asking them if you can.

trial noun *plural* trials
1 When you give something a trial, you try it to see how well it works.

2 When there is a trial, a prisoner and witnesses are questioned in a court to decide whether the prisoner has done something wrong.

triangle noun *plural* triangles
a shape with three straight edges and three angles

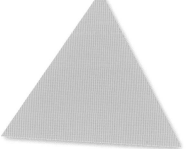

tribe noun *plural* tribes
a group of people who live together and are ruled by a chief

trick noun *plural* tricks
1 something that you do to cheat someone or make them look silly *I thought my friends were planning to play a trick on me.*
2 something clever that you have learned to do *Can you do any card tricks?*

trick verb tricks, tricking, tricked
To trick someone means to make them believe something that is not true.

trickle verb trickles, trickling, trickled
When water trickles, it moves very slowly.

tricycle noun *plural* tricycles
a bicycle with three wheels

tried verb past tense of try

trigger noun *plural* triggers
the part of a gun that you pull with your finger to fire it

trim verb trims, trimming, trimmed
To trim something means to cut it so that it looks neat and tidy.

trip verb trips, tripping, tripped
If you trip, you catch your foot on something and nearly fall over.

trip noun *plural* trips
a short journey

triumph noun *plural* triumphs
If something is a triumph, it is a great success.

trod, trodden verb past tense of tread

trolley noun *plural* trolleys
a large container on wheels that you can put things in and push along

troops noun
soldiers

trophy noun *plural* trophies
a cup that you can win

tropical adjective
A tropical place has a very hot, wet climate. *A lot of endangered animals live in tropical rainforests.*

trot verb trots, trotting, trotted
When a horse trots, it runs but does not gallop.

trouble noun *plural* troubles
1 If something causes trouble for you, it causes problems for you or upsets you.
2 If you are in trouble, you have a problem or someone is cross with you. *You'll be in trouble when dad sees this mess!*

trough noun *plural* troughs (say **troff**)
a long, narrow container that holds food or water for farm animals

trousers noun
a piece of clothing that you wear over your legs and bottom

trout noun *plural* trout
a fish that lives in rivers and lakes and can be cooked and eaten

a
b
c
d
e
f
g
h
i
j
k
l
m
n
o
p
q
r
s
t
u
v
w
x
y
z

A
B
C
D
E
F
G
H
I
J
K
L
M
N
O
P
Q
R
S
T
U
V
W
X
Y
Z

truant noun *plural* truants (say **troo**-ant)
To play truant means to stay away from school when you should be there.

truce noun *plural* truces
an agreement between two people to stop fighting or arguing for a while

truck noun *plural* trucks
a small lorry

trudge verb trudges, trudging, trudged
When you trudge along, you walk along slowly, with heavy steps.

true adjective truer, truest
Something that is true is real and not made up or pretended.

trumpet noun *plural* trumpets
A trumpet is a musical instrument made of brass. You blow into it and press down buttons to make different notes.

trunk noun *plural* trunks
1 The trunk on a tree is the thick stem that grows up out of the ground.
2 An elephant's trunk is its long nose.
3 A trunk is a large box that you use for carrying things on a journey.

trust verb trusts, trusting, trusted
If you trust someone, you believe that they are good and honest and will not hurt you or tell you lies.

truth noun
The truth is something that is true. *Is he telling the truth?*

truthful adjective
Someone who is truthful tells the truth.

try verb tries, trying, tried
1 If you try to do something, you make an effort to do it. *I tried to climb that tree, but I couldn't.*
2 If you try something, you do it or use it to see what it is like. *Have you ever tried ice skating?*

T-shirt noun *plural* T-shirts
A T-shirt is a piece of clothing that you wear on the top half of your body. It has a round neck and short sleeves.

tub noun *plural* tubs
a container *We bought a tub of ice cream.*

tube noun *plural* tubes
1 a long, thin container that you can squeeze a thick liquid out of
2 a long, round, hollow thing *The picture was rolled up in a tube.*

tuck verb tucks, tucking, tucked
If you tuck a piece of clothing in, you push the ends of it into another piece of clothing.

Tuesday noun *plural* Tuesdays
the day after Monday

tug verb tugs, tugging, tugged
When you tug something, you pull it hard.

tumble verb tumbles, tumbling, tumbled
To tumble means to fall. *He tumbled off the wall.*

tuna noun *plural* tuna
a large sea fish that you can eat

tune noun *plural* **tunes**
a group of musical notes which make a nice sound when they are played in order

tunnel noun *plural* **tunnels**
a long hole under the ground that you can walk or drive through

turban noun *plural* **turbans**
a long piece of material that you wear wrapped round your head

turkey noun *plural* **turkeys**
a large bird that is kept on farms for its meat

turn verb **turns, turning, turned**
1 When you turn round, you move round. *I turned round to see who was behind me.*
2 When you turn something, you move it round. *He turned the key in the lock.*
3 To turn means to become. *A lot of leaves turn red and orange in the autumn.*
4 To turn into something means to change and become that thing. *Tadpoles turn into frogs.*

turn noun *plural* **turns**
If it is your turn to do something, you are the person who should do it next.

turtle noun *plural* **turtles**
a sea animal that looks like a tortoise

tusk noun *plural* **tusks**
An elephant's tusks are its two very long, pointed teeth.

TV noun *plural* **TVs**
a television

twelve noun
the number 12

twenty noun
the number 20

twice adverb
If something happens twice, it happens two times.

twig noun *plural* **twigs**
a very small, thin branch on a tree

twin noun *plural* **twins**
Twins are two children who are born to the same mother at the same time.

twinkle verb **twinkles, twinkling, twinkled**
If something twinkles, it shines with little flashes of light.

twirl verb **twirls, twirling, twirled**
To twirl means to spin round and round.

twist verb **twists, twisting, twisted**
1 When you twist something, you turn it round. *She twisted the lid off the jar.*

2 When you twist things together, you turn them round each other so that they become fixed together.

two noun *plural* **twos**
the number 2

a
b
c
d
e
f
g
h
i
j
k
l
m
n
o
p
q
r
s
t
u
v
w
x
y
z

A B C D E F G H I J K L M N O P Q R S **T U** V W X Y Z

two-dimensional adjective
A two-dimensional shape is flat rather than solid. A square is a two-dimensional shape.

type noun plural types
A type is a kind or sort *What type of car have your parents got?*

type verb types, typing, typed
When you type, you write with a computer keyboard.

typical adjective
Something that is typical is normal and usual.

tyre noun plural tyres
a circle of rubber that goes round the outside of a wheel

Uu

ugly adjective uglier, ugliest
Something that is ugly is horrible to look at.

umbrella noun plural umbrellas
a round cover that you hold over your head to keep the rain off you

unable adjective
If you are unable to do something, you cannot do it. *The rocks were heavy and we were unable to move them.*

unbelievable adjective
If something is unbelievable, it is so strange that you cannot believe it.

uncertain adjective
If you are uncertain about something, you are not sure about it. *She was uncertain what to do next.*

uncle noun plural uncles
Your uncle is the brother of your mother or father, or your aunt's husband.

uncomfortable adjective
1 If you are uncomfortable, part of your body hurts or is not relaxed.
2 If a chair or bed is uncomfortable, it does not feel nice when you sit on it or lie on it.

unconscious adjective
(say un-**kon**-shuss)
When you are unconscious, you are in a very deep sleep and cannot understand what is happening around you. *If you bang your head, sometimes you might be unconscious for a few minutes.*

under preposition
1 below *The cat is under the table.*
2 less than *You can't drive if you are under 17.*

underground adjective
Something that is underground is under the ground. *They escaped and hid in an underground cave.*

underground noun
An underground is a railway that runs through tunnels under the ground. *You can travel around London on the Underground.*

undergrowth noun
bushes and plants that grow thickly together under trees

underline verb underlines, underlining, underlined
When you underline a word, you draw a straight line underneath it.

underneath preposition
under *The cat was sitting underneath the table.*

understand verb understands, understanding, understood
If you can understand something, you know what it means or how it works. *I don't understand what you're saying.*

undo verb undoes, undoing, undid, undone
1 When you undo something, you open it so that it is no longer tied or fastened. *I can't undo my laces.*

2 When you undo a change you have made on a computer, you change it back.

undress verb undresses, undressing, undressed
When you undress, you take your clothes off.

unemployed adjective
Someone who is unemployed does not have a job.

uneven adjective
Something that is uneven is not smooth or flat. *The road was quite uneven and bumpy.*

unexpected adjective
If something is unexpected, it is surprising because you did not expect it to happen.

unfair adjective
If something is unfair, it is not fair or right because it treats some people badly.

unfairly adverb
If something is done unfairly, it is done in a way that is not fair or right. *She was treated unfairly.*

unfortunate adjective
If something is unfortunate, it happens because of bad luck.

ungrateful adjective
If you are ungrateful, you do not thank someone when they have helped you or given you something.

unhappy adjective unhappier, unhappiest
If you are unhappy, you are sad and not happy.

unhealthy adjective
1 If you are unhealthy, you are not strong and healthy.
2 Things that are unhealthy are not good for you and can make you ill.

a
b
c
d
e
f
g
h
i
j
k
l
m
n
o
p
q
r
s
t
u
v
w
x
y
z

A
B
C
D
E
F
G
H
I
J
K
L
M
N
O
P
Q
R
S
T
U
V
W
X
Y
Z

unicorn noun *plural* unicorns
(say **yoo**-ni-corn)
an animal in stories that has one long, straight horn growing from the front of its head

uniform noun *plural* uniforms
a special set of clothes that everyone in the same school, job, or club wears

unique adjective (say yoo-**neek**)
If something is unique, there is nothing else like it. *This picture is unique.*

unit noun *plural* units
1 (in mathematics) Units are ones. When you add or subtract big numbers, you work with hundreds, tens, and units.
2 A unit is something that you use for measuring or counting things. Centimetres and metres are units of length.

unite verb unites, uniting, united
When people unite, they join together and work together.

universe noun
everything in space, including the earth, the sun, and all the stars and planets

university noun *plural* universities
a place where you can go to study after you have left school

unkind adjective unkinder, unkindest
Someone who is unkind is nasty or cruel to another person.

unleaded adjective
Unleaded petrol does not have any lead in it.

unless conjunction
if something does not happen *I won't go unless you come with me.*

unlock verb unlocks, unlocking, unlocked
When you unlock something, you open its lock with a key. *We need a key to unlock the door.*

unlucky adjective unluckier, unluckiest
If you are unlucky, you have bad luck. *We were very unlucky to lose that game.*

unnecessary adjective
If something is unnecessary, you do not need it.

unpack verb unpacks, unpacking, unpacked
When you unpack things, you take them out of a bag, box, or suitcase.

unpleasant adjective
Something that is unpleasant is nasty or horrible. *The meat had a rather unpleasant taste.*

unpopular adjective
If something is unpopular, not many people like it. If someone is unpopular, not many people like them.

unsafe adjective
Something that is unsafe is dangerous and not safe.

unselfish adjective
If you are unselfish, you think about other people and are not selfish.

untidy adjective untidier, untidiest
A place that is untidy is messy and not tidy.

untie verb unties, untying, untied
When you untie a piece of rope or string, you undo a knot in it.

until conjunction, preposition
up to a certain time *I stayed up until midnight.*

untrue adjective
Something that is untrue is not true or correct.

unusual adjective
Something that is unusual is strange and not normal or usual.

up adverb preposition
towards a higher place *She ran up the hill.*

upper case adjective
Upper case letters are capital letters.

ABCDE
ABCDE

upright adjective
Something that is upright is standing up straight.

uproar noun
If there is an uproar, a lot of people shout and make a noise.

upset adjective
If you are upset, you are sad or crying.

upset verb upsets, upsetting, upset
1 To upset someone means to make them feel sad and disappointed.
2 To upset something means to knock it over. *Someone had upset a bottle of water.*

upside-down adjective
If something is upside-down, it is turned over so that the bottom is at the top.

upwards adverb
When something goes upwards, it goes towards a higher place. *The rocket zoomed upwards.*

urgent adjective
If something is urgent, you have to do it immediately.

us pronoun
You use **us** when you are talking about yourself and at least one more other person. *Would you like to come to the shops with us?*

use verb uses, using, used
1 When you use something, you do a job with it. *We used a bucket to carry water in.*
2 If you used to do something, you did it in the past but you do not do it now. *I used to go to swimming lessons.*

use noun plural uses
If something has a use, you can use it to make something or do a job. *I'm sure we can find a use for these old wheels.*

useful adjective
Something that is useful is good and helpful.

useless adjective
If something is useless, you cannot use it.

user-friendly adjective
A machine that is user-friendly is easy to understand and use.

usual adjective
Something that is usual is normal and happens quite often. *I got up at my usual time of eight o'clock.*
usually adverb If you usually do something, you do it normally and quite often. *She usually goes to bed after ten o'clock.*

a
b
c
d
e
f
g
h
i
j
k
l
m
n
o
p
q
r
s
t
u
v
w
x
y
z

A B C D E F G H I J K L M N O P Q R S T U **V** W X Y Z

Vv

vacant adjective
A place that is vacant has no one in it.

vaccination noun *plural* vaccinations
(say vak-si-**nay**-shun)
an injection that stops you getting an illness

vacuum cleaner noun
plural **vacuum cleaners**
a machine that cleans floors by sucking up dust and dirt

vague adjective vaguer, vaguest
Something that is vague is not clear or certain.

vain adjective vainer, vainest
1 If you are vain, you think too much about how nice you look and how clever you are.
2 If you try in vain to do something, you try to do it but do not manage it.

valley noun *plural* valleys
low land between two hills

valuable adjective
Something that is valuable is worth a lot of money, or is very useful. *Some of these paintings are very valuable.*

value noun
The value of something is how much money it is worth, or how important or useful it is.

van noun *plural* vans
a type of car with a large, covered part at the back for carrying things in

vandal noun *plural* vandals
someone who deliberately breaks things that belong to other people

vanilla noun
something that is added to ice cream and other sweet food to make it taste nice

vanish verb vanishes, vanishing, vanished
If something vanishes, it disappears.

vapour noun *plural* vapours
A vapour is a mass of tiny drops of liquid in the air. Steam is a vapour.

variety noun *plural* varieties
1 A variety of things is a lot of different things. *We have a variety of colours to choose from.*
2 One variety of something is one type. *They sell over twenty varieties of ice cream.*

various adjective
Various things means a lot of different things. *There were various things to eat.*

vase noun *plural* vases
a pot that you put flowers in

vast adjective
Something that is vast is very big.

vegetable noun plural vegetables
A vegetable is a part of a plant that we can eat. Potatoes, carrots, and beans are vegetables.

vegetarian noun plural vegetarians
a person who does not eat meat

vehicle noun plural vehicles
(say **vee**-ik-al)
A vehicle is anything that can travel on land and take people or things from one place to another. Cars, vans, buses, trains, and lorries are vehicles.

veil noun plural veils
a piece of thin material that some women or girls wear over their face or head

vein noun plural veins (say **vain**)
Your veins are the narrow tubes inside your body that carry blood to your heart.

velvet noun
a type of thick, soft cloth

verb noun plural verbs (in grammar)
A verb is a word that describes what someone or something is doing. Words like *eat* and *bring* are verbs.

verdict noun plural verdicts
When the jury in a court of law reach a verdict, they decide whether someone is guilty or not guilty.

verse noun plural verses
1 One verse of a song or poem is one part of it that is not the chorus.
2 Verse is poetry.

version noun plural versions
One version of something is one form of it, which is slightly different from all the other forms. *I'm worried that I may have lost the latest version of my story.*

vertical adjective
Something that is vertical is standing or pointing straight up.

very adverb
extremely *That was a very silly thing to do!*

vessel noun plural vessels
a ship or boat

vest noun plural vests
a piece of clothing that you wear on the top half of the body under your other clothes

vet noun plural vets
a doctor for animals

via preposition
When you go via a place, you go through that place to get somewhere else.

vibrate verb vibrates, vibrating, vibrated
When something vibrates, it shakes. *The whole house vibrates when a lorry goes past.*

vicious adjective (say **vish**-uss)
Someone who is vicious is violent and cruel. *He wasn't a vicious dog, he was just scared.*

victim noun plural victims
someone who has been hurt, robbed, or killed *We must help the victims of this terrible earthquake.*

victory noun plural victories
A victory is when you win a game or battle.

video verb videos, videoing, videoed
When you video a television programme, you record it on a video so that you can watch it.

a
b
c
d
e
f
g
h
i
j
k
l
m
n
o
p
q
r
s
t
u
v
w
x
y
z

A
B
C
D
E
F
G
H
I
J
K
L
M
N
O
P
Q
R
S
T
U
V
W
X
Y
Z

view noun *plural* views

The view from a place is everything that you can see from that place. *We had a beautiful view of the sea from our window.*

village noun *plural* villages

A village is a small group of houses and other buildings in the country. A village is smaller than a town.

vinegar noun

a sour liquid which you use in cooking to give a sharp, sour taste to food

violin noun *plural* violins

A violin is a musical instrument made of wood with strings across it. You hold a violin under your chin and play it by pulling a bow across the strings.

virtual adjective

A virtual place is one that you can look at on a computer screen. You feel as if you are really in the place because you can use the controls to move around inside it.

virus noun *plural* viruses

a tiny living thing that can make you ill if it gets into your body

visible adjective

If something is visible, you can see it. *Stars are only visible at night.*

vision noun

Your vision is how well you can see things. *Glasses will improve your vision.*

visit verb visits, visiting, visited

When you visit a person, you go to see them. When you visit a place, you go there to see what it is like.

vital adjective

Something that is vital is very important.

vitamin noun *plural* vitamins

A vitamin is something that is found in your food. Your body needs vitamins to stay strong and healthy. *Oranges are full of vitamin C.*

vivid adjective

1 Vivid colours are very bright.
2 A vivid dream or memory is so clear that it seems real.

vocabulary noun

all the words that someone knows and uses *You must try to improve your vocabulary as you get older.*

voice noun *plural* voices

Your voice is the sound you make with your mouth when you are speaking or singing.

volcano noun *plural* volcanoes

a mountain or other place on the earth's surface from which hot, liquid rock sometimes bursts from inside the earth

volume noun *plural* volumes

1 The volume of something is how much space it takes up. *We measured the volume of liquid in the bottle.*
2 The volume of a sound is how loud it is. *Please could you turn down the volume on your radio?*
3 one book that is part of a set of books *I have read all three volumes of this story.*

voluntary adjective

If something is voluntary, you can choose to do it if you want, but you do not have to do it.

volunteer verb volunteers, volunteering, volunteered
If you volunteer to do a job, you offer to do it.

volunteer noun plural volunteers
someone who offers to do a job

vote verb votes, voting, voted
When you vote, you say which person or thing you choose.

voucher noun plural vouchers
a piece of printed paper you can use instead of money to pay for something

vowel noun plural vowels
Vowels are the letters, a, e, i, o, u, and sometimes y. All the other letters of the alphabet are consonants.

voyage noun plural voyages
a long journey in a boat or spacecraft

vulture noun plural vultures
a large bird that eats dead animals

Ww

wade verb wades, wading, waded
When you wade through water, you walk through it.

wag verb wags, wagging, wagged
When a dog wags its tail, it moves it quickly from side to side because it is happy or excited.

wagon noun plural wagons
a cart with four wheels that is pulled by horses

wail verb wails, wailing, wailed
If you wail, you give a long, sad cry.

waist noun plural waists
Your waist is the narrow part in the middle of your body.

wait verb waits, waiting, waited
If you wait, you stay in a place until someone comes or until something happens.

wake verb wakes, waking, woke, woken
When you wake up, you stop sleeping. *I woke up at six o'clock.*

walk verb walks, walking, walked
When you walk, you move along on your feet. *I walked down the road to my friend's house.*

a b c d e f g h i j k l m n o p q r s t u v w x y z

A
B
C
D
E
F
G
H
I
J
K
L
M
N
O
P
Q
R
S
T
U
V
W
X
Y
Z

walk noun *plural* walks
When you go for a walk, you walk somewhere.

wall noun *plural* walls
1 The walls of a building are the parts that hold up the roof and separate the building into different rooms.
2 A wall is something built from bricks or stone around a garden or field.

wallet noun *plural* wallets
a small, flat, case that you carry money in

wallpaper noun
colourful paper that you stick onto the walls of a room to make it look nice

wand noun *plural* wands
a stick that you use for casting magic spells or doing magic tricks

wander verb wanders, wandering, wandered
When you wander about, you walk about in no particular direction.

want verb wants, wanting, wanted
If you want something, you would like to have it or do it. *Do you want a drink?*

war noun *plural* wars
When there is a war, two countries fight against each other.

wardrobe noun wardrobes
a cupboard where you hang clothes

warm adjective warmer, warmest
Something that is warm is quite hot. *It was a warm, sunny day.*

warn verb warns, warning, warned
If you warn someone about a danger, you tell them about it. *'Don't get too excited or you'll fall out of the tree,' I warned.* — Jeremy Strong, *The Hundred Mile An Hour Dog*

wary adjective warier, wariest
If you are wary of something, you are slightly nervous or frightened of it.

wash verb washes, washing, washed
1 When you wash something, you clean it with water.
2 When you wash up, you wash the plates, knives, and forks at the end of a meal.

washing noun
clothes that need to be washed or are being washed

washing machine noun
plural washing machines
a machine for washing clothes

wasp noun *plural* wasps (say **wosp**)
A wasp is an insect with black and yellow stripes on its body. Wasps can sting you.

waste noun
something that is left over and cannot be used *The factory used to pour all the waste substances into the river.*

waste verb wastes, wasting, wasted
If you waste something, you use more of it than you really need to.

watch verb watches, watching, watched
When you watch something, you look at it. *Mum, watch me!*

watch noun *plural* watches
a small clock that you wear on your wrist

water noun
Water is the clear liquid that is in rivers and seas. All living things need water to live.

water verb waters, watering, watered
1 When you water a plant, you pour water onto it to help it to grow.
2 When your eyes water, tears come into them. *The smoke made my eyes water.*

waterfall noun *plural* waterfalls
part of a river where the water falls down over rocks

waterproof adjective
Something that is waterproof is made of material that does not let water through. *Bring a waterproof coat in case it rains.*

watertight adjective
Something that is watertight is closed so tightly that no water can get through.

wave verb waves, waving, waved
1 When you wave, you lift up your hand and move it from side to side.
2 When something waves, it moves backwards and forwards or from side to side. *The flags were waving in the wind.*

wave noun *plural* waves
Waves in the sea are the parts that move up and down across the top of it.

wax noun
the substance that candles are made from

way noun *plural* ways
1 The way to a place is the roads or paths you follow to get there.
2 The way you do something is how you do it. *What's the best way to cook potatoes?*

we pronoun
You use **we** when you're talking about yourself and one or more people. *We are all going to my granny's house for tea.*

weak adjective weaker, weakest
1 Someone who is weak is not very strong.
2 Something that is weak will break easily.
3 A weak drink has a lot of water in it and so does not have a very strong taste.

wealthy adjective wealthier, wealthiest
Someone who is wealthy is rich.

weapon noun *plural* weapons
A weapon is something that a person can use to hurt or kill someone. Knives and guns are weapons.

wear verb wears, wearing, wore, worn
(rhymes with *air*)
1 When you wear clothes, you have them on your body.
2 When something wears out, it becomes so old that you cannot use it any more.

weary adjective wearier, weariest
(say **weer**-ee)
If you feel weary, you feel very tired.

a
b
c
d
e
f
g
h
i
j
k
l
m
n
o
p
q
r
s
t
u
v
w
x
y
z

A
B
C
D
E
F
G
H
I
J
K
L
M
N
O
P
Q
R
S
T
U
V
W
X
Y
Z

weather noun

The weather is what it is like outside, for example whether the sun is shining, or it is rainy, or windy.

weave verb weaves, weaving, wove, woven

To weave cloth means to make it from threads.

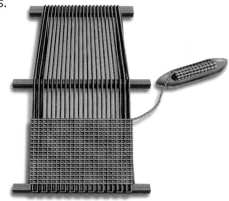

web noun plural webs

1 A web is a thin net that a spider spins to trap insects.
2 (in ICT) The web is the World Wide Web, where information is kept on computers all over the world and people can use it by using the Internet.

webbed adjective

Animals with webbed feet have skin between the toes of their feet.

webcam noun plural webcams

a camera that films things that are happening and broadcasts them live over the Internet

website noun plural websites

a place on the Internet where you can find information about something

wedding noun plural weddings

the time when a man and woman get married

Wednesday noun plural Wednesdays

the day after Tuesday

weed noun plural weeds

Weeds are wild plants that grow in a garden or field when you do not want them to.

week noun plural weeks

a period of seven days *I'll see you next week.*

weekend noun plural weekends

The weekend is Saturday and Sunday.

weep verb weeps, weeping, wept

When you weep, you cry.

weigh verb weighs, weighing, weighed (say **way**)

1 When you weigh something, you use a machine to find out how heavy it is.
2 The amount that something weighs is how heavy it is. *How much do you weigh?*

weight noun plural weights (say **wait**)

1 The weight of something is how heavy it is. *We measured the weight of each child in the class.*
2 Weights are pieces of metal that you use for weighing things.
3 Weights are heavy pieces of metal that people lift to make their bodies stronger.

weird adjective weirder, weirdest (say **weerd**)

Something that is weird is very strange.

welcome verb welcomes, welcoming, welcomed

If you welcome someone, you show that you are pleased when they arrive.

well noun plural wells
a deep hole in the ground from which you can get water or oil

well adverb better, best
1 If you do something well, you do it in a good or successful way. *I can play the piano quite well now.*
2 If you do something well, you do it a lot. *Shake the bottle well before you open it.*
as well also *Can I come as well?*

well adjective
If you are well, you are healthy and not ill. *I hope you are well.*

went verb past tense of go

wept verb past tense of weep

west noun
West is the direction where the sun sets in the evening. W stands for west on a compass.

wet adjective wetter, wettest
1 Something that is wet is covered or soaked in water.
2 When the weather is wet, it rains. *We had to stay in because it was wet outside.*

whale noun plural whales
A whale is a very large sea animal. Whales are mammals and breathe air, but they live in the sea like fish.

what adjective, pronoun
Use this word when you are asking about something. *What is your name?*

wheat noun
Wheat is a plant that farmers grow. It is used to make flour.

wheel noun plural wheels
Wheels are the round objects that cars, buses, bicycles, and trains go along on.

wheelbarrow noun
plural wheelbarrows
a small cart that you push along and use for carrying things

wheelchair noun plural wheelchairs
a chair on wheels for a person who cannot walk very well

when adverb, conjunction
Use this word when you are talking about the time that something happens. *When will the others be here?*

where adverb, conjunction
Use this word when you are talking about the place that something happens. *Where do you live?*

whether conjunction
if *The teacher asked whether I had finished my work.*

which determiner, pronoun
Use this word when you are choosing one thing or talking about one particular thing. *Which dress do you like best?*

while conjunction
during the time that something else is happening *I'll lay the table while you make the tea.*

whimper verb whimpers, whimpering, whimpered
To whimper means to cry softly because you are frightened or hurt. *The puppy whimpered in his basket because he wanted to be in the room with the children.*

a
b
c
d
e
f
g
h
i
j
k
l
m
n
o
p
q
r
s
t
u
v
w
x
y
z

whine verb whines, whining, whined
1 To whine means to make a long, high, sad sound.
2 If you whine about something, you complain about it.

whip noun *plural* whips
a long piece of rope or leather that is used for hitting people or animals

whip verb whips, whipping, whipped
1 To whip a person or animal means to hit them with a whip.
2 When you whip cream, you stir it quickly until it goes thick.

whirl verb whirls, whirling, whirled
To whirl round means to turn round and round very fast.

whirlpool noun *plural* whirlpools
a place in a river or sea where the water spins round and round very quickly and pulls things down with it

whirlwind noun *plural* whirlwinds
a strong wind that spins round and round very quickly as it moves along

whirr verb whirrs, whirring, whirred
When a machine whirrs, it makes a gentle humming sound.

whisk verb whisks, whisking, whisked
When you whisk eggs or cream, you stir them round and round very fast.

whisker noun *plural* whiskers
An animal's whiskers are the long, stiff hairs near its mouth.

whisper verb whispers, whispering, whispered
When you whisper, you speak very quietly.

whistle verb whistles, whistling, whistled
When you whistle, you make a high sound by blowing air through your lips.

whistle noun *plural* whistles
something that you can blow into to make a loud, high sound

white adjective whiter, whitest
1 Something that is white is the colour of snow.

2 Someone who is white has a skin that is naturally pale in colour.
3 White bread is made with just the white part of the wheat grain, not the whole grain.

whiteboard noun *plural* whiteboards
a large board with a smooth white surface that you can write on with special pens

who pronoun
which person *Who broke my mug?*

whole adjective
1 A whole thing is all of it, with nothing left out.
2 in one piece *The bird swallowed the fish whole.*

wholemeal adjective
Wholemeal bread is brown bread.

whose adjective, pronoun
belonging to which person *Whose coat is this?*

why adverb
Use this word when you are talking about the reason that something happens. *Why are you late?*

wicked adjective
Someone who is wicked is very bad or cruel.

wide adjective wider, widest
Something that is wide measures a lot from one side to the other. *We had to cross a wide river.*

widow noun *plural* widows
a woman whose husband has died

widower noun *plural* widowers
a man whose wife has died

width noun *plural* widths
The width of something is how wide it is.

wife noun *plural* wives
A man's wife is the woman he is married to.

wig noun *plural* wigs
false hair that some people wear on their head

wild adjective wilder, wildest
1 Wild animals and plants live or grow in a natural way and are not looked after by people.
2 Wild behaviour is rough and not calm.

wildlife noun
wild animals

will verb would
If you will do something, you are going to do it in the future. *I will be there at ten o'clock.*

will noun *plural* wills
something that a person writes down to tell other people what they want to happen to their things after they have died

willing adjective
If you are willing to do something, you are happy to do it. *We are all willing to help.*

win verb wins, winning, won
When you win a game, competition, or battle, you beat the other people or teams.

wind noun *plural* winds
(rhymes with *tinned*)
Wind is air that moves over the earth. *Everything was blowing about in the wind.*

wind verb winds, winding, wound
(rhymes with *find*)
1 To wind something round means to twist or turn it round. *She wound her scarf round her neck.*
2 If a road or river winds, it has a lot of bends in it.
3 When you wind up a clock or clockwork toy, you turn a key so that it will work.

windmill noun *plural* windmills
a building with large sails that move in the wind and use the power of the wind to make a machine work

window noun *plural* windows
1 an opening in a wall that is filled with glass to let the light in *We had to climb in through the window.*
2 (in ICT) one area of a computer screen where you can see information or a document

windscreen noun *plural* windscreens
the big window at the front of a car

a
b
c
d
e
f
g
h
i
j
k
l
m
n
o
p
q
r
s
t
u
v
w
x
y
z

wind turbine noun
plural **wind turbines**
a tall thin building that has large sails which move in the wind to produce electricity.

windy adjective windier, windiest
When the weather is windy, there is a strong wind.

wine noun *plural* wines
a drink that is made from grapes

wing noun *plural* wings
1 A bird's wings are the parts that it moves up and down when it is flying.
2 The wings on an aeroplane are the parts that stick out on each side and help the aeroplane to fly smoothly.

wink verb winks, winking, winked
When you wink, you close one eye.

winner noun *plural* winners
The winner of a game or competition is the person or team that wins.

winter noun *plural* winters
the time of the year when the weather is cold and it gets dark early in the evenings

wipe verb wipes, wiping, wiped
When you wipe something, you rub it gently to clean it.

wire noun *plural* wires
A wire is a long, thin strip of metal. Electricity goes along wires, and wires are also used to hold things in place.

wireless adjective
Something that is wireless can send and receive signals without using wires. *You can get a wireless Internet connection for your computer.*

wise adjective wiser, wisest
Someone who is wise understands a lot of things and knows the most sensible thing to do.

wish verb wishes, wishing, wished
If you wish that something would happen, you say that you would really like it to happen. *I wish I had lots of money.*

wish noun *plural* wishes
When you make a wish, you say what you would like to happen.

witch noun *plural* witches
a woman in stories who uses magic

with preposition
1 If one thing is with another thing, the two things are together. *We had apple pie with cream.*
2 using *You can cut paper with scissors.*

wither verb withers, withering, withered
If a plant withers, it becomes dry and dies.

within preposition
inside *You must stay within the school grounds.*

without preposition
not having *The family was left without any money.*

witness noun *plural* witnesses
someone who sees a crime or an accident happen

wizard noun *plural* wizards
a man in stories who uses magic

wobble verb wobbles, wobbling, wobbled
To wobble means to move and shake about. *The ladder began to wobble.*

woke, woken verb past tense of wake

wolf noun *plural* wolves
a wild animal that is like a large, grey dog

woman noun *plural* women
a grown-up female person

won verb past tense of win

wonder noun
When you have a feeling of wonder, you feel amazed and very glad.

wonder verb wonders, wondering, wondered
If you wonder about something, you ask yourself about it. *I wonder who wrote that letter?*

wonderful adjective
Something that is wonderful is amazing and fantastic.

won't verb
will not *I won't put up with this bad behaviour!*

wood noun *plural* woods
1 Wood is the hard material that trees are made of. You can burn wood as fuel or use it for making things.

2 A wood is an area of land where a lot of trees grow. *Don't go into the woods on your own.*

wool noun
the thick, soft hair that sheep have on their bodies

word noun *plural* words
1 a group of sounds or letters that mean something
2 If you give your word, you promise.

word class noun *plural* word classes
(in grammar)
A word class is a name that we give to different types of words. Adjectives, nouns, and verbs are different word classes.

word processor noun
plural word processors
A word processor is a computer program that you use when you want to write something.

wore verb past tense of wear

a
b
c
d
e
f
g
h
i
j
k
l
m
n
o
p
q
r
s
t
u
v
w
x
y
z

work noun
a job that you have to do *Please get on with your work quietly.*

work verb works, working, worked
1 When you work, you do a job or do something useful.
2 If a machine works, it does what it is meant to do. *This light doesn't work.*
3 When you work out the answer to a question, you find the answer.

world noun
The world is all the countries and people on the earth.

World Wide Web noun
The World Wide Web is the system for keeping information on computers all over the world so that people can use it by using the Internet.

worm noun *plural* worms
a long, thin animal with no legs that lives in the soil

worn verb past tense of wear

worry verb worries, worrying, worried
When you worry, you feel upset and nervous because you think something bad might happen.

worse adjective
1 If one thing is worse than another, it is less good. *My first painting was bad, and my second one was even worse!*
2 When you feel worse, you feel more ill than before.

worship verb worships, worshipping, worshipped
To worship a god means to show your love and respect.

worst adjective
The worst person or thing is the one that is worse than any other. *I'm the worst swimmer in my class.*

worth adjective
1 If something is worth an amount of money, you could sell it for that amount of money. *How much are these old coins worth?*
2 If something is worth doing or having, it is good or useful. *This film is well worth seeing.*

would verb *see* will verb

wound noun *plural* wounds
(rhymes with *spooned*)
a cut on your body

wound verb wounds, wounding, wounded (rhymes with *spooned*)
To wound someone means to hurt them.

wound verb past tense of wind verb
(rhymes with *round*)

woven verb past tense of weave

wrap verb wraps, wrapping, wrapped
When you wrap something, you put cloth or paper around it. *I forgot to wrap your present.*

wreath noun *plural* wreaths
a circle of flowers or leaves twisted together

wreck verb wrecks, wrecking, wrecked
To wreck something means to break it or destroy it completely.

wreck noun *plural* wrecks
a car, ship, or aeroplane that has been damaged in an accident

wrestle verb wrestles, wrestling, wrestled
When people wrestle, they fight with each other by holding each other and trying to force each other to the ground.

wriggle verb wriggles, wriggling, wriggled
When you wriggle, you twist and turn with your body.

wrinkle noun plural wrinkles
Wrinkles are small lines in your skin that often appear as you get older.

wrist noun plural wrists
Your wrist is the thin part of your arm where it is joined to your hand.

write verb writes, writing, wrote, written
When you write, you put letters and words onto paper so that people can read them.

writing noun
1 A piece of writing is something that you have written.
2 Your writing is the way you write.

wrong adjective
1 Something that is wrong is not right or correct. *He gave the wrong answer.*
2 Something that is wrong is bad. *Stealing is wrong.*

wrote verb past tense of write

Xx

X-ray noun plural X-rays
a photograph that shows the bones and other things inside your body so that doctors can see if there is anything wrong

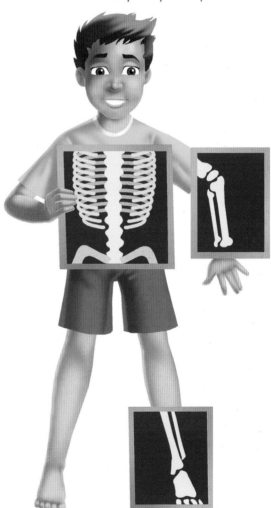

xylophone noun plural xylophones
(say **zye**-lo-fone)
a musical instrument with a row of wooden or metal bars that you hit with small hammers

a b c d e f g h i j k l m n o p q r s t u v **w** **x** y z

255

A
B
C
D
E
F
G
H
I
J
K
L
M
N
O
P
Q
R
S
T
U
V
W
X
Y
Z

Yy

yacht noun *plural* **yachts** (say **yot**)
a boat with sails that people use for racing or for pleasure

yard noun *plural* **yards**
1 We can measure length in yards. One yard is just under one metre.
2 a piece of ground that is next to a building and has a wall round it

yawn verb **yawns, yawning, yawned**
When you yawn, you open your mouth and breathe in deeply because you are tired.

year noun *plural* **years**
a period of twelve months, or three hundred and sixty-five days

yell verb **yells, yelling, yelled**
If you yell, you shout very loudly.

yellow adjective
Something that is yellow is the colour of a lemon.

yelp verb **yelps, yelping, yelped**
If an animal yelps, it gives a cry because it is in pain.

yes adverb
You use yes to agree or accept something or as an answer meaning 'I am here'.

yesterday noun, adverb
the day before today

yet adverb, preposition
1 until now *He hasn't arrived yet.*
2 If you do not want to do something yet, you do not want to do it until later.
3 but *It was the middle of winter, yet it was quite warm.*

yogurt noun
a thick liquid that is made from milk and has a slightly sour taste

yolk noun *plural* **yolks** (rhymes with *joke*)
The yolk of an egg is the yellow part inside it.

you pronoun
The person or people that you are talking to and nobody else. *Can I ask you a question? Would you like a cup of tea?*

young adjective **younger, youngest**
Someone who is young is not very old.

your determiner
belonging to you *Can you take your books away? I've told your mum that you don't have to do your homework tonight.*

yourself pronoun **yourselves**
The person that you are talking to and nobody else. *Would you like to try making pizza yourself?*

youth noun *plural* **youths**
1 a youth is a boy or young man
2 Your youth is the time in your life when you are young.

yo-yo noun *plural* **yo-yos**
a toy that spins round on a piece of string

Zz

zap *verb* zaps, zapping, zapped
When you zap between channels on the television, you keep changing channels.

zebra *noun* *plural* zebras
an animal that looks like a horse and has black and white stripes on its body

zebra crossing *noun*
plural zebra crossings
a place where there are black and white stripes across a road to show that cars must stop to let people cross the road

zero *noun* *plural* zeros
the number 0

zigzag *noun* *plural* zigzags
a line with a lot of sudden, sharp turns in it like this

zip, zipper *noun* *plural* zips, zippers
A zip joins two pieces of cloth. It has two lines of teeth that come together and grip each other when you close it.

zone *noun* *plural* zones
an area of land that has a special use

zoo *noun* *plural* zoos
a place where different kinds of wild animals are kept so that people can go and see them

zoom *verb* zooms, zooming, zoomed
To zoom means to move along very quickly. *Harry put on a burst of speed and zoomed towards the other end of the pitch.* — J. K. Rowling, *Harry Potter and the Chamber of Secrets*

a
b
c
d
e
f
g
h
i
j
k
l
m
n
o
p
q
r
s
t
u
v
w
x
y
z

Use this guide to help check your punctuation:

punctuation mark		when it's used	example
	full stop	at the end of a statement	It's raining today.
	question mark	at the end of a question	What's your favourite colour?
	exclamation mark	at the end of an exclamation	I don't believe it!
	comma	to separate items in a list	Yesterday, when I went shopping, I bought flour, eggs, butter, and sugar.
	apostrophe	to show that some letters are missing	I can't. He won't. They'll be here. It's time.
		to show ownership of something	John's coat. Anya's watch. The boys' books. The girls' pens.
	speech marks	to show the words someone says	'What's the time?' asked Raj. Tara replied, 'It's almost time to go home.' "Thank you for inviting me today," said Raj. Tara replied, "You are welcome."

All the words in a sentence tell you different information. The kinds of words are grouped together into word classes. Common words classes are:

word class	what the word does in a sentence	example
noun	names things	The cat sat on the mat.
verb	tells you what is happening Verbs tell you about doing, being, and having.	The cat sat on the mat and washed its face.
adjective	gives you more information about the noun which is often descriptive	The fluffy, grey cat sat on the ragged, dirty mat and licked its furry paws.
adverb	gives you more information about the verb It tells you how, when, and where events are happening.	Meanwhile, the fluffy, grey cat sat quietly on the ragged, dirty mat and solemnly licked its furry paws.
preposition	tells you where things are	Meanwhile, the fluffy, grey cat sat quietly on the ragged, dirty mat and solemnly licked its furry paws with its pink tongue.

Words we use a lot

These words are words we use often. Some of them have unusual spellings so it is useful to spot them here so that it is easy to recognize them when reading a new piece of text. You can also check their spelling when you use them in your writing.

a

about	and
above	another
across	any
after	anyone
again	are
all	aren't
almost	around
along	as
also	ask
always	at
am	away
an	

b

back	better
be	between
because	big
been	both
before	brother
began	brought
begin	but
below	by

c

call	children
called	come
came	comes
can	coming
can't	could
change	

d

dad	doesn't
day	doing
did	done
didn't	don't
different	down
do	during
does	

e

earth	everyone
every	eyes

f

father	found
first	friends
following	from
for	

g

get	gone
getting	good
go	got
goes	great
going	

h

had	help
hadn't	her
half	hers
has	here
have	he's
haven't	high
having	him
he	his
head	how
heard	

i

I	is
if	isn't
I'm	it
in	its
inside	it's (it is)
into	

j

just

k

knew	know

l

last	live
leave	lived
light	look
like	lost
little	

m

made	morning
make	mother
many	much
may	mum
me	must
might	my
mine	myself
more	

n

name	night
near	no
never	not
new	now
next	number

o

of	or
off	other
often	our
on	ours
once	out
one	outside
only	over
opened	own

p

play	put

r

ran	round
right	

s

said	some
saw	something
second	sometimes
see	sound
seen	started
she	still
should	stopped
show	such
sister	suddenly
small	sure
so	

t

take care	those
taken	thought
than	three
that	through
the	to
their	today
theirs	together
them	told
then	too
there	took
these	tries
they	turn
think	turned
this	

u

under	upon
until	us
up	used

v

very

w

walk	white
walked	who
walking	whole
wasn't	why
want	will
watch	window
was	with
we	without
went	woke
were	woken
what	won't
when	work
where	would
which	write
while	

y

year	you
yes	your

Prefixes

prefix	meaning	example
anti-	against or opposite	anticlockwise, antibiotic (*a medicine that works against an infection in your body*)
co-	together with someone else	co-pilot, co-author
de-	to take something away	debug, de-ice, defrost
dis-	opposite	dislike, disagree, disobey
ex-	in the past, but not now	ex-policeman, ex-wife
in- (also im-)	opposite	incorrect, insane, impossible, impolite
micro-	very small	microchip, microcomputer
mid-	in the middle	midday, midnight, midsummer
mini-	very small	minibus, miniskirt
mis-	badly or wrongly	misbehave, misspell
non-	opposite	non-fiction, non-smoker, non-stop
over-	too much	oversleep, overweight
pre-	before	prehistoric (*before the beginning of history*) pre-school (*before a child is old enough to go to school*)
re-	again, for a second time	rebuild, reheat, reopen
semi-	half	semicircle, semi-final, semi-detached
sub-	under	submarine (*a ship that goes under the sea*), subway (*a path that goes under a road*)
super-	more than or bigger than	superhero, superhuman, superstar
un-	opposite	unable, uncomfortable, undress
under-	not enough	underfed, underweight

Suffixes

for making nouns

-hood	child childhood, father fatherhood
-ity	stupid stupidity, able ability, pure purity
-ness	happy happiness, kind kindness, lazy laziness
-ment	enjoy enjoyment, move movement, replace replacement
-ship	friend friendship, champion championship, partner partnership
-sion	divide division, persuade persuasion
-tion	subtract subtraction, react reaction

for making nouns that mean a person who does something

-er, -or	paint painter, write writer, act actor
-ist	science scientist, art artist, violin violinist

for making feminine nouns

-ess	actor actress, lion lioness

for making adjectives

-able	enjoy enjoyable, break breakable, forgive forgivable
-ful	hope hopeful, colour colourful, care careful, pain painful
-ible	eat edible, reverse reversible
-ic	science scientific, photograph photographic, allergy allergic
-ish	child childish
-ive	attract attractive, compete competitive, explode explosive
-less	care careless, fear fearless, hope hopeless
-like	child childlike, life lifelike
-y	hunger hungry, thirst thirsty, anger angry, hair hairy

for making adverbs

-ly	quick quickly, slow slowly, careful carefully, normal normally

for making verbs

-ate	active activate, pollen pollinate
-en	damp dampen, short shorten, length lengthen
-ify	solid solidify, pure purify
-ize, -ise	apology apologize, fossil fossilize

Numbers

1	one	first	21	twenty-one	twenty-first
2	two	second	22	twenty-two	twenty-second
3	three	third	30	thirty	thirtieth
4	four	fourth	40	forty	fortieth
5	five	fifth	50	fifty	fiftieth
6	six	sixth	60	sixty	sixtieth
7	seven	seventh	70	seventy	seventieth
8	eight	eighth	80	eighty	eightieth
9	nine	ninth	90	ninety	ninetieth
10	ten	tenth	100	a hundred	hundredth
11	eleven	eleventh	101	a hundred and one	hundred and first
12	twelve	twelfth	102	two hundred	two hundredth
13	thirteen	thirteenth			
14	fourteen	fourteenth			
15	fifteen	fifteenth			
16	sixteen	sixteenth			
17	seventeen	seventeenth			
18	eighteen	eighteenth			
19	nineteen	nineteenth			
20	twenty	twentieth			

Shapes

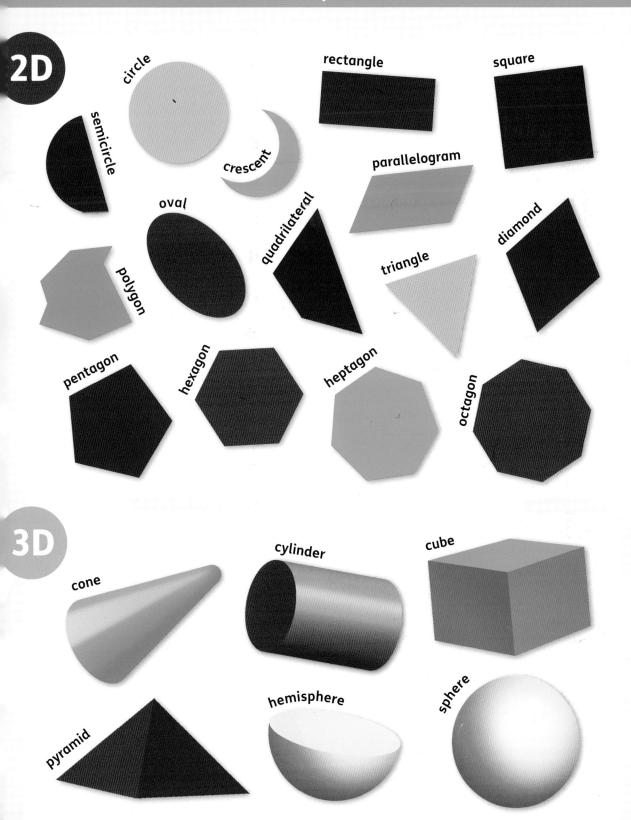

2D

circle

rectangle

square

semicircle

crescent

parallelogram

oval

quadrilateral

diamond

triangle

polygon

pentagon

hexagon

heptagon

octagon

3D

cone

cylinder

cube

pyramid

hemisphere

sphere

9:00

nine o'clock

9:05

five past nine

9:10

ten past nine

9:15

nine fifteen
quarter past nine

9:20

nine twenty
twenty past nine

9:25

nine twenty-five

9:30

nine thirty
half past nine

9:35

nine thirty-five
twenty-five to ten

9:40

nine forty
twenty to ten

9:45

nine forty-five
quarter to ten

9:50

nine fifty
ten to ten

9:55

nine fifty-five
five to ten

12:00

midday (noon)

24:00

midnight

fortnight	14 days
month	28–31 days
year	12 months or 365 days
leap year	366 days
decade	10 years
century	100 years

morning

the time before midday, the letters a.m. stand for *ante meridiem* which is Latin for 'before noon'

midday or noon

the time when the Sun is at its highest is 12 midday or noon

afternoon

the time after midday is afternoon, the letters p.m. stand for *post meridiem* which is Latin for 'after noon'

Days

Monday

Tuesday

Wednesday

Thursday

Friday

Saturday

Sunday

Months

January	31 days
February	28 or 29 days
March	31 days
April	30 days
May	31 days
June	30 days
July	31 days
August	31 days
September	30 days
October	31 days
November	30 days
December	31 days

> 30 days has September,
> April, June, and November
> All the rest have 31
> And February's great with 28
> And Leap Year's February's
> fine with 29

Seasons

spring

summer

autumn

winter

apple

pear

peach

orange

nectarine

rhubarb

tangerine

apricot

banana

tomato

gooseberry

cherry

plum

blackberry

star fruit

kiwi fruit

raspberry

raisin

grapefruit

passion fruit

strawberry

grape

nut

date

lemon

pineapple

mango

melon

Fruit & vegetables

spring onion

sweetcorn

radish

courgette

pepper

garlic

celery

spinach

cucumber

onion

pea

mushroom

parsnip

beetroot

aubergine

lettuce

cabbage

avocado

yam

squash

runner bean

swede

broccoli

potato

leek

pumpkin

turnip

carrot

cauliflower

267

Parts of the body

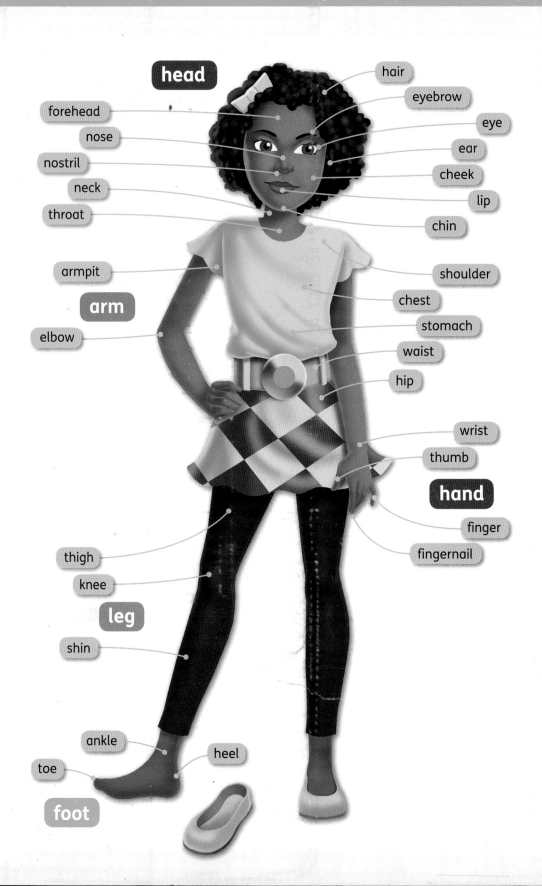

head

hair

eyebrow

forehead

eye

nose

ear

nostril

cheek

neck

lip

throat

chin

armpit

shoulder

arm

chest

elbow

stomach

waist

hip

wrist

thumb

hand

finger

fingernail

thigh

knee

leg

shin

ankle

heel

toe

foot